CAMBRIDGE COMPANIONS TO LITERATURE

The Cambridge Companion to Greek Tragedy
edited by P. E. Easterling

The Cambridge Companion to Old English Literature
edited by Malcolm Godden and Michael Lapidge

The Cambridge Companion to Medieval Romance
edited by Roberta L. Kreuger

The Cambridge Companion to Medieval English Theatre
edited by Richard Beadle

The Cambridge Companion to English Renaissance Drama
edited by A. R. Braunmuller and Michael Hattaway

The Cambridge Companion to Renaissance Humanism
edited by Jill Kraye

The Cambridge Companion to English Poetry, Donne to Marvell
edited by Thomas N. Corns

The Cambridge Companion to English Literature, 1500–1600
edited by Arthur F. Kinney

The Cambridge Companion to English Literature, 1650–1740
edited by Steven N. Zwicker

The Cambridge Companion to Writing of the English Revolution
edited by N. H. Keeble

The Cambridge Companion to English Restoration Theatre
edited by Deborah C. Payne Fisk

The Cambridge Companion to British Romanticism
edited by Stuart Curran

The Cambridge Companion to Eighteenth-Century Poetry
edited by John Sitter

The Cambridge Companion to the Eighteenth-Century Novel
edited by John Richetti

The Cambridge Companion to Victorian Poetry
edited by Joseph Bristow

The Cambridge Companion to the Victorian Novel
edited by Deirdre David

The Cambridge Companion to American Realism and Naturalism
edited by Donald Pizer

The Cambridge Companion to the Classic Russian Novel
edited by Malcolm V. Jones and Robin Feuer Miller

The Cambridge Companion to the French Novel: from 1800 to the Present
edited by Timothy Unwin

The Cambridge Companion to Modernism
edited by Michael Levenson

The Cambridge Companion to Australian Literature
edited by Elizabeth Webby

The Cambridge Companion to American Women Playwrights
edited by Brenda Murphy

The Cambridge Companion to Modern British Women Playwrights
edited by Elaine Aston and Janelle Reinelt

The Cambridge Companion to Virgil
edited by Charles Martindale

The Cambridge Companion to Dante
edited by Rachel Jacoff

The Cambridge Companion to Proust
edited by Richard Bales

The Cambridge Companion to Chekhov
edited by Vera Gottlieb and Paul Allain

The Cambridge Companion to Ibsen
edited by James McFarlane

The Cambridge Companion to Brecht
edited by Peter Thomson and Glendyr Sacks

The Cambridge Chaucer Companion
edited by Piero Boitani and Jill Mann

The Cambridge Companion to Shakespeare
edited by Margareta de Grazia and Stanley Wells

The Cambridge Companion to Shakespeare on Film
edited by Russell Jackson

The Cambridge Companion to Spenser
edited by Andrew Hadfield

The Cambridge Companion to Ben Jonson
edited by Richard Harp and Stanley Stewart

The Cambridge Companion to Milton
edited by Dennis Danielson

The Cambridge Companion to Samuel Johnson
edited by Greg Clingham

The Cambridge Companion to Keats
edited by Susan J. Wolfson

The Cambridge Companion to Jane Austen
edited by Edward Copeland and Juliet McMaster

The Cambridge Companion to Charles Dickens
edited by John O. Jordan

CAMBRIDGE COMPANIONS TO CULTURE

THE CAMBRIDGE
COMPANION TO
TOM STOPPARD

EDITED BY
KATHERINE E. KELLY

Texas A&M University

CAMBRIDGE
UNIVERSITY PRESS

PUBLISHED BY THE PRESS SYNDICATE OF THE UNIVERSITY OF CAMBRIDGE
The Pitt Building, Trumpington Street, Cambridge, United Kingdom

CAMBRIDGE UNIVERSITY PRESS
The Edinburgh Building, Cambridge CB2 2RU, UK
40 West 20th Street, New York, NY 10011-4211, USA
477 Williamstown Road, Port Melbourne, VIC 3207, Australia
Ruiz de Alarcón 13, 28014 Madrid, Spain
Dock House, The Waterfront, Cape Town 8001, South Africa

http://www.cambridge.org

First published 2001
Reprinted 2002

Printed in the United Kingdom at the University Press, Cambridge

Typeface Adobe Sabon 10/13pt   *System* QuarkXpress®   [SE]

A catalogue record for this book is available from the British Library

Library of Congress Cataloguing in Publication data

The Cambridge companion to Tom Stoppard / edited by Katherine E. Kelly.
   p.   cm.
Includes bibliographical references and index.
ISBN 0 521 64178 0 (hardback) – ISBN 0 521 64592 1 (paperback)
   1. Stoppard, Tom – Criticism and interpretation.   I. Title: Tom Stoppard.
II. Kelly, Katherine E., 1947–
PR6069.T6 Z615 2001
822'.914 – dc21 00-069777

ISBN 0 521 64178 0 hardback
ISBN 0 521 64592 1 paperback

*This book is dedicated to
my family and friends who
showed me the way forward*

CONTENTS

CONTENTS

ILLUSTRATIONS

ENOCH BRATER is Professor of English and Theater at the University of Michigan in Ann Arbor. His published work includes *Beyond Minimalism: Beckett's late style in the theater*, *Why Beckett*, *The Drama in the Text: Beckett's late fiction*, and the edited volumes, *Around the Absurd*, *The Theatrical Gamut*, *Beckett at 80/Beckett in Context*, and *Approaches to Teaching Beckett's "Waiting for Godot."* Widely published in the fields of American and European drama, he is also author of the forthcoming *The Stages of Arthur Miller* and *Arthur Miller's America: theater and culture in a century of change.*

JOHN BULL is Professor of Film and Drama at the University of Reading. A former Chair of the Standing Committee of University Drama Departments, he has directed many classic and contemporary plays, including two of his own. His many publications in the field of modern drama include *New British Political Dramatists* and *Stage Right: crisis and recovery in contemporary British mainstream theatre*. His most recent book is *Vanbrugh and Farquhar*, and he is working on a six-volume project on British and Irish dramatists since World War Two.

PAUL DELANEY, professor of English at Westmont College, is the author of *Tom Stoppard: the moral vision of the major plays* (London, 1990) and the editor of *Tom Stoppard in Conversation* (Ann Arbor, 1994) and *Brian Friel in Conversation* (Ann Arbor, 1999).

PAUL EDWARDS teaches English at Bath Spa University College. His book, *Wyndham Lewis: painter and writer*, was published by Yale University Press in 2000. He is also the editor of *Blast: Vorticism, 1914–1918* (Ashgate, 2000) and of several critical editions of books by Wyndham Lewis.

ELISSA S. GURALNICK is Professor of English at the University of Colorado at Boulder, where she codirects the University Writing Program. She is the author of "Radio Drama: the stage of the mind," *Virginia Quarterly*

Review, 61 (winter 1985); and *Sight Unseen: Beckett, Pinter, Stoppard, and other contemporary dramatists on radio* (Athens, Ohio, 1996). In addition, she has published articles on Robert Browning, Mary Wollstonecraft, and Oscar Wilde. She is coauthor of two children's books: *The Weighty Word Book* and *The Stolen Appaloosa and other Indian stories*.

KATHERINE E. KELLY is Associate Professor of English at Texas A&M University, where she teaches Modern British Drama, Modernism, and Film. She is the author of *Tom Stoppard and the Craft of Comedy* (Ann Arbor, 1991) and general editor of *Modern Drama by Women 1880s–1930s: an international anthology* (London, 1996). She coedited *British Playwrights 1880–1956: a research and production sourcebook* (Greenwood Press, 1996) and has published widely on modern playwrights, including George Bernard Shaw, the Actresses' Franchise League, and Elizabeth Robins. She is currently working on a study of the modernity of modern drama.

JOSEPHINE LEE teaches in the English Department at the University of Minnesota, Twin Cities. She is author of *Performing Asian America: race and ethnicity on the contemporary stage* (Temple University Press, 1997) and a coeditor with Imogene Lim and Yuko Matsukawa of *Recollecting Early Asian America: readings in cultural history* (Temple University Press, forthcoming). She has written on various aspects of modern and contemporary British, Irish, and American theater and performance. She is currently at work on a critical study of racial politics and American theater.

JILL L. LEVENSON, professor of English at Trinity College, University of Toronto, is editor of the Oxford (and World's Classics) *Romeo and Juliet*. In addition to writing about other Shakespearean plays and early modern drama outside of Shakespeare, she edited the international quarterly journal *Modern Drama* for more than ten years and is presently chair of its Editorial Advisory Board. She is currently writing a book on Shakespeare and modern drama for Oxford University Press.

MELISSA MILLER has worked with the Theatre Arts Collection at the Harry J. Ransom Humanities Research Center since 1990. Her exhibitions, publications, and dramaturgy have included research on British Theatre since the 1940s, realism, Tennessee Williams, and Shakespeare.

IRA B. NADEL, professor of English at the University of British Columbia, is the author of *Biography: ficton, fact and form*; *Joyce and the Jews*, and *Various Positions: a life of Leonard Cohen*. He has edited *The Cambridge Companion to Ezra Pound*, and Wilkie Collins's formerly lost first novel, *Iolani, or Tahiti as It Was*. He is currently writing a biography of Tom Stoppard.

PETER J. RABINOWITZ divides his time between music and narrative theory. He is the author of *Before Reading: narrative conventions and the politics of interpretation* and coauthor, with Michael Smith, of *Authorizing Readers: resistance and respect in the teaching of literature*; he is also coeditor, with James Phelan, of *Understanding Narrative*. His published articles cover a wide range of subjects, from Dostoevsky to Mrs. E.D.E.N. Southworth, from detective fiction to the ideology of musical structure, from Mahler to Scott Joplin. A professor of comparative literature at Hamilton College, he is also an active music critic, and a contributing editor of *Fanfare*.

NEIL SAMMELLS is Dean of Humanities at Bath Spa University College, England. His *Tom Stoppard: the artist as critic* (London) was published in 1988. He has coedited with Paul Hyland two collections of essays: *Irish Writing: exile and subversion* (London, 1991) and *Writing and Censorship in Britain* (London, 1992). A third collection, edited with Richard Kerridge, and called *Writing the Environment*, was published by Zed Books in 1998. He is editor of *Irish Studies Review* and general editor of Longman's interdisciplinary writing series, Crosscurrents. He is currently writing a book on Oscar Wilde to be published by Longman.

MICHAEL VANDEN HEUVEL is Associate Professor of Theatre and Drama at the University of Wisconsin–Madison. He is the author of *Performing Drama/Dramatizing Performance: alternative theater and the dramatic text* (Ann Arbor, 1991) and *Elmer Rice: a research and production sourcebook* (Greenwood Press, 1996). His articles on American experimental theater, interactions between theater and science, and cultural theory have appeared in *Theatre Journal*, *Journal of Dramatic Theory and Criticism*, *Theatre Topics*, *New Theatre Quarterly*, and elsewhere.

HERSH ZEIFMAN, professor of English and Drama at York University, Toronto, has published widely on contemporary British and American drama. A former coeditor of *Modern Drama* and former president of the Samuel Beckett Society, he is the editor of *Contemporary British Drama, 1970–90* (1993) and *David Hare: a casebook* (1994).

TOBY ZINMAN teaches at the University of the Arts in Philadelphia, where she is both Professor of English and Dramaturg for the School of Theatre. She has also served as a Fulbright Professor at Tel Aviv University. Her books include *David Rabe* (New York, 1991) and *Terrence McNally* (New York, 1997). In addition to frequent scholarly articles on contemporary drama, she is the theater critic for Philadelphia's *City Paper* and writes for *Variety*, *American Theatre*, and the *New York Times*.

ACKNOWLEDGMENTS

I would like to thank the contributors to this volume and my editor, Victoria Cooper, for staying with this project in spite of the delays and uncertainties accompanying illness and prolonged treatment. I am also grateful to Donald Cooper and Ken Friedman, whose luminous photographs offer readers a glimpse of some of the most memorable stagings of Stoppard's plays. Photofest, providers of theatrical photographs, has also helped with images in this collection. The Harry J. Ransom Humanities Research Center in Austin, Texas, was generous in providing us with access to the Stoppard archives, and my colleagues and chairman, J. Lawrence Mitchell, in the Department of English at Texas A&M University were constant in supporting and encouraging my efforts to complete this book.

PAUL DELANEY

Chronology

1937   Stoppard born Tomáš Straüssler (3 July), the second son of Eugen and Martha Straüssler in Zlín, Czechoslovakia, where his father was a physician for Bata, a shoe manufacturer.

1939   The day the Nazis invade Czechoslovakia (14 March), the Straüsslers leave Zlín, with other Jewish doctors who worked for Bata, to go to Singapore.

1942   Briefly attends an English convent school in Singapore. When women and children are evacuated prior to the Japanese invasion, four-year-old Tomáš along with his mother and brother leaves for India; his father remains behind and is killed.

1943–46 Attends an English-speaking boarding school run by American Methodists in Darjeeling; his mother serves as manager of the local Bata shoe shop.

1945   Mother marries Kenneth Stoppard, a British Army major (November).

1946   Family moves to England (February) and three weeks later Major Stoppard adopts his two stepsons, giving them his surname; Tommy Straüssler becomes Tom Stoppard.

1946–51 Attends the Dolphin School, Nottinghamshire.
1951–54 Attends the Pocklington School, Yorkshire.
1950   Stoppard family moves to Bristol.
1954–58 Stoppard becomes a journalist on the *Western Daily Press*. Kenneth Tynan serves as drama critic on the *Observer*.
1954–60 Stoppard attends productions at the Bristol Old Vic.
1955   First British production, directed by Peter Hall, of Samuel Beckett's *Waiting for Godot*, which Stoppard cites as the catalyst for modern British drama.

1956   The Royal Court production of John Osborne's *Look Back in Anger* acclaimed by critic Kenneth Tynan. The Berliner Ensemble, directed by Bertolt Brecht, visits London.

1958–60   Stoppard works as a journalist on the *Bristol Evening World*.

1958   The 24-year-old Peter O'Toole's performance as Hamlet at the Bristol Old Vic impresses Stoppard.

1959   Peter Hall founds the Royal Shakespeare Company.

1960   On holiday for his 23rd birthday, Stoppard decides to quit his job as a journalist to try his hand as a playwright; writes *A Walk on the Water*.

1960–61   Writes *The Gamblers* (a one-act play) and *The Stand-Ins* (later revised as *The Real Inspector Hound*).

1962–63   Theatre critic at *Scene* magazine in London.

1963   *A Walk on the Water* televised.

Writes *I Can't Give You Anything But Love, Baby* and *Funny Man* (unproduced television plays).

Becomes romantically involved with Jose Ingle.

1964   *The Dissolution of Dominic Boot* and *"M" is for Moon Among Other Things* on radio.

Three short stories published.

Writes *This Way Out With Samuel Boot* (unproduced television play).

In Berlin on a Ford Foundation grant, writes *Rosencrantz and Guildenstern Meet King Lear*, a one-act play.

A Walk on the Water staged in Hamburg, Germany.

1965   Marries Jose Ingle (26 March).

The Gamblers, first produced stage play, performed at Bristol University in a two-act version.

A Paragraph for Mr. Blake (an adaptation of Stoppard's short story "The Story") televised.

Writes *How Sir Dudley Lost the Empire* (unproduced television play).

Writes the first of seventy episodes of "A Student's Diary," a radio serial about an Arab medical student in London broadcast by the BBC World Service in Arabic.

1966   *If You're Glad I'll Be Frank* on radio.

Stoppard's first son, Oliver, born on 4 May.

Translation (with Nicholas Bethell) of Slawomir Mrozek's *Tango* staged by the RSC.

A Separate Peace televised.

Rosencrantz and Guildenstern Are Dead staged on the Edinburgh Festival Fringe; Ronald Bryden's review in the *Observer* prompts Kenneth Tynan, literary manager at the National Theatre, to cable Stoppard requesting a script.

Lord Malquist and Mr Moon, a novel, published.

1967　*Teeth* televised.

Rosencrantz and Guildenstern Are Dead staged by the National Theatre, making Stoppard the youngest playwright to have a play performed by the NT.

Another Moon Called Earth televised; *Albert's Bridge* on radio.

Rosencrantz and Guildenstern Are Dead opens on Broadway, the first National Theatre production to transfer to New York.

1968　*Enter a Free Man* (a revised version of *A Walk on the Water*) staged.

Rosencrantz wins the Tony award for best play.

The Real Inspector Hound staged.

Neutral Ground televised.

1969　First stage productions of *Albert's Bridge* and *If You're Glad I'll Be Frank* at the Edinburgh Festival.

Stoppard's second son, Barnaby, born 20 September.

Exhibition at the Tate Gallery of the works of René Magritte, who died in 1967.

Stoppard leaves Jose and takes their two sons.

1970　*Where Are They Now?* on radio.

Stoppard begins divorce and custody proceedings.

Expands *The Dissolution of Dominic Boot* into *The Engagement* (televised in the US and shown in cinemas in the UK).

After Magritte staged.

Stoppard, with his two sons, moves in with Dr. Miriam Moore-Robinson.

1971　*Dogg's Our Pet* staged.

1972　Divorce from Jose Stoppard, *née* Ingle, granted and Stoppard wins custody of his two sons.

Jumpers, staged by the National Theatre, begins Stoppard's long-term theatrical partnership with director Peter Wood.

Marries Dr. Miriam Moore-Robinson (11 February); their first child, William, is born 7 March.

First New York production of *The Real Inspector Hound* and *After Magritte*.

One Pair of Eyes televises an episode entitled "Tom Stoppard Doesn't Know."

Artist Descending a Staircase on radio.

1973　Adaptation of Federico Garcia Lorca's *The House of Bernarda Alba* staged.

Stoppard directs Lynn Redgrave in Garson Kanin's *Born Yesterday*.

1974 First New York production of *Jumpers*.

Travesties staged by the RSC.

Stoppard's fourth son, Edmund, born 16 September.

First New York production of *Enter a Free Man*.

1975 *The Boundary*, cowritten with Clive Exton, televised.

First New York production of *Travesties*.

Coauthors screenplay of Thomas Wiseman's *The Romantic Englishwoman*.

Adaptation of Jerome K. Jerome's *Three Men in a Boat* televised.

1976 *Dirty Linen* staged and becomes the first lunchtime play to transfer to the West End.

Travesties wins two Tony Awards including best play.

Stoppard meets Victor Fainberg, confined for five years in a Soviet psychiatric hospital for protesting the invasion of Czechoslovakia, whose experiences contribute to *Every Good Boy Deserves Favour*.

Speaks out on behalf of Soviet dissidents.

Jumpers returns to the repertoire as the National Theatre opens its new facility on the South Bank.

The (15 Minute) Dogg's Troupe Hamlet performed outside the NT.

Vladimir Bukovsky, referred to in *Every Good Boy* as "my friend C," is released from Soviet prison and sent to the West.

1977 First New York production of *Dirty Linen*.

Czech dissidents publish Charter 77; Czech playwright Václav Havel and other signers are arrested and charged with subversion. Stoppard publishes letters to the editor about Havel's arrest.

Meets with Soviet dissidents in Moscow and Leningrad.

Every Good Boy Deserves Favour receives one performance with the London Symphony Orchestra.

Visits Czechoslovakia and publishes an account of the repression of the Chartists.

The National Union of Journalists' call for newspapers to be closed shops prompts Stoppard to publish a letter to the editor denouncing the suppression of freedom of expression.

Professional Foul televised.

In the Prague trial of the Chartists, Havel is given a suspended sentence but other Czech dissidents receive prison terms.

1978   *Every Good Boy Deserves Favour* revived with a chamber orchestra in London and given its first US production.

Dissidents Anatoly Shcharansky and Alexander Ginzburg put on trial by Soviet authorities; Stoppard protests at the treatment of Soviet Jews.

Night and Day staged.

Adapts Vladimir Nabokov's *Despair* for film.

1979   Stoppard serves as chairman of the worldwide "Let Misha Go" campaign, resulting in Soviet authorities releasing the thirteen-year-old boy to join his mother in England.

Dogg's Hamlet, Cahoot's Macbeth tours England and the US.

Undiscovered Country, an adaptation of Arthur Schnitzler's *Das Weite Land*, staged at the National Theatre.

First New York production of *Every Good Boy Deserves Favor*.

Havel and five other dissidents sentenced to prison terms.

First New York production of *Night and Day*.

1980   Stoppard participates in a staged recreation in Munich of Havel's 1979 trial.

In preparation for the 22nd Olympiad, Soviet authorities launch the heaviest crackdown on dissenters in fifteen years; Stoppard supports the Olympic boycott movement.

Writes screenplay of *The Human Factor*, adapted from the novel by Graham Greene.

1981   *On the Razzle* (adapted from Johann Nestroy's *Einen Jux will er sich machen*) staged in a National Theatre production that includes Felicity Kendal cast as a boy.

Publishes an "Open Letter to President Husák" about being denied a visa to return to Czechoslovakia.

In Poland, martial law imposed as General Jaruzelski's regime outlaws the trade union Solidarity and arrests its leaders including Lech Walesa.

1982   Stoppard begins to write a television play, which will become *Squaring the Circle*, about Solidarity.

Every Good Boy Deserves Favour revival with the London Symphony Orchestra.

The Real Thing, starring Felicity Kendal and Roger Rees, staged.

On the Razzle receives US premiere.

The Dog It Was That Died on radio.

1983   *The Love for Three Oranges* (translation of libretto for Prokofiev's opera) performed.

Havel is released from prison.

The Nobel Peace Prize is awarded to Lech Walesa.

1984   First New York production of *The Real Thing* wins five Tony awards including best play and runs until May 1985.

Squaring the Circle televised.

Rough Crossing (freely adapted from Ferenc Molnár's *Play at the Castle*) staged at the National Theatre.

1985   Receives Oscar nomination for cowriting the screenplay of *Brazil*.

Revises *Jumpers* for West End revival with Felicity Kendal.

Directs *The Real Inspector Hound* at the National Theatre.

1986   Organizes "Roll Call at the NT," a 24-hour reading outside the National Theatre by various notables (Senator Bill Bradley flew over for the event) of the names of 10,000 Russian Jews denied the freedom to emigrate.

Dalliance (adapted from Schnitzler's *Liebelei*) staged.

Translates *Largo Desolato* by Havel for the Bristol Old Vic.

1987   First London and US productions of Stoppard's translation of *Largo Desolato*.

Writes screenplay for *Empire of the Sun* (dir. Steven Spielberg), adapted from J. G. Ballard's novel.

1988   *Hapgood* staged after a six-month wait for Felicity Kendal to return to the stage following the birth of her child.

While retaining their country home in Iver, Stoppard purchases a Chelsea Harbour luxury apartment separate from his wife's in-town flat.

First stage production of the radio play *Artist Descending a Staircase*.

Writes screenplay (unproduced) of Laurens van der Post's novel *A Far Off Place*.

1989   Writes television version of *The Dog It Was That Died*.

Filming of *Rosencrantz and Guildenstern are Dead* is canceled when Sean Connery withdraws from the cast.

Stoppard revises *Hapgood* for first US production in Los Angeles.

First New York production of *Artist Descending a Staircase*.

Makes uncredited contributions to the screenplays of *Always* and *Indiana Jones and the Last Crusade*.

Appointed to the Board of the National Theatre.

Václav Havel is elected interim president of Czechoslovakia and subsequently reelected to the presidency in 1990.

1990 First New York production of *Rough Crossing*.

Rosencrantz and Guildenstern are Dead, written and directed by Stoppard, wins the Golden Lion at the Venice Film Festival.

Stoppard and actress Felicity Kendal are linked romantically in a relationship that will last eight years; Stoppard and his wife agree to a legal separation.

Writes screenplay for *The Russia House* (starring Sean Connery), adapted from the novel by John le Carré.

Lech Walesa becomes president of Poland.

1991 Film version of *Rosencrantz and Guildenstern are Dead* released.

In the Native State on radio.

Visits Darjeeling for the first time since leaving India forty-five years earlier.

Writes screenplay for *Billy Bathgate*, adapted from the E. L. Doctorow novel.

1992 Divorces Miriam Stoppard.

The Real Inspector Hound and *The 15–Minute Hamlet* revived on Broadway.

With Marc Norman writes screenplay for *Shakespeare in Love* but filming is canceled in October when Julia Roberts withdraws from the cast.

1993 *A Separate Peace* televised.

Arcadia staged at the National Theatre.

Writes new narration for Franz Lehár's *The Merry Widow*.

Travesties revived by the RSC, making Stoppard the first living playwright to have plays running concurrently in London at the NT and the RSC.

Stoppard's archives deposited at the University of Texas at Austin.

Arcadia on radio with the original NT cast.

Writes screenplay (unproduced) for *Hopeful Monsters*, a novel by Nicholas Mosley.

1994 Learns from a Czech relative that his family had been Jewish and that he had three aunts who, along with his grandparents, died in the Holocaust

West End transfers for the RSC revival of *Travesties* and the NT production of *Arcadia*.

First New York production of *Hapgood*.

Adapts *Three Men in a Boat* for radio.

Writes screenplay (unproduced) for a full-length animated film version of *Cats*, the Andrew Lloyd Webber musical.

1995   *Indian Ink* (stage adaptation of the radio play *In the Native State*) opens in London starring Felicity Kendal.

When *Arcadia* opens in New York while *Hapgood* is still running, Stoppard becomes the first playwright to have plays concurrently on both stages at Lincoln Center. *Arcadia* nominated for a Tony Award for best play.

Rosencrantz and Guildenstern Are Dead revived at the National Theatre.

Begins adapting *Hapgood* for the screen, having given the film rights to Stockard Channing who played the title role in New York.

1996   Stoppard's mother dies, age 85, in October; a few days later Stoppard's stepfather writes to his 59-year-old stepson and asks the playwright to stop using "Stoppard" as his name.

1997   Stoppard's version of Chekhov's *The Seagull* directed by Sir Peter Hall.

Stoppard's stepfather dies.

The Invention of Love staged at the National Theatre.

Knighted at Buckingham Palace, Sir Tom Stoppard becomes the first dramatist thus honored since Sir Terence Rattigan in 1971.

1998   *The Real Inspector Hound* revived in London.

Returns, with his brother Peter, to Zlín for the first time since his family fled Czechoslovakia 59 years earlier.

Adaptation of *Poodle Springs* by Raymond Chandler televised.

Felicity Kendal ends eight-year romantic relationship with Stoppard.

The Invention of Love transfers to the West End.

Stoppard becomes the first living non-Francophone playwright to have a play (*Arcadia*) staged at the Comédie-Française.

Revises screenplay of *Shakespeare in Love* for a film starring Gwyneth Paltrow and Joseph Fiennes.

Spends a month trying to find a way to adapt *Arcadia* as a film.

1999   *Shakespeare in Love* wins three Golden Globes including best screenplay and seven Academy Awards including best screenplay and best picture.

Donmar Warehouse revives *The Real Thing* in an award-winning production with Stephen Dillane and Jennifer Ehle.

Makes uncredited contributions to the screenplay for *Sleepy*

Hollow (dir. Tim Burton), adapted from the short story by Washington Irving.

Writes screenplays for *Vatel*, a French film to star Gérard Depardieu; and for *Enigma*, to be produced by Mick Jagger adapted from the novel by Robert Harris.

Reports that he is at work on a play dealing with the role of the artist in nineteenth-century Russia.

2000 First US production of *The Invention of Love* in San Francisco.

Begins calling the six-hour play he is writing on nineteenth-century Russia, a trilogy.

Tweaks his translation of *The Seagull* for its first US production in San Diego.

Begins romantic relationship with former model Marie Helvin.

The Donmar Warehouse production of *The Real Thing* transfers to New York and wins Tony Awards for best revival, best actor and best actress.

Vatel, with screenplay co-written by Stoppard, released.

Enigma (dir. Michael Apted), with screenplay by Stoppard, filmed.

2001 First New York production of *The Invention of Love*.

Stoppard's trilogy set in nineteenth-century Russia to be staged at the National Theatre.

KATHERINE E. KELLY

Introduction: Tom Stoppard in transformation

This book takes a new look at Tom Stoppard's drama, fiction, and screen-writing nearly forty years after his work began appearing before audiences. Most contributors agree that the Stoppard style in 2000 is recognizable but fundamentally changed from his self-conscious dandyism of the 1960s and early 1970s. As Stoppard has continued to write, his later work has not only extended his early preoccupation with memory, uncertainty, and ethics but also deepened the sense of human consequence growing from ethical conflict and intellectual doubt. In the past ten years, as many of the book's chapters suggest, Stoppard has overcome the charge of emotional coldness, especially the claim that he had failed to represent human love. In slowly dropping his emotional guard, he has imbued his writing with a depth of compassion hinted at in the early work through his consistent appeals to humor.

These chapters are written to introduce both first-time and experienced readers of Stoppard's novel and plays to the critical tradition that has grown up alongside them from the late 1960s to the present. Most offer the added value of viewing the earlier work through the lens of the later, suggesting both a continuous shifting of Stoppard's technique and dramatic architec-ture and a continuity of theme over four decades of writing. In showing us, for example, how a 1967 play like *Rosencrantz and Guildenstern Are Dead* (*R&GAD*) both prepares for and inhabits the 1998 screenplay *Shakespeare in Love*, the chapters encourage us to read Stoppard's writing as a series of transformational exchanges between texts quoted in the plays, between the history and fiction represented by the plays, and between the writing early and later in his career. This exchange, initiated by the author but completed by "knowing" readers and spectators, is the secret to the pleasure of Stoppard's plays. It is the hope of this collection to intensify that pleasure for all who use it.

Stoppard's habit of recycling prior texts, which informs virtually all of his work, draws the reader and spectator into the process of transformation by presenting them with familiar literary language (and visual imagery) made strange by an unfamiliar dramatic context. We both hear and then re-hear quotations from the literary past as Stoppard selectively mines the "imaginary museum" of western art. In the earliest of his full-length plays, he taught his spectators how to listen and how to view his characteristic uses of stage speech and action. Since *R&GAD* the Stoppard spectator knows to listen for texts behind the text and enjoys the game of recognizing echoes of Dada poetry, Shakespearean sonnets, and Wittgensteinian philosophy, as well as visual and aural puns from modern painting and music. The Stoppard spectator, that is, collaborates in anticipating and then recognizing familiar but transformed texts as these evoke and critique major works of the western tradition. Transformation is not, then, an operation performed by the author alone or a virtuoso display passively admired by a static spectator. Rather, it is Stoppard's method for revising the artistic past and its customary expectations in league with a literate audience whose recognition and enjoyment of textual mingling completes the transformational process.

Both the plays and the author's life have been marked by a comingling – of idioms, of nations, of families, and of identities. Paul Delaney's opening biographical chapter brings the nature of this mixing and doubling squarely into focus. Following Stoppard's lead, Delaney describes twinning, a persistent thematic coursing through the plays, as the "sense that inside any self may be some other self waiting to be revealed." In this regard, textual doubling and its linguistic transformations can be understood to mimic the biological doubling expressed by the twins – identical and unidentical – that appear repeatedly in the plays. Delaney suggests that the Stoppard canon to date offers "a classic case of self-revelation in (its) recurrent concern with unidentical twins," a concern Delaney links to Stoppard's early and enforced globe-trotting. Born Tomáš Straüssler (Tomik to his family) in 1937 in Zlin, Czechoslovakia, he was forced to flee the invading Nazis with his parents and brother at the age of one and a half. They settled in Singapore for three years when the Japanese invasion again forced them to move on, this time to India. But Stoppard's father, Dr. Eugen Straüssler, stayed behind and was killed. Four-year-old Tomáš, his brother, and mother arrived in Darjeeling, India, having lost their father/husband, their native country, and an adopted nation. Two years later, Mrs. Straüssler married Kenneth Stoppard, a British Army major, and three months after that, the family moved to England. Major Stoppard adopted the two boys, giving them his last name. Upon arrival in England, Stoppard felt an "English" self emerge and he embraced the country as a permanent home. Fifty-one years later, when he was knighted in December of 1997, Stoppard felt "instantly proud. I have felt English almost from the day I arrived, but the knighthood puts some kind of seal on that emotion." But that emotion and its accompanying sense of identity were complicated again by Stoppard's patriotic stepfather, the sponsor of his British citizenship and an anti-Semite. Contacted by a Czech relative in 1994, the playwright eventually discovered the Jewish identity of his biological parents and aunts and uncles. Suddenly, as he titled his 1999 *Talk* magazine memoir, he "turned out to be Jewish." His stepfather, in deference to whom Stoppard's mother had kept their Jewish identity quiet, had already been unsettled by Stoppard's support, ten years earlier, of Russian Jews. Shortly after Stoppard's mother died in 1996, Major Stoppard requested that Tom no longer use his last name, explaining his objection to Tom's "tribalization" by which he meant, Stoppard explained, "mainly my association . . . with the cause of Russian Jews." Stoppard was now a different and very particular kind of hybrid Englishman – honored for his achievements with a knighthood but rejected by his "English father" as alien and "other," and embraced by his lost Czech family as a welcome member. Delaney's chapter and chronology trace how Tomáš–Tomik–Tommy–Tom–Sir Tom "turns out to be his own unidentical twin."

Stoppard's multi-layered identity finds expression in his long-term interest in cultural conflict and hybridity. Josephine Lee's chapter charts Stoppard's portrayal of postcolonial Indian subjects in the 1991 radio drama, *In the Native State*, and its 1995 stage adaptation, *Indian Ink*. Lee identifies these plays, Stoppard's self-described attempts to explore "the ethics of empire," as more politically astute than his earlier stage play, *Night and Day* (1978), set in Kambawe, a fictional African country and former British colony. Noting that the latter plays continue to "emphasize the perspective of the British characters," Lee points to Stoppard's new effort "to create Indian characters who are more fully developed" than their African counterparts in the earlier play. On the subject of character development, Lee quotes Stoppard, who wrestles with the contradictions of creating Indian characters not from "life" but from the fictional stereotypes of British film and novel. "The difficulty," he explains, is "to avoid writing characters who (seem) to have already appeared in *The Jewel in the Crown* and *Passage to India* . . . and so I mean there is this slight embarrassment about . . . merely mimicking the Indian characters in other people's work." He avoids "mere mimickry" here as elsewhere, by raising within the play itself the question of ethnicity and authenticity in art. Flora Crewe, the young Englishwoman lecturing on English art in Jummapur, asks the Indian painter Nirad Das, who is preparing to paint her portrait, "Can't you paint me without thinking of Rossetti or Milais? Especially without thinking of Holman Hunt?"[1] Nirad Das would appear to share Stoppard's limitation but not his self-consciousness. Lee recognizes another kind of limitation in the play, one of which the author may have been less aware. In equating Flora's poetry with a feminized, erotic, and irrational "India" under masculine English control, Stoppard repeats the familiar equation of India with the exotic, the feminine, the chaotic, and the primitive in need of British regulation and governance. Yet, Lee continues, "he also juxtaposes these stereotypes with a more difficult, complex, and still emergent notion of national identity." This attempt to create an emergent national identity marks the beginning of Stoppard's exploration of imperialist ethics and takes him deeper into the dramatic treatment of cultural difference.

One of the strengths of the chapters of this book is their willingness to look not only at Stoppard's successes but also at his partial successes and at his failures. Peter J. Rabinowitz's analysis of Stoppard's only published novel, *Lord Malquist and Mr Moon* (1966), explains its failure in terms that reverberate interestingly in discussions of the emotional range of his stage characters. Rabinowitz relies on distinguishing two kinds of audiences – the authorial audience, which reads the novel as a fiction and therefore at an emotionally cool remove, and the narrative audience, which suspends disbelief and reads the novel as if it were provisionally "real." In explaining why the novel fails to move its readers, Rabinowitz argues that Stoppard tips the balance too far towards the (aloof) authorial audience and away from the (emotionally involved) narrative audience. As a consequence, the novel produces indifference rather than sympathy in its readers. By focusing the audience's attention squarely on the novel's style not as an expression of its characters but as a self-conscious display by its author, Stoppard inhibits the reader's sense of emotional attachment to the characters. Moon's death at the novel's end, writes Rabinowitz, "appears a mere formal necessity in a way that saps the novel's emotional power."

On the level of ideas, Rabinowitz argues, the novel also falls short of the stage plays. Adopting a cubist technique of "additive realism," the authorial level of the novel offers a "ceiling view" of reality composed of the characters' hopelessly partial individual views. Using images of mirrors and glass, Stoppard shows us Moon trying to understand the global view of his predicament. But Moon, who struggles with inarticulateness, cannot know as much as the narrator knows. What Rabinowitz calls the "cruel skepticism" advanced by the characters' limitations collides with their individual tragedies to prevent the reader from taking their misfortunes seriously. As Stoppard continued to work in stage and film media, his use of a dramatized narrator, such as Henry Carr in *Travesties* (1974), showed greater confidence and skill in shaping the reader/spectators' emotional involvement in the characters' dilemmas. In spite of its failure, this early (and only) experiment in novel-writing introduced Stoppard to narrative complexity, to popular culture as a source of comedy, and to stock characters such as the hapless Moon and elegant Malquist, who would repeat in his later works.

Elissa Guralnick's chapter on the radio and television plays demonstrates just how self-consciously Stoppard approached writing for various media both early and later in his career. In writing for broadcast media, Guralnick notes that Stoppard "probes (its) very nature," attempting to "discover what constitutes a stage on air and on screen, then [inducing] each stage to speak its own oblique language." Profiting from BBC Radio's commitment to high-quality radio drama, Stoppard and his contemporaries found a prestige outlet and a mass audience for small-scale plays crafted for the ear. Radio encouraged Stoppard to adopt motifs such as time that could be developed cleverly to appeal to the "blind" auditor. As Guralnick explains, an early radio play such as *If You're Glad I'll be Frank* (1966) "actualizes time – the only physical dimension literally present in a radio broadcast – in order to convey the heartbreaking emptiness of its lonely expanses." This "genuine radio play" (in that no other medium could persuasively produce it) marks an advance over others in investing the play's meaning in its medium. The play wittily draws attention to heroine Gladys both as a machine – the speaking clock – and as a human being with memories, longings and fears. Guralnick praises this play in particular as a "subtle but pervasive mimesis, produced by (the) artful exploitation of radio's performance space." In his best radio pieces, Stoppard plays with the spectator's tendency to call up images evoked by his language. Television, on the other hand, raises questions about the tension between documentary accuracy and the fictional manipulation of historical "truth." In the television medium, Guralnick singles out *Squaring the Circle* (1984) as "that rarest of entities: a play so specifically imagined for television that the medium functions as part of the message." While focusing on the formal characteristics of Stoppard's plays for radio and television, Guralnick's discussion of Stoppard's television plays as political tools overlaps John Bull's later treatment of Stoppard's politics, in which he analyzes a television play like *Squaring the Circle* for its political rather than its formal properties.

In his chapter, "Stoppard and Film," Ira Nadel also focuses on Stoppard's work for a particular medium, in this case, film. In this first extended treatment of Stoppard's screenplays and script doctoring, Nadel brings archival evidence to bear in order to demonstrate the centrality of screenwriting to Stoppard's output and to the evolution of his approach to the difficulties of writing for this medium. Nadel begins with Stoppard's film reviews written for Bristol newspapers, reviews that "became a testing ground for an aesthetic." Intriguingly, one of these early reviews – of Dalton Trumbell (writer) and Stanley Kubrick's (director) *Spartacus* – appeared under the name "Tomik Sträussler," returning us to the identity motif discussed in the chapters by Delaney, Zinman, Levenson, Edwards, and Zeifman. By 1961, Nadel shows us that Stoppard has synthesized his opinions on film, both as a fan and as a critic, in a long review essay of *Breakfast at Tiffany's*, in which the following appears: "(t)he dichotomy of minority art and popular rubbish is slowly making way for popular art – *Saturday Night and Sunday Morning* has been one of the biggest money makers this year." Of course, as both script doctor and screenwriter, Stoppard shuttled between popular and "high art" writing over the next forty years, ambivalent about learning a new medium that treated the screenwriter as no more than "a privileged tourist on a set while the film is being made."

Nadel speculates that Stoppard contributed to the contemporary screenplay by demonstrating that a precise form of spoken dialogue can raise the value and the interest in a film. But film, in its turn, has sharpened the playwright's sense of structure, scene, and visual realization. Nadel points to the cinematic quality of the opening scene of *The Invention of Love* (1997), in which A. E. Housman confronts Charon as he arrives to ferry him across a darkened misty landscape, and Housman utters the striking line, "I'm dead then. Good." In spite of his growth as a screenwriter, playwright Stoppard has never fully accommodated himself to the medium. Nadel quotes him explaining, "What you write you almost never see on the screen since screenwriting by definition invites interference by others." But in the theatre, "the director is there to serve the writer. It's more or less the opposite of the movies." The recent success, *Shakespeare in Love* (1999), takes its place alongside other (cowritten) Stoppard screenplays as primarily a director's property but with extraordinary dialogue instantly recognizable as Stoppardian.

Like his screenwriting, Stoppard's playwriting has benefited from a series of surprising teachers. In analyzing his early stage plays, Neil Sammells identifies Oscar Wilde as a crucial influence, a "mentor," with a "collectivist ethic" (evidenced by Wilde's *The Soul of Man Under Socialism*) that Stoppard refused to adopt. Arguing that Stoppard's best writing is that which most closely aligns with Wilde's avoidance of naturalism, Sammells attributes a "militant conservatism" in the later plays to the playwright's failure to adhere to his mentor's political and aesthetic philosophy. Sammells points to Stoppard's interest in the singular, the eccentric, the individualist in his early plays, most of whose comic heroes resist an organized power (usually represented in seriocomic terms as vaguely totalitarian, e.g. *Jumpers*' [1972] Rad-Libs). Sammells argues that the early stage plays develop an "inverted" Wildean aesthetic with an "inverted politics." That is, Stoppard's uses of parody to question dramatic form and language disappoint because they preserve at their center "an insistent construction of individualism in conservative political terms." This resistance to a collectivist ethic Sammells associates with a "nostalgic rejection of a new 'leftist' collectivism in postwar British politics and culture." Stoppard's "little men," he suggests, share this political coloration with the world of the Ealing comedies, films produced from the late 1930s to the late 1950s, in which modest individuals form close-knit communities and prevail against adversity.

Sammells' discussion of Stoppard's politics invites comparison with John Bull's chapter, which also critiques the playwright's political evolution from early, to middle, to later plays, but concludes that in *The Invention of Love*, Stoppard has "found a way of arguing for the supremacy of the individual" using a new definition of freedom that permits chaos as one of its elements. His "conservatism," in other words, has developed cracks.

Sammells identifies Stoppard's ideal audience with Wilde's and Joe Orton's, all of them explicitly middle-class, commercial playwrights "trying to meet, satisfy and ambush the expectations of a specific theatregoing public," a public composed of "the middle-brow adherents of the West End." Toby Zinman's chapter on the major stage plays precisely characterizes the qualities in Stoppard's writing that have repeatedly attracted these audiences and readers. *Travesties*, *Night and Day* (1978), and *The Real Thing* (1982) share "word-intoxicated characters" in a drama that is intellectual rather than psychological, fast-paced rather than leisurely, complex rather than spare, dialectical rather than linear. Noting that Stoppard has claimed structure to be more important than dialogue in his writing (reflecting lessons learned as a scriptwriter?), Zinman describes three structural characteristics shared by these major stage plays – an opening "faux" scene taken by the audience to be true; a doubled, trebled, or quadrupled structure; and a set design that functions as part of the play. Each of these structural features involves the audience in first assessing and then reassessing its reading of the action as it progresses.

Zinman's discussion of *Night and Day* takes up the question of postcolonial discourse treated in Josephine Lee's chapter. Stoppard doubles military maneuvers with sexual maneuvers, as Ruth Carson, the bored wife of mine owner Jeffrey Carson in postcolonial African Kambawe, daydreams about a new lover in the form of Jacob Milne, a young and idealistic British freelance reporter. Stoppard works through the postcolonial dynamic by using mine owner Carson as a double for England: as England is to Africa, so Carson is to the marriage – "displaced but not replaced, still very much present." Ruth stands in for Kambawe itself, represented in the play by African servant Francis, submissive but opportunistic.

In Zinman's new reading, *Night and Day* amounts to an extended treatment of postcolonial politics that, admittedly, views colonialism from the British perspective, but encourages a critical assessment of that perspective.

In her discussions of both *Travesties* and *The Real Thing,* Zinman draws attention to the structural and linguistic doubling noted in Delaney's biographical essay. In conclusion, Zinman sees the three major plays she has discussed as building towards the "greatness of *Arcadia,*" where a rigorous and carefully structured intellectual debate combines with fully humanized characters to give us the best of high comedy.

In his chapter on Stoppard's politics, John Bull also sees an evolution in Stoppard's political positioning. Echoing Rabinowitz's claim about Stoppard's first novel, Bull argues that the early work "refuses to present a reliable voice: uncertainty is all." But by 1974, Stoppard was "slowly but gradually being drawn into taking a direct political stand." When he met Czech playwright, Václav Havel, in 1977, two strands of his literary heritage – the British absurdist (ahistorical) strand and the Eastern European (politicized) strand – merged in his writing. In a suggestive reading of the 1984 television film, *Squaring the Circle,* Bull finds these two impulses coexisting in the form of a narrator with a self-conscious but not entirely reliable knowledge of the film's recounting of the rise of Poland's Solidarity movement. Intersecting Delaney's discussion of twinning and Lee's consideration of postcolonial tension in Stoppard's plays, Bull finds that the playwright's sense of cultural bifurcation enlivens plays like *In the Native State* and *Squaring the Circle,* where the narrator stands, like the Housman of *The Invention of Love,* between two shores, a native of neither. In agreement with most contributors, Bull finds the 1993 play, *Arcadia,* the best of his full-length work to date. Using the political arguments underpinning his chapter, Bull places *Arcadia* at the center of Stoppard's mature "political credo": "the individual is more . . . than just a construction of the political state; all ideologies will crumble in the face of individual will; but the result is not an ungovernable chaos, (it is) rather a set of unpredictable patterns." One of the determiners of those patterns turns out to be sexual desire, a theme fully developed by Hersh Zeifman in a later chapter. Bull identifies erotic passion in the play as providing opposition to a rigidly determinist view of the human and nonhuman universe. This opposition is an essential force in what Bull sees as Stoppard's definition of freedom in the most recent full-length stage plays, a definition recalling the playwright's adherence to conservatism with a small *c* – a reverence for tradition and for the efforts of the individual within the limits of tradition qualified by an opposition to the imposing of order on human chaos.

Given Stoppard's dialectical habit of mind, his attraction to intellectual qualification, uncertainty and to irresolvable questions, it comes as no surprise that Jill Levenson finds Stoppard's lifelong uses of Shakespeare to be composed of a "series of conflicting statements made by conflicting characters."

Levenson points to two Shakespearean tragedies as "the keys" to understanding the most profound borrowings from the playwright Stoppard has mischievously called "The Champ." *Rosencrantz and Guildenstern Are Dead* (*R&GAD*) draws deeply upon *Hamlet*, while *Dogg's Hamlet, Cahoot's Macbeth* (1979) heavily rewrites its title plays. In contrast to assessments of Stoppard as privileging the writer-as-individual, Levenson's analysis suggests that he occasionally uses others' texts irreverently and finally views all texts as shifting and unstable grounds of meaning. She quotes the playwright, "(Plays) are organic things. They change their composition in relation to the time they exist . . . and in relation to oneself." Levenson also quotes Clive James, who has described Stoppard's plays as "fields of force," changing in relation to one another. These metaphors of shift and instability bear directly on Stoppard's varied uses of Shakespeare, some reverent and some mocking, as well as on the nature of the intertexts arising from Stoppard's literary borrowing. Not only do the texts change each other but the changes provoke the spectator to reconsider the monumentality of Shakespeare-the-icon. Levenson argues that *Dogg's Hamlet, Cahoot's Macbeth* goes the furthest towards dethroning the Bard both in the speeches selected and in the method of quotation, juxtaposing chunks of Shakespeare's texts with Stoppard's, permitting the spectators to "hear" their own resulting textual conversations.

Turning to the most recent use of Shakespeare, Levenson draws attention to moments in *Shakespeare in Love* where Stoppard slyly refashions "Shakespeare-the-World-Champ" as a double for his earlier self (twinning – again), the provincial journalist moving to London to make it as a writer. The film's casual anachronisms – the juxtaposing of advertising logos and quill pens, for example – share with the stage play, *Arcadia* (1993), the momentary abandoning of linear time in favor of multiple time zones, one of the legacies of Stoppard's fascination with modern science.

In his chapter on science in *Hapgood* (1988) and *Arcadia*, Paul Edwards, in agreement with many contributors, sees a fusing of emotion and intellect in Stoppard's more recent work. In Stoppard's hands, "science should, through the sideways slant of its analogies, illuminate the human world, and . . . show it in a more . . . emotional light than could be achieved through more direct treatment." Inverting the usual association of science with abstract intellect, Edwards points to the powerful role played by analogy in Stoppard's science plays. The challenge in these plays, as Edwards expresses it, is to balance feeling and thinking, to convey the technical details of difficult theories in a way that reveals their human consequences. As a "deeply Romantic writer," Stoppard cannot articulate directly the "emotional heart of his plays." It must be "smuggled in" behind the "glittering surface where words and ideas are juggled by a master showman." *Hapgood*, Stoppard's attempt to demonstrate dramatically Richard Feynman's description of the dual nature of light (both particle and wave), failed to achieve critical or popular success. But its technical achievements, Edwards argues, paved the way for the triumph of *Arcadia*. The weakness of *Hapgood* – its remoteness from everyday life – is turned to advantage in *Arcadia*, set in a distant world of social privilege that blends with a contemporary world of struggling lovers.

Twinning and doubling take center stage in both plays, marking them as characteristically Stoppardian and linking them structurally and thematically to the earlier writing. Edwards builds for readers a scaffold of explanation sturdy enough to help us through the complexities of particle wave physics in *Hapgood* and chaos theory in *Arcadia* but not so heavy that it immobilizes us with information. If any Stoppard plays require reader supports, these do, and Edwards has constructed them with care. As an interpreter, he offers a persuasive reading of both plays, especially of the central role of death in *Arcadia*, the subject of the key phrase, "Et in Arcadia Ego." The "overcoming of time" at the play's conclusion is finally "a triumph of art, not of science, and like all such triumphs it is . . . the more poignant for being useless."

Extending what Edwards calls "Stoppard the Romantic," Hersh Zeifman's chapter, "Stoppard in Love," explores the erotics of *Arcadia* and *The Invention of Love*, dismissing critical clichés about the coldness of Stoppard's plays: "there was always an emotional pulse beating steadily beneath all that surface erudition and irony." In Zeifman's argument, Stoppard turned a corner with the *The Real Thing*, shedding inhibitions and opening his work to self-revelation. Joking that he had been a "repressed exhibitionist" in his younger days, Stoppard agreed, "The older I get, the less I care about self-concealment." And these are, as Zeifman illustrates, the plays of a mature artist. All of the themes and structural devices occupying the earlier works crystallize in these two plays, as doubling and twinning extend not only to characters but to action, theme, and chronology. In *Arcadia*, writes Zeifman (as *In the Native State*) love is heat; in *The Invention of Love*, it is ice. *Invention*, like *Travesties*, is a "memory play." *Arcadia* blends memory and desire through dancing as a metaphor for a world "without predictable pattern or meaning," but a world nevertheless transformed by love. *Invention*'s Housman, frozen in repressed desire, meets his opposite in Oscar Wilde, who dared to love. And in this way, the play shows us both halves of the Stoppard hero – the Romantic individualist celebrated (and punished) for his authenticity and the repressed Classicist refusing the chaos of feeling.

In Zeifman's reading, this play, above all, exposes Housman's refusal to love not only through the contrasting figure of Oscar Wilde but also by two poignant images, the first of Housman's beloved Mo running towards us in the distance but never getting any closer, and the other a replay of AEH's memory of his student days at Oxford, captured by a parodic scene in which "three men in a boat (one of them Mo) row into view, small dog yapping." This scene, duplicated from Jerome K. Jerome's comic novel by that title, triggers a very different response from similar moments of humorous parody in earlier plays. In line with the dominant tone of pathos and regret, the boat and its precious cargo provoke sadness and longing from the "half-alive" Housman. It is tempting to imagine the regret infusing *The Invention of Love* as an artistic transposing of Stoppard's yearning for his father: "I have nothing that came from my father," he wrote in the *Talk* memoir, "nothing he owned or touched, but here is his trace, a small scar."[2] Touching the hand of a woman whose wound had been stitched by his father, Stoppard recalls, "I am surprised by grief, a small catching-up of all the grief I owe." Without ceasing to be cerebral, Stoppard has constructed a world of feeling in his later plays that unites thought and emotion, comedy and tragedy.

Stoppard's audiences have shared this growth in expressive range. Enoch Brater's chapter, "Tom Stoppard's Brit/Lit/Crit" asks how the audience helps create the experience of the Stoppard play. Relying on spectators who are "with him all the way," Stoppard invites them to complete the comedy, whether it lies in a one-line joke or a dense allusion to other writing. In identifying those who seek out Stoppard's plays, Brater tells us what we already knew but frequently forget: his audience "is literate in precisely the same way that shares and appreciates and above all recognizes his telling points of reference . . . This is drama for the A-level and AP-English crowd . . . the same audience that knows [the] traditional canon backwards and forwards."

Brater gives a theatrically informed reading of Stoppard's literary borrowing. Beginning with *R&GAD*, he connects the subversions of textual parody with similar reversals in staging, arguing that "the geography of Stoppard's play" will scramble the traditional assignment of action to stage location. *Hamlet* is presented "in the distance," off stage and behind the scenes. Shakespeare's tragedy takes on the status of a play-within-the-play as its former bit players move to center stage. Brater argues that in recognizing Beckett's Didi and Gogo as the models for Rosencrantz and Guildenstern, the audience learns to "fill in the blanks" of Stoppard's play with the chilling context of Beckett's.

Reinforcing Zeifman's discussion of *The Real Thing* as a play transitioning into the world of feeling, Brater notes that this play draws on the literary past for both the intellectual and emotional resonance it carries for the spectators. *Arcadia's* double time scheme makes greater claims on and offers greater rewards to the audience "savvy enough to know that on stage things are never *then* and *now* but always and enigmatically *there*." Stoppard has consistently given the literate, middle-class spectator a role to play in completing his comedy. In some plays, like the overly complex *Hapgood*, he miscalculated that role. But Brater shows how, over time, his growth as a playwright has included a keener sense of how much and what kind of knowledge to expect of his audiences.

Michael Vanden Heuvel's chapter takes us further into the landscape of expectation surrounding Stoppard's plays – is it informed by modern or postmodern assumptions? Vanden Heuvel's answer ("both") has been prepared for repeatedly in chapters describing Stoppard the author and his plays as hybrid, as "double-visioned," as ambivalent, and divided. In Vanden Heuvel's view, Stoppard betrays a strong interest and sympathy for the aesthetic, ideological, and intellectual positions associated with postmodern art but remains indifferent to the radical claims of postmodern social theory. His plays defy an either/or logic in relation to postmodern ideas and aesthetics. On the one hand, he returns repeatedly to themes related to postmodernism's preoccupation with textual openness and the play of signifiers; on the other hand, he rejects the "postmodern" label for his work. His major plays both mimic and critique the "helter-skelter flow of capital, images, and signs that characterize late capitalism." Stoppard is well positioned to critique such conditions and their effects, argues Vanden Heuvel, living as he does in a period of late capitalism with its "fetishization of information, signs, and the circulation of images" that has invaded the contemporary world with theatricality. Stoppard's "hypertheatricality" coexists uneasily with his self-declared identity as a "moral" writer "unwilling to give himself completely over to the very ideas about which he writes so compellingly."

Resonating with the political assessments of the playwright offered by John Bull and Neil Sammells, Vanden Heuvel's argument nevertheless manages to demonstrate the complex and paradoxically unclassifiable nature of this conservative (small *c*), seriocomic writer. His success owes as much to Stoppard's "moderate position between the extremes of the so-called 'crises in the humanities' debates as it does to his talent for dialogue." Vanden Heuvel offers Stoppard as "living and theatrical proof that humanism and postmodernism, like classicism and romanticism, may . . . constitute and animate one another."

Whether we read Stoppard as a high modern or postmodern writer, his major plays from *R&GAD* to *The Invention of Love* set us temporarily in the imaginative space of Prospero's island, in a dream, a metaphor, and a true history all at once. In layering the textual and theatrical past with the present, Stoppard invites the spectator to undergo a transformation much like that of his texts and his characters – to discover that inside his plays other plays are "waiting to be revealed."

NOTES

My thanks to Susan Egenolf and Lynne Vallone for their close reading of this Introduction.

1 Tom Stoppard, *Indian Ink* (London and Boston: Faber and Faber 1995), p. 44.
2 Tom Stoppard, "On Turning out to be Jewish," *Talk* (September 1999), p. 241.

I
BACKGROUND

I

PAUL DELANEY

Exit Tomáš Straüssler, enter Sir Tom Stoppard

Tomáš Straüssler (Tomik to his parents) arrived in India as a four-year-old Czech refugee in 1942; but in early 1946 the eight-year-old who left India as Tommy Straüssler would become Tom Stoppard.[1] By then he had a new father, British Army Major Kenneth Stoppard, whom his mother had married after her husband had died in Singapore following the Japanese invasion. He had a new language, English, which he had learned at Mount Hermon, a Darjeeling school run by American Methodists. He had a new nationality – neither American nor Indian nor Czech but British. He had a new identity in a land where he and his brother would be "starting over as English schoolboys."[2] And he had a new name. Three weeks after arriving in England, the Straüssler brothers received, from their stepfather, the surname Stoppard.

After *Rosencrantz and Guildenstern Are Dead* opened to acclaim – and a welter of interpretations – both in London and on Broadway, its 29-year-old author would jokingly refer to himself as "a bounced Czech" and dismiss his biographical background as irrelevant to his play about Elizabethan courtiers. But to describe what it felt like to have his play examined for hidden meanings, the Czech émigré who had arrived from Singapore to attend an American school in India before relocating with a new name to Derbyshire significantly invoked the metaphor of going through customs. When a customs officer ransacks *Rosencrantz* and "comes up with all manner of exotic contraband like truth and illusion, the nature of identity, what I feel about life and death," Stoppard confesses, "I have to admit the stuff is there but I can't for the life of me remember packing it." Noting that "one is . . . the beneficiary and victim of one's subconscious: that is, of one's personal history, experience and environment," Stoppard pointed to his own identity as a concrete example of such a subconscious influence:

> My mother married again and my name was changed to my stepfather's when
> I was about eight years old. This I didn't care one way or the other about; but

then it occurred to me that in practically everything I had written there was something about people getting each other's names wrong, usually in a completely gratuitous way, nothing to do with character or plot.[3]

Over thirty years later, the 61-year-old author of *The Invention of Love* could look back on his career and say that he "could write an awfully good book about *The Plays of Tom Stoppard*! To me, it's so obvious. Many of my plays are about unidentical twins, about double acts. Twins, in *Hapgood*. There are the two Housmans here."[4] *The Invention of Love* shows us Housman as young and old, as poet and critic, as passionate lover and repressed celibate. *Hapgood* dramatizes the coolly professional buttoned-down title character and a woman who appears to be her raucous, impetuous twin in a play that uses quantum mechanics as a metaphor for the ineluctable duality of human personality. But Stoppard was also by this time the author of *Arcadia* in which romantic impetuosity and classical restraint are as interwoven in personal temperament as in poetry. Even *Rosencrantz and Guildenstern Are Dead* contains, in the contrast between its two title characters, a sense of the multiple possibilities of identity. "They both add up to me in many ways in the sense that they're carrying out a dialogue which I carry out with myself," Stoppard says. "One of them is fairly intellectual, fairly incisive; the other one is thicker, nicer in a curious way, more sympathetic. There's a leader and the led. Retrospectively, with all benefit of other people's comments and enthusiasms and so on, it just seems a classic case of self-revelation even though it isn't about this fellow who wrote his first novel."[5] Given the benefit of Stoppard's canon to date, we may see a classic case of self-revelation in his recurrent concern with unidentical twins, his pervasive sense that inside any self may be some other self waiting to be revealed.

Indeed, Stoppard talks about moving from Darjeeling to Derbyshire almost as the discovery of a new self. "I came here when I was eight," Stoppard says, "and I don't know why, I don't particularly wish to understand why but I just seized England and it seized me. Within minutes it seems to me, I had no sense of being in an alien land and my feelings for, my empathy for English landscape, English architecture, English character, all that, has just somehow become stronger and stronger."[6] The Czechoslovakia he never knew, the Singapore he could only dimly recall, the American school in Darjeeling where he had been "old enough to know it was not my natural surroundings,"[7] all receded. "As soon as we all landed up in England, I knew I had found a home," Stoppard says, "I embraced the language and the landscape."[8]

After settling in Derbyshire, Stoppard attended the Dolphin School in Nottinghamshire and then the Pocklington School in Yorkshire. Although he says he has often dreamed of India, his prep school years are associated with feeling "depressed, longing for the holidays, and a bit homesick, usually to do with the severity of one or two of the teachers."[9] In *Arcadia*, Stoppard would depict a sixteen-year-old whose love for learning leads her to grieve the loss of the library at Alexandria and to question the Newtonian model of the universe. But when he was that age, Stoppard couldn't wait to abandon academe. "The chief influence of my education on me was negative," Stoppard says. "I left school thoroughly bored by the idea of anything intellectual . . . I'd been totally bored and alienated by everyone from Shakespeare to Dickens besides."[10] Leaving school age seventeen after completing O-levels in Greek and Latin, Stoppard got a job as a reporter on the *Western Daily Press* in Bristol, where his family was then living. "When I left school," Stoppard says, "I wanted to be a great journalist. My first ambition was to be lying on the floor of an African airport while machine-gun bullets zoomed over my typewriter."[11] Stoppard's fascination with journalism would eventually find its way into his 1978 play *Night and Day*, dealing with British newspapermen facing bullets while on assignment in Africa.

In the meantime, Stoppard was discovering theatre. As a prep school student, he had been taken to see Laurence Olivier's film of *Hamlet* (1948) and was "very bored . . . It didn't seem to be a very exciting film, until they got to the swordfight."[12] But while working as a journalist, Stoppard started attending productions at the Bristol Old Vic. In 1958 the 24-year-old Peter O'Toole's performance as Hamlet "had a tremendous effect on me," Stoppard says. "It was everything it was supposed to be. It was exciting and mysterious and eloquent. I used to dash back from evening jobs, or rather get the reporter on the rival newspaper to cover for me, to catch the end of it."[13] Although he had been serving as a second-string theatre critic throughout his stint as a journalist, by 1960 Stoppard had decided he wanted to write for the theatre. Besides his own fascination with O'Toole's Hamlet, the theatre was a center of intellectual ferment in Britain. Peter Hall directed the first British production of Samuel Beckett's *Waiting for Godot* in 1955 and was about to found the Royal Shakespeare Company; John Osborne's *Look Back in Anger* was staged at the Royal Court in 1956 followed by a London visit of Bertolt Brecht's Berliner Ensemble; and Kenneth Tynan was churning the intellectual waters in his capacity as drama critic for the *Observer*. "After 1956 everybody of my age who wanted to write, wanted to write plays," says Stoppard. In the summer of 1960 while on holiday in Capri to celebrate his twenty-third birthday, Stoppard was struck with the sense "that

I was never going to start writing unless I did something active about it." When he returned, he handed in his notice, making sure he had two weekly columns to pay for room and board while he wrote his first play, *A Walk on the Water*. "I was working in a sort of panic because," Stoppard says, "it seemed incredibly important that I hadn't done any of the things by the age of 23 that I'd intended doing by the age of 21; so I was doing everything two years late, and really had to get down to it."[14]

Although *A Walk on the Water* would eventually be televised, the play's greatest significance for Stoppard was that it brought him to the attention of Kenneth Ewing, who has continued as Stoppard's agent throughout his career. After sending Ewing his play, Stoppard received "one of those Hollywood-style telegrams that change struggling young artists' lives,"[15] though it would be three years before the play was produced. Meanwhile, he applied for a job on a new London magazine called *Scene* and to his amazement was offered the position of theatre critic. He moved to London and reviewed dozens of shows during the seven months of the magazine's existence. When the chronically underfunded magazine could not pay its writers, Stoppard borrowed money from friends and went fly-fishing in Scotland. Back in London, he lived a hand-to-mouth existence, borrowing money from Ewing because his bank account was, perpetually, overdrawn. But even in those days, Ewing says, Stoppard "always travelled by taxi, never by bus. It was as if he knew that his time would come."[16] In the summer of 1963, Stoppard sold *A Walk on the Water* to ITV for £350 and went on a ten-week holiday in the Mediterranean with his girlfriend Isabel Dunjohn. But by fall a penniless Stoppard was considering hack work on the *TV Times*. *A Walk on the Water* was filmed in November to be Play of the Week in March; but in late November Stoppard received a call saying the play would be aired that night – with no advance publicity – to replace a play deemed inappropriate so soon after President Kennedy's assassination. *A Walk on the Water* sank without a trace. Stoppard continued to pound out unproduced scripts for television plays and one-acts for BBC Radio.

Then came "the idea." On a ride back from an unsuccessful attempt to pitch one of Stoppard's efforts, a sixty-minute television play called *I Can't Give You Anything But Love, Baby*, Ewing and Stoppard were talking about a production of *Hamlet* at the Old Vic.[17] "[Ewing] said there was a play to be written about Rosencrantz and Guildenstern after they got to England," says Stoppard. "What happened to them once they got there? I was attracted to it immediately."[18] Ewing mused aloud that the two courtiers might have found King Lear on the throne, raving mad at Dover. In 1964 while in Berlin on a Ford Foundation grant, Stoppard wrote *Rosencrantz and Guildenstern*

Meet King Lear, a one-act play in which Hamlet and the Player change identities on the boat and "the Player is captured by Pirates and goes off to fulfill
Hamlet's role in the rest of Shakespeare's play."[19] Years later Stoppard would
write a screenplay about Shakespeare as a penniless writer trying to come up
with a plot for "Romeo and Ethel, the Pirate's Daughter." Clearly, Stoppard
can identify with a penniless young writer struggling with pirates.

Stoppard can also identify with a penniless young writer struggling with
love. Before leaving for Germany on the Ford Foundation grant, he had
become romantically involved with Jose Ingle. While Stoppard in Germany
had Rosencrantz and Guildenstern at sea bound for England, he was debating where to disembark upon his own return to England. Should he return
to London as Jose wished or to Bristol where he could live more cheaply and
"write like a madman till April"[20] to fulfill a contract for a novel (eventually
Lord Malquist and Mr Moon). Although the relationship with Jose seemed
more fully formed in her mind than in his, Stoppard returned to London in
October 1964, took a flat with two other Ford fellows, and instead of
writing like a madman till April, married Jose on 26 March 1965.

In May the Royal Shakespeare Company took a year's option on
Stoppard's play about Rosencrantz and Guildenstern which then existed in
a two-act version. With high hopes Stoppard wrote a third act as requested.
But a year later the RSC returned Stoppard's script, leaving Rosencrantz and
Guildenstern as much at sea as ever. Meanwhile the newly wed Stoppard was
attempting to make ends meet by writing five fifteen-minute episodes each
week for a BBC World Service serial – broadcast in Arabic – about the experiences of a Palestinian medical student in London. Although critics have
repeated Kenneth Tynan's assertion that none of the scripts survive, tran-
scripts of "A Student's Diary" are preserved on microfilm at the BBC Written
Archives Centre. In the first, the announcer introduces Amin Osman crossing the English Channel "on his way to London with high hopes of being
accepted as a medical student." For a young man anticipating "a new
country" with "new experiences," the announcer intones, "the prospect is
exciting":

> ANNOUNCER. So as the boat ploughs through the twenty-two stormy miles
> between Calais and Dover, one might well guess Amin's emotions . . . which,
> as it happens, can be expressed in a single sentence . . .
> AMIN. (*with measured deliberation*) I think I'm going to be sick.[21]

For Amin or for Rosencrantz as for Tomáš all boats seem bound for England.
A month after Amin's arrival in England was broadcast on 3 April 1966,
Stoppard's son Oliver was born. When the RSC and the Royal Court both

rejected *Rosencrantz and Guildenstern Are Dead*, Ewing sent the play to the Oxford Playhouse which passed the script to undergraduates looking for something to perform on the Edinburgh Festival Fringe. Ewing reluctantly agreed to allow the amateur production to proceed. When Stoppard went to Edinburgh in August he found "a stage the size of a ping pong table"[22] for a production panned by the *Scotsman* and the *Scottish Daily Express* (in a review headlined "What's It All About Tom?"[23]). Then Ronald Bryden's review in the *Observer* hailed *Rosencrantz* as an "erudite comedy, punning, far-fetched, leaping from depth to dizziness" that was "the most brilliant debut by a young playwright since John Arden's."[24] After reading Bryden's review, Kenneth Tynan, then literary manager for the National Theatre, cabled Stoppard to request a copy of the script. The National asked for a fortnight to decide and paid £50 for a six months' option, while saying they might not be able to schedule the play until October 1967 (and Stoppard worried that *Rosencrantz and Guildenstern* could be dead if a play of greater interest came along in the meanwhile).

Negotiating to publish the play and fielding inquiries from several countries regarding possible productions, Stoppard remained beseiged by creditors and continued to write installments of his Arab serial for the BBC. Going home one day, he threw himself once again on the mercy of his agent, who agreed to loan Stoppard £40. The heretofore penniless playwright "turned right around and hailed a taxi," Ewing says, "I went home on a bus."[25] Cancellation of a production of *As You Like It* meant Rosencrantz and Guildenstern could tread the boards of the Old Vic in April 1967, making Stoppard the youngest playwright to have a play performed by the National Theatre. Harold Hobson hailed the production as "the most important event in the British professional theatre of the last nine years,"[26] that is, since the London debut of Harold Pinter. On the South Bank of the Thames, Stoppard's ship had come in. In October, Rosencrantz and Guildenstern disembarked once more, landing on Broadway as the first National Theatre production to transfer to New York. The play by a previously unknown 29-year-old would win the Tony award for best play of the year on Broadway.

After the triumph of *Rosencrantz*, it was a foregone conclusion that the National Theatre would produce Stoppard's next play unless he completely lost his way. But after *Rosencrantz* lifted the pressure of achieving success, Stoppard began to feel the pressure of not being a one-hit wonder. Although he turned out superbly crafted entertainments like *The Real Inspector Hound* along with radio plays and short pieces, his next major play, *Jumpers*, would not be staged until five years after *Rosencrantz*. Stoppard's second son, Barnaby, was born in September 1969; but all was not well at home. Overshadowed by Stoppard's international acclaim, Jose had a nervous breakdown. "In her cups, she would tell Tom's friends how she had really written *Rosencrantz and Guildenstern*," a friend would say years later. "And all the time, Tom was behaving with a kind of chivalric constancy. His friends were throwing up their hands because he was spending all his time looking after the children and doing the washing up. Then came the time when he decided it was over, at which point he behaved with a kind of frightening clarity, taking the two kids with him and setting up a new home with Miriam."[27]

Stoppard left Jose in December 1969; began divorce and custody proceedings in early 1970; and, with his two sons, moved in with Dr. Miriam Moore-Robinson in August 1970. Stoppard's divorce was not granted until January 1972; he married Miriam on 11 February; and their first son, William, was born on 7 March 1972. The couple would have a second son, Edmund, born 16 September 1974, and would rear all four boys throughout two decades together as a family. Besides being a medical doctor, Miriam Stoppard became a television personality (whose fame with the British public exceeded her husband's), and the author of numerous books of advice on health care, beauty, and sexual issues. With two high-flying careers, the Stoppards purchased a large Victorian house in Iver Heath and then Iver Grove, a Georgian mansion set on seventeen acres in Iver. Stoppard seemed to thrive not only on the life of the country squire but also on the stability of his family life. He would write in the afternoons or late at night so he could be with his children when they got home from school.

In the meanwhile, *Jumpers*, which opened at the National Theatre during the same fortnight that Stoppard divorced Jose and married Miriam, introduced Stoppard to what would become a long-term theatrical partnership with the director Peter Wood. Wood was reluctant to direct *Jumpers*, saying he "was a little affronted by the play" because his Catholicism "at first made me question its facetiousness about belief."[28] In fact, in creating *Jumpers* – the play Kenneth Tynan described as "a farce whose main purpose is to affirm the existence of God"[29] – Stoppard says, "I wanted to write a theist play, to combat the arrogant view that anyone who believes in God is some kind of cripple, using God as a crutch."[30] But while Stoppard wanted to write "about a man who really believed that good and bad were absolute moral truths," he acknowledges that such "internal subject matter" in *Jumpers* had "so much mayonnaise on it that it was very hard to taste the roast beef at all."[31] With bursts of flashing lights, a trapeze striptease, the projection of televised images onto a gargantuan screen, and a concluding musical number that might bring down the house in Las Vegas, *Jumpers* offered lots of mayonnaise. But Wood and Stoppard found they quite enjoyed working together and would share numerous theatrical roast beef sandwiches over the years. Stoppard would turn to Wood to direct *Travesties* (in London and New York), *Night and Day* (in London and New York), *The Real Thing, Rough Crossing*, a 1985 West End revival of *Jumpers, Dalliance, Hapgood* (in London and Los Angeles), *The Dog It Was That Died*, and *Indian Ink*. The playwright would attend virtually all rehearsals. Stoppard wanted to let audiences have the satisfaction of figuring out some things for themselves; Wood wanted audiences to understand what was going on even if they had to be told. Between the playwright's reluctance to be overly obvious and the director's concern about being overly obscure, the two formed a complementary team.

But Stoppard also took on challenges from the sheer insatiable desire to do the impossible. "You see, ultimately, before being carried out feet first, I would like to have done a bit of absolutely everything," Stoppard says. "Really, without any evidence of any talent in those other directions, I find it very hard to turn down offers to write an underwater ballet for dolphins or a play for a motorcyclist on the wall of death."[32] Thus when conductor André Previn asked if Stoppard might want to write a play that included a symphony orchestra, it was an offer the playwright couldn't refuse. *Every Good Boy Deserves Favour* began as a play about a Florida grapefruit millionaire who owned an orchestra. But about the time Stoppard realized the symphony could be in the mind of his protagonist, he was meeting with political prisoners who had been confined in Soviet psychiatric hospitals for their political beliefs. By the time *Every Good Boy* was performed, the play had been transposed to a Soviet psychiatric hospital where a prisoner of political conscience is confined alongside a patient whose psychiatric symptoms consist of believing he has a symphony orchestra. *Every Good Boy* was a fantasia compared to the realistic format of *Professional Foul* televised later in 1977. But in both, Stoppard was dealing more directly with overtly political issues as he would in *Night and Day* (1978), *Dogg's Hamlet, Cahoot's Macbeth* (1979) and *Squaring the Circle* (1984). Besides the new emphasis in his plays, Stoppard was also speaking out against Soviet abuse of Jewish dissidents, Czech violations of human rights, and limitations on journalists' freedom of expression in Britain. However, he pointed to thematic continuities between his so-called "political plays" and his earlier work, insisting that despite their differences in form, both *Professional Foul* and *Jumpers* address themselves to the same moral questions: "Both are about the way human beings are supposed to behave towards each other."[33]

Besides thematic connections, Stoppard's involvement in an array of projects shows other continuities, one of which is simply how much he enjoys working with a coterie of people on the task of mounting a production. "Rehearsing a play is more or less the best time in my life," Stoppard says, adding that by the end of the process "you're sort of a family of a kind." Besides Stoppard's partnership with Wood as director and Carl Toms as designer, such actors as Michael Hordern, Diana Rigg, John Wood, and Roger Rees show up again and again in Stoppard plays. "By the time you open a play you are very close to the people you're working with," says Stoppard, "even the ones you've never met before." [34]

In the course of one such job, Stoppard's adapation of a Nestroy play as *On the Razzle* (1981), another actor would join Stoppard's theatrical team. Years later in his screenplay for *Shakespeare in Love*, Stoppard would show the already married Shakespeare falling in love with a young woman named Viola who would become the muse of his plays after an inauspicious first meeting in which she is dressed in male attire attempting to pass herself off in the theatre as a boy. After joining the coterie of Stoppardian actors, Felicity Kendal would eventually become the playwright's companion, the leading lady of his casts, and the one whose evocation of such characters as Flora Crewe, Hapgood and Hannah Jarvis would lead some to describe her as his muse. But his first association with Kendal was in *On the Razzle* where the already married Stoppard encountered a pert actress with an alluringly husky voice who, a year after appearing in the BBC *Twelfth Night* as Viola, was in male attire attempting once again to pass herself off in the theatre as a boy, in a "dogsbody" role as the stock clerk Christopher.

A year later Kendal would star in Stoppard's *The Real Thing*, dedicated to his wife, about an adulterous relationship between a playwright and an actress whom he met "in this poncy business" of theatre. Kendal – who married the Jewish, Texas-born theatrical director Michael Rudman in 1983 – had become Stoppard's leading lady on stage although it would be some while before life would imitate art. Stoppard revised *Jumpers* for a spectacular 1985 West End revival with Kendal as a striking Dotty. Although he wrote *Hapgood* with Kendal in mind, cast members were amazed when Stoppard delayed the production for six months so she could play the title role after giving birth. Kendal was divorced in late February 1991 and Stoppard in February 1992. But by November 1990 the two were linked romantically in a relationship that would continue for eight years. Recorded in early February 1991, Stoppard's radio play *In the Native State* – dedicated "For Felicity Kendal" who starred as Flora Crewe – seemed in some ways to be not only for and by but also about Kendal.

In the Native State deals with India, where Stoppard and Kendal spent their childhoods, and focuses on the free-spirited Flora Crewe who scandalizes prim Brits and Indian Anglophiles with her delight in native Indian art and interest in the *rasa* of erotic love. Although the play as performed contains only brief excerpts of Flora Crewe's poetry, Stoppard says completion of *In the Native State* was delayed because he became so caught up in writing the young woman's sensual poetry. The next major project Stoppard turned to, shortly after becoming romantically involved with Felicity Kendal, was a screenplay called *Shakespeare in Love*. With the sets already built and filming set to begin in October 1992, the production was cancelled when Julia Roberts withdrew from the cast, delaying the film by six years.

In the meanwhile Stoppard had completed *Arcadia*, the stage play that may well be his masterpiece. Opening at the National Theatre in April 1993 with a well-balanced ensemble, *Arcadia* would win both the *Evening Standard* and Olivier awards for best play of the year. It would run for two years, eventually transferring to the West End two months after a major RSC revival of *Travesties* starring Antony Sher also transferred to the West End. With *Arcadia* still running, Stoppard opened *Indian Ink* (1995), a stage adaptation of *In the Native State* that again starred Felicity Kendal as Flora Crewe. As Irina Arkadina in Stoppard's translation of Chekhov's *The Seagull* (May 1997), Kendal would make her eighth appearance in a Stoppard production.

On 12 December 1997, Stoppard went to Buckingham Palace to be knighted, the first playwright thus honored since Sir Terence Rattigan in 1971. Since Stoppard had been Tomáš and Tom but never Thomas, the newly dubbed knight of the realm would, as the leading article in *The Times* put it, "Arise, Sir Tom."[35] As he arose, the sixty-year-old knight's thoughts were of coming to Britain as an eight year old. "I was instantly proud," said Stoppard. "I have felt English almost from the day I arrived, but the knighthood puts some kind of seal on that emotion." His one regret was that his mother had died a year earlier: "She would have liked it very much."[36]

Sir Tom did not mention the more recent death of his stepfather who, as an Anglophile, might have been expected to take pride in a Stoppardian knighthood. During the last years of his mother's life, however, the playwright had been discovering more of his background than his mother had ever revealed. From a Czech relative, Stoppard learned that rather than having one Jewish grandparent as he had supposed, he had four Jewish grandparents, all of whom had died at the hands of Nazis, that both his father and mother had been Jewish, and that he had three aunts whom he had never heard of who died in concentration camps. Titling a 1999 article "On Turning Out To Be Jewish," the 62-year-old Stoppard discloses some wonderment at his altered sense of self. He talks about his state of mind "now that I'm Jewish," and a sentence that begins "before I was Jewish"[37] expresses not religious conversion but a certain amazement at who, after six decades, he turns out to be. His recovery of his Straüssler Jewish past became all the more poignant when he was asked to return what he had supposed for half a century to be his for life. A few days after his mother died, Stoppard says his stepfather "wrote to me to say that he had been concerned for some time about my 'tribalization,' by which he meant mainly my association, 10 years earlier, with the cause of Russian Jews, and he asked me to stop using 'Stoppard' as my name."[38]

From Tomáš Straüssler, Czech émigré, to Sir Tom Stoppard, one of the greatest playwrights in the English language, covers a territory almost too vast to span in one lifetime. But *Shakespeare in Love* would remind us of the inexplicable distance between juvenilia and genius. Indeed, the journey from "Romeo and Ethel, the Pirate's Daughter" to *Romeo and Juliet* is scarcely less plausible than the journey from "Rosencrantz and Guildenstern Meet King Lear" to *Arcadia*. In Stoppard's screenplay for *Shakespeare in Love*, which won seven Academy Awards, the experience of Shakespeare as lover and Shakespeare as playwright intersect as the off-stage world and the onstage world reflect and inform each other in a swirling kaleidoscope. In Stoppard's career the reflections and intersections of life and art also form a swirling kaleidoscope as he has doubled and redoubled his explorations of double acts. From Tomáš or Tomik to Tommy to Tom and then Sir Tom; from Straüssler to Stoppard and then, if his step-father had had his way, back to Straüssler; from Czech to British while belatedly "turning out to be Jewish," Tom Stoppard turns out to be his own unidentical twin in a way he could not have imagined. Or, to rephrase that, the playwright who throughout his career had written about unidentical twins, about double acts, turns out to be his own unidentical twin in a way he had *always* imagined.

NOTES

1 Tom Stoppard, "On Turning Out to be Jewish," *Talk* (September 1999), p. 243.
2 Tom Stoppard, "Going Back," *Independent Magazine*, 23 March 1991, p. 29.
3 Tom Stoppard, "Something to Declare," *Sunday Times*, 25 February 1968, p. 47.
4 Alastair Macaulay, "The Man Who Was Two Men," *Financial Times*, 31 October 1998, p. 7.

5 Giles Gordon, "Tom Stoppard," *Transatlantic Review*, 29 (summer 1968), reprinted in Paul Delaney, ed., *Tom Stoppard in Conversation* (Ann Arbor: University of Michigan Press, 1994), p. 19.

6 Paul Allen, *Third Ear*, BBC Radio Three, 16 April 1991, reprinted in Delaney, ed., *Stoppard in Conversation*, p. 246.

7 Michael Pye, "A Very English Kind of Celebrity," *Daily Telegraph*, 31 March 1995, p. 25.

8 Diana Maychick, "Stoppard Ascending," *New York Post*, 26 November 1989, reprinted in Delaney, ed., *Stoppard in Conversation*, p. 233.

9 Mel Gussow, *Conversations with Tom Stoppard* (London: Nick Hern, 1995), p. 132.

10 Roger Hudson, Catherine Itzin and Simon Trussler, "Ambushes for the Audience," *Theatre Quarterly* 4 (May 1974), reprinted in Delaney, ed., *Stoppard in Conversation*, p. 53.

11 Jon Bradshaw, "Tom Stoppard, Nonstop," *New York*, 10 January 1977, reprinted in Delaney, ed., *Stoppard in Conversation*, p. 91.

12 Jasper Rees, "'So, Mr. Stoppard, What Is Your New Play About?,'" *Independent*, 2 December 1995, p. 3.

13 Ibid.

14 Hudson, "Ambushes," p. 54.

15 Ibid., p. 55.

16 Kenneth Tynan, *Show People: Profiles in Entertainment* (New York: Simon and Schuster, 1979), p. 66.

17 John Patrick Fleming, "Defining Stoppard," Ph.D. dissertation, University of Texas at Austin, 1996, p. 58; Hudson, "Ambushes," pp. 56–57; Bradshaw, "Tom Stoppard, Nonstop," p. 94.

18 Bradshaw, "Tom Stoppard, Nonstop," p. 94.

19 Stoppard quoted by Fleming, "Defining Stoppard," p. 72.

20 Stoppard quoted by Fleming, ibid., p. 70.

21 Tom Stoppard, *A Student's Diary: Episode 1*, BBC World Service, 3 April 1966, p. 1. Transcript: BBC Written Archives Centre.

22 Gordon, "Tom Stoppard," p. 17.

23 Colin Donald, "On the Dazzle," *Scotsman*, 5 November 1996, p. 18.

24 Ronald Bryden, "Wyndy Excitements," *Observer*, 28 August 1966, p. 15.

25 Stephen Schiff, "Full Stoppard," *Vanity Fair*, 52.5 (May 1989), reprinted in Delaney, ed., *Stoppard in Conversation*, p. 219.

26 Harold Hobson, "A Fearful Summons," *Sunday Times*, 16 April 1967, p. 49.

27 Schiff, "Full Stoppard," p. 220.

28 Peter Lewis, "Doubles Match That's Lasted 20 Years," *Sunday Telegraph*, 12 February 1995, p. 6.

29 Tynan, *Show People*, p. 93.

30 Oleg Kerensky, *The New British Drama* (London: Hamish Hamilton, 1977), p. 170.

31 Melvyn Bragg, *The South Bank Show*, London Weekend Television, 26 November 1978, reprinted in Delaney, ed., *Stoppard in Conversation*, p. 121.

32 Bradshaw, "Tom Stoppard, Nonstop," p. 98.

33 Hugh Hebert, "A Playwright in Undiscovered Country," *Guardian*, 7 July 1979, reprinted in Delaney, ed., *Stoppard in Conversation*, p. 127.

34 Bragg, *The South Bank Show*, pp. 118, 119.
35 "Arise, Sir Tom," *The Times*, 13 December 1997, p. 23.
36 Robin Young, "Wood and Stoppard Honoured at Palace," *The Times*, 13 December 1997.
37 Stoppard, "On Turning Out To Be Jewish," p. 241.
38 Ibid., p. 243.

2

JOSEPHINE LEE

In the Native State and *Indian Ink*

Stoppard has long demonstrated a certain interest in dramatizing political and cultural differences. Plays such as *Professional Foul, Every Good Boy Deserves Favour*, and *Hapgood* play off the Cold War politics of Eastern Europe (Czechoslovakia and the former Soviet Union in the 1970s and 1980s), as do shorter plays such as *The Dog It Was That Died* and *Cahoot's Macbeth*. Significantly, the delineation of cultural differences in these plays is mainly subordinated to discussion of the repression and censorship of the artist or writer as individual. These plays emphasize the perspectives of English characters in these exotic settings or mark non-English characters as decidedly "foreign," sometimes picturing, as in *Every Good Boy Deserves Favour*, repressive situations in ways that ultimately foster a sense of English nationalism. *Night and Day* (1978) might serve as a good example. Set in a volatile political situation in Kambawe, a "fictitious African country, formerly a British colony" (p. ix), it focuses mainly on the personal and professional dilemmas of veteran journalist Dick Wagner, photographer George Guthrie, idealistic young reporter Jacob Milne, mine owner Geoffrey Carson and his bored wife Ruth, these taking precedence over any psychological development of the African characters. The second act appearance of President Mageeba promises an interesting characterization; in an interview with Wagner, the British-educated Mageeba articulately delivers his perspectives on his country's postcolonial politics and the role of the press. However, this conversation soon comes to an end. Mageeba reveals the danger barely concealed by this well-spoken exterior as he suddenly strikes Wagner; the interview ends entirely when Guthrie enters bringing news of Milne's violent death in military crossfire. Mageeba's presence ultimately serves only to establish the degree of uncertainty suffered by the English and Australian journalists and expatriates.

But the 1991 radio play *In the Native State* and the 1995 stage play *Indian Ink* seem to mark a change in the way Stoppard writes about culture, power, and difference. Although the plays do emphasize the perspective of the

British characters, at the same time there seems to be a concerted effort to create Indian characters who are more fully developed. Stoppard integrates dramatic tropes and devices familiar from his other plays – a fascination with the politics of art, an interest in language games and debates, a gradual revelation of the past by characters operating in the present as "detectives" – into a more sustained effort to explore "the ethics of empire,"[1] the colonial interaction between England and India.

In the Native State charts the visit in 1930 of poet Flora Crewe to Jummapur, one of the "native states" still governed by Indian royalty in collaboration with British rule. On a speaking tour of India, where she lectures on "Literary Life in London," Flora writes a series of poems and letters to her sister while having her portrait painted by Nirad Das, a local artist and literati. The free-spirited Flora meets a number of men who take an interest in her, including local British military officer David Durance and the Harrow-educated Rajah; yet it is Das with whom she has the most intense romantic relationship. Das draws Flora both in an unfinished "official" portrait and in the nude. These are the only surviving pictures of Flora, who dies on her Indian excursion later that year.

This plot is paralleled with a set of dialogues taking place in the mid-1980s: a teatime conversation between Das's son Anish and Flora's now-elderly sister, Mrs. Swan. Flora's poetry has attracted the attention of feminist scholars. One in particular, a would-be biographer, places the "official" portrait of Flora on the cover of a published volume of her letters. Anish Das, an artist educated and living in England, sees the book and recognizes the unidentified woman whose nude portrait he has inherited from his dead father.

Indian Ink makes a number of significant additions to the radio version. Stoppard plays up the mystery of Das's relationship with Flora as well as elaborating on the nature of his later political imprisonment. Stoppard also expands the role of the over-eager American scholar, Eldon Pike, whose attempts to find out the nature of Das's portrait lead him to India. The stage play ends as the radio play does, with a flashback to the young Mrs. Swan's visit to Flora's grave, where she meets her future husband; and a quotation from Emily Eden's 1866 account of her travels in India, *Up the Country*.

One way to read the play is as another of Stoppard's dramatized debates. A series of positions on the "ethics of empire" and the colonial history of India can be traced, beginning with the conflicting perspectives articulated by Anish Das and Mrs. Swan. Anish's heroic romanticization of the struggle for Indian nationhood and independence is juxtaposed with Mrs. Swan's insistence that "We made you a proper country! And when we left you fell straight to pieces like Humpty Dumpty!"[2] Likewise, the events of 1930 in Jummapur also provide a forum for various reflections on dimensions of colonialism.

Here Stoppard turns his preoccupation with artist characters to draw attention to the cultural dimensions of British imperialism, questioning how British rule imposed English education, arts, and language upon an already vigorous culture and established civilization. This long history of linguistic and cultural indoctrination can be seen in the numerous "Anglicized" Indian characters who idolize English literature, paint in oils, and collect European cars and furniture. Stoppard describes Das as "the Indian who loves things English – literature and his references are English and he obviously is in a kind of thrall to English culture."[3] Lord William Bentick's acceptance of Thomas Macaulay's infamous 1835 "Minute," arguing for the education of Indians in English, helped institute an educational system in India whose lasting effects are noted by Dilip in *Indian Ink*: "Yes, it's a disaster for us! Fifty years of Independence and we are still hypnotized! Jackets and ties must be worn! English-model public schools for the children of the elite, and the voice of Bush House is heard in the land" (*Indian Ink*, p. 59). Das tells Flora that "the bloody Empire finished off Indian painting!" (*Indian Ink*, p. 44); significantly, fifty years later his son, trained in London, doesn't consider himself a "particularly Indian" painter (*In the Native State*, p. 3; *Indian Ink*, p. 14).

The economic forces underlying Britain's colonization of India also enter into Stoppard's dramatic discussion. India's colonization had its formal beginnings in 1600 with the formation of the British East India Company, a monopoly of London merchants given exclusive trading rights by Queen Elizabeth I; their influence expanded through the subsequent two centuries as the power of the Mughal emperors declined. The underpinnings of colonial enterprise, V. I. Lenin insists in his *Imperialism, the Highest Stage of Capitalism* (1916), have all to do with the increasing need for natural resources and labor in the capitalistic expansion of modern industrial European nations. Furthermore, although imperial nations introduced the imperatives of industrialization, modernization, and capitalism to their colonies, they did not encourage indigenous enterprise nor did they foster the future capacity to compete in a modern industrial environment. These colonies remained underdeveloped even as they were modernized, in many cases continuing their dependence on foreign capital even after their later independence. Both of these dimensions of Indian colonization are stressed in the play. Das mentions Mr. Chamberlain's lecture on industrial England's exploitation of India's resources: "The women here wear saris made in Lancashire. The cotton is Indian but we cannot compete in the weaving" (*Indian Ink*, p. 44). Mr. Coomaraswami's criticisms of empire argue Britain's failure to follow through on the modernization of India: "'Where are the cotton mills? The steel mills? No investment, no planning. The Empire has failed us!'" (*Indian Ink*, p. 44).

Indian colonization is not just a matter of the forceful imposition of military rule and the institutionalization of economic and cultural hierarchies. It involves the appropriation of an already-existing Indian feudalism. In 1858, following the Indian Mutiny, the East India Company was dissolved, and its powers handed over to the crown. Moreover, the 1858 proclamation protected the hereditary power of native princes in exchange for their complicity with British rule. The proclamation pledged to respect "the rights, dignity and honour of native Princes" and "the feelings of attachment with which the natives of India regard the lands inherited by them from their ancestors." It also promised "to protect them in all rights" and to pay "due regard" "in framing and administering the law . . . to the ancient rights, usages and customs of India."[4] This strategy was calculated to preserve a semblance of self-government and thus divide political opposition to British rule. Gail Ching-Liang Low notes that "Saxon domination," as Lord Canning, the first viceroy of India, put it, "required the cooperation of sections of the Indian public in order to ensure its uninterrupted rule"; in his words,

> I believe there is but one way of meeting this danger, and that is to bring the influential classes – the native states first and afterwards our own chief subjects – into that condition and temper in which, when the moment comes, we may as completely as possible throw the reins on their necks and entrust to them the keeping of internal peace and order.[5]

Stoppard's choice to focus on one of the "native states" allows him to examine how well this tactic worked, particularly in the plays' depiction of the Rajah's guarded, yet still symbiotic, relationship with the Residency. It is the Rajah who suppresses dissent from nationalists, and fears that independence will mean the end of both the native states, and the "end of the unity of the subcontinent" (*Indian Ink*, p. 61).

This background allows Stoppard to dramatize a debate on colonial history, where characters provide a series of cogent arguments. The English Durance supports the idea of colonialism as benevolent paternal rule, imagining English and Indians in a relationship of peaceful coexistence and mutual respect. He supports "Indianization," the transition to self-rule that nonetheless preserves the existing social hierarchy; he notes, for instance, that Brahmins and other members of the Indian ruling classes will gradually inherit more powerful positions. Others such as Flora have a much more critical stance on British rule: "(i)t beats me how we're getting away with it, darling, I wouldn't trust some of them to run the *Hackney* Empire" (*Indian Ink*, p. 51). A largely implicit yet significant voice in the discussion can be heard through the references to the emerging nationalism that was to result in independence in 1947: the 1857 Indian Mutiny; Indian-led nationalist and independence movements, such as the nonviolent civil disobedience campaigns led by Mahatma Gandhi; as well as the many instances of local protest and unrest in the first half of the twentieth century, such as that in which Das presumably participates after his affair with Flora.

Stoppard weaves this historical background and its interpretation into more subtle aspects of his theatre. Both *In the Native State* and *Indian Ink* raise questions about colonialism and culture not only through dramatic debate but also through the creation of particular characterizations and imaginary spaces. In a 1991 interview, Stoppard made a telling comment about the challenges of writing *In the Native State*:

> the difficulty, particularly in this decade by the way, is not to write Indians who sound like Indians, which is hard enough, but to avoid writing characters who appear to have already appeared in *The Jewel in the Crown* and *Passage to India*. I mean the whole Anglo-Indian world has been so raked over and presented and re-presented by quite a small company of actors who appear in all of them . . . and so I mean there is this slight embarrassment about actually not really knowing much about how to write an Indian character and really merely mimicking the Indian characters in other people's work. Because my own memory of living in India really hasn't been that much help because my conscious knowledge of how Indians speak and behave has actually been derived from other people's fictions.
>
> (Allen in Delaney, ed., *Stoppard in Conversation*, pp. 242–243)

What Stoppard seems to be indicating here is not only the problem of writing believable characters from a different cultural background but also the degree to which these characters – particularly given his method of writing – are always already established in overdetermined ways, influenced by the pervasive images appearing in novels, television, and film. His worry that the discourse, the field of representation, has been saturated by certain images, thus preventing access to a more "authentically Indian" characterization, is quite different from his apparently rather casual acceptance of stereotypes in his earlier work ("What I like to do is take a stereotype and betray it, rather than create an original character. I never try to invent characters. All my best characters are clichés").[6] This negotiation of cultural clichés becomes a key question for Stoppard, for whom the "real" India is inseparable from the fictions influenced by the history of power and representation.

Thus to understand *In the Native State* and *Indian Ink*, one must think about a set of images and characterizations to which Stoppard is – consciously or not – responding, as well as whether or not he ultimately "betrays" these types. Such powerful images – which define an extensive field of representation – indicate, express, and disseminate deeper values of cultural self-definition. Stoppard spent several years of his childhood in

Jummapur, where he sets his two plays. Yet he suggests that he can take very little from his own experience, saying of *In the Native State* that "there's almost nothing of my experience in it, not even indirectly."[7] Stoppard's "geography" should thus not be read as based on a literal recreation of space but rather as the creation of a set of evocative imaginative and literal spaces, each of which manifests this history of power.

Lisa Lowe suggests that an aspect of the colonial process was to ingrain certain notions of "Indianness" defined *against* ideas of the quintessentially "English": "As Englishmen constructed a myth of their own omniscience, there also evolved the myth of the 'real India.'"[8] In Stoppard's plays there are also several versions of the "real" India that raise difficult questions about the responsibilities of representation. To some extent, Stoppard reiterates all too familiar images of India as an exotic, feminized, disorganized, and barbaric place in need of the British Empire's regulation, governance, and cultural reform. Yet he also juxtaposes these stereotypes with a more difficult, complex, and still emergent notion of national identity. Both appear in the creation of fictional landscapes that are evoked in the characters' descriptions.

To some extent Stoppard mocks those who hold patently stereotyped ideas about Indians – the inhabitants of the Resident's club who quote Kipling's poetry. Yet what he creates through the descriptions of English characters like Flora, Durance, and Mrs. Swan, who express a more complex and nuanced experience of India, are supposedly "authentic" visions of India that nonetheless also evoke racial and gendered difference in very predictable ways.

Flora's poetry suggests a feminized, erotic, and irrational "India" under masculine English control.[9] A quotation from her poem "Heat" opens *In the Native State* with a series of sensual images that associate the Indian climate with female sexuality and eventual decay. Flora's voice speaks successive descriptions of "heat" as associated with female lust: "Yes, I am in heat like a bride in a bath, / without secrets," to an image of the poet, "think of a woman in a blue dress . . . writing about the weather," to explicit animal sexuality, "Or think, if you prefer, of bitches, / cats, goats, monkeys at it like knives / in the jacaranda" (*In the Native State*, p. 1). Later, her poem associates such heat with the death and decay of the poet: "a corpse in a ditch . . . each hair / a lily stem straggling out of a poisoned swamp"

> Heat has had its way with me,
> yes, I know this ditch, I have been left for dead before,
> my lips gone slack and the wild iris
> flickers in the drooling cavity, insects
> crawl like tears from behind my eyes –
>
> (*In the Native State*, p. 20)

1 A scene from the American Conservatory Theater production of *Indian Ink* –
Susan Gibney (Flora Crewe) and Art Malik (Nirad Das).

In the stage play *Indian Ink,* the voiceover of her poems is condensed, and
the suggestion of crude animal sexuality is omitted, but the basic progres-
sion of images remains the same. Both versions conclude the poem with an
aestheticized image of "heat" that imagines sexual desire sublimated into art
("a pearl at my throat, / lets go and slides like a tongue-tip down a
Modigliani" [*In the Native State*, p. 77; *Indian Ink*, p. 75]), but then returns
to the association of female sexuality (in an image of the womb) and the
Indian landscape:

> (Heat) spills into the delta, now in the salt-lick,
> lost in the mangroves and in the airless moisture,
> a seed-pearl returning to the oyster –
> > *et nos cedamus amori* – (*Indian Ink*, p. 75;
> > *In the Native State*, p. 77)

Richard Dyer offers an evocative interpretation of the "dissolving, form-
less nature" so often evoked in describing female sexuality as well as the

traditional female body. For Dyer, particular female bodies in film, influenced by early 1950s descriptions of the "vaginal orgasm," are often imaged as soft, blurred, or "oceanic."[10] Flora's "Heat" adapts this association to a feminized image of India.

Flora's poetry is the plays' strongest statement of how India becomes imagined as sexualized, feminized, illicit, and transgressive. Despite comments that insist on the rigidity of Indian patriarchy (Das's reminder that Flora's sister, had she been Indian, would have been dearly punished for her affair with the married Mr. Chamberlain), India is associated with the open sexuality of female bodies and, significantly, with Flora's personal and poetic liberation. The story of Krishna's love affair with "a married lady, Radha, who was the most beautiful of the herdswomen" and who "would often escape from her husband to meet him in secret" (*In the Native State*, p. 22; *Indian Ink*, p. 28) attracts her. When Flora asks Das, "Were Krishna and Radha punished in the story?" he simply replies, "What for?" It is his nonchalance that inspires her to comment: "I should have come here years ago" (p. 47). The association of India with the realm of the openly sexualized is rearticulated throughout the mention of Indian erotic art, both in Das's nude portrait of her and in the Rajah's gift.

The imagining of India as an eroticized and feminized body engages on the one hand in the "romanticising of healthy primitivity," while on the other it identifies India with contagion, filth, and disease, making "a metaphoric connection between organic, climatic and moral degradation."[11] This imaginary space is attractive but also risky in its promise of adventure, wilderness, and danger. Durance comments to Flora, "People here drop like flies – cholera, typhoid, malaria – men, women and children, here one day, gone the next" (*In the Native State*, p. 56; *Indian Ink*, p. 52). This contradiction is maintained in numerous descriptions. The beauty and freshness of the natural wilderness are contrasted with the ills of modern civilization; Mrs. Swan remarks, "I can't get the tea here to taste as it should. I expect it's the water. A reservoir near Staines won't have the makings of a good cup of tea compared to the water we got in the Hills. It came straight off the Himalayas" (*In the Native State*, p. 19; *Indian Ink*, p. 26). Eldon Pike, on the other hand, refuses the Indian soft drinks unfamiliar to him. Durance's description marks out the thrilling yet at the same time disgusting aspects of the "real" India, praising the "wonderful" smell of the Indian countryside: "You should smell chappatis cooking on a camel-dung fire out in the Thar Desert. Perfume!" (*In the Native State*, p. 61; *Indian Ink*, p. 56).

Durance pictures an earlier state of India as an Eden before Eve, a homoerotic fantasy of virgin territory inhabited only by men:

I'll tell you where it all went wrong with us and India. It was the Suez Canal.
It let the women in . . . When you had to sail round the Cape this was a man's
country and men mucked in with the natives. The memsahibs put a stop to
that. The memsahib won't muck in, won't even be alone in a room with an
Indian.   (*In the Native State*, p. 61; *Indian Ink*, p. 56)

Durance's reflections and recollections of the "real" India are consistent
with, as Renato Rosaldo puts it, a kind of "imperialist nostalgia" which pictures an "authentic" body of India that is both deliciously beautiful and
thrillingly dangerous. This conceals "complicity with often brutal domination."[12] Significantly, it is the presence of women that "contaminates" the
purity of masculine bonding. Eldon Pike presents perhaps most memorably
the culmination of associating India with the contaminated feminine reproductive body, as he describes a beggar-woman:

she had this baby at the breast, I mean, she looked *sixty,* and – well, this is the
thing, she had a stump, you see, she had no hand, just this stump, up against
the glass, and it was . . . raw . . . so when the light changed, the stump left this
. . . smear . . .   (*Indian Ink*, p. 58)

Flora's own fate embodies the fear of contamination associated with India
and its feminized erotic. The unconventional English woman, Flora revels
in her consumption of India, eating unpeeled fruit and living amongst the
natives. Her lack of caution is contrasted with the eating habits at the
Club, where they serve "soup, boiled fish, lamb cutlets, sherry trifle and
sardines on toast" (*In the Native State*, p. 54; *Indian Ink*, p. 51). Yet the
free-spirited Flora both thrives in and eventually suffers from this environment. Her carefree disregard of proper English manners and her embrace
of India, while heroic, is associated both with her lack of control, her
sexual excesses, and her untimely death. When Mrs. Swan describes her
visit to Flora's grave, she recollects a pristine landscape: "I have never seen
such blossom, it blew everywhere. There were drifts of snow-white
flowers piled up against the walls of the graveyard. I had to kneel on the
ground and sweep the petals off her stone to read her name" (*In the
Native State*, p. 81; *Indian Ink*, p. 80). This recollection reiterates earlier
connections made between India, female sexuality, reproductive excess,
and death.

Each of Stoppard's characterizations, whether English, Indian, or
American, is inextricably tied up with this delineation of imagined cultural
space. While Stoppard's English characters are preoccupied with defining
"India," his Indian characters show the contradictions of their own colonial
history. Both *In the Native State* and *Indian Ink* end with the same quotation from Emily Eden's *Up the Country*:

Twenty years ago no European had ever been here, and there we were with a band playing, and observing that St Cloup's Potage à la Julienne was perhaps better than his other soups, and that some of the ladies' sleeves were too tight according to the overland fashions for March, and so on, and all this in the face of those high hills, and we one hundred and five Europeans being surrounded by at least three thousand mountaineers, who, wrapped up in their hill blankets, look on at what we call our polite amusements, and bowed to the ground if a European came near them. I sometimes wonder they do not cut all our heads off and say nothing more about it.

(*In the Native State*, p. 85; *Indian Ink*, p. 83)

The characterizations of Das and other Indian characters help answer the question of why the native "mountaineers" do not simply cut off the heads of the British. Colonial rule is maintained both through martial and ideological control.

The values disseminated by the English characters to justify their rule are absorbed all too well by some of the Indian characters. Macaulay's famous "Minute on Education" (1835) imagines "a class of interpreters between us and the millions whom we govern – a class of persons Indian in blood and colour, but English in tastes, in opinions, in morals and in intellect."[13] Yet the transformation of the Indian "interpreter" into Englishman is inevitably partial and incomplete; the racial barriers could not fully admit Indians as Englishmen. Stoppard's plays reflect this paradoxical situation. The colonial directive imagined the "native" in need of improvement, education, and assimilation. However, at the same time there was also a corresponding need to protect racial integrity from the others; to foster the belief that the native was inherently unassimilable, primitive, and irrational. Although natives were supposedly reformed by receiving the proper literary education, serving in the military, and playing cricket, they would always remain imperfect copies of the white British.

Homi Bhabha describes the "mimic man" created within colonial situations who both resembles and yet must remain inevitably different from the colonizer, the product of "the desire for a reformed, recognizable Other, as *a subject of a difference that is almost the same, but not quite.*"[14] Such versions of "mimic men" are those such as Stoppard's Das and the Harrow-educated Rajah; they are slavishly devoted to English literature and European cars, yet remain undeniably unassimilable. Flora describes the scene at her poetry reading: "it's so moving, they read the *New Statesman* and *Time and Tide* and the *TLS* as if they were the Bible in parts . . . and they know who wrote what about whom; it's like children with their faces jammed to the railings of an unattainable park" (*In the Native State*, p. 31; *Indian Ink*, p. 6). Das seems to embrace all things British: he desires "to write like Macaulay" (*In the Native State*, p. 11; *Indian Ink*, p. 19) and imagines a fictional London populated by his favorite writers and artists. As Durance tells Flora, Anglicized Indians from the higher castes have begun to occupy positions of power within the military and government.

The extent to which the Indian can actually become British is, however, limited, as attested to by the display of "Indian English" in the play. Das, Coomaraswami, and the Rajah speak English fluently, but it is a version of English whose verbosity marks it as inauthentic English, an exotic hybrid. The hyperbolic and metaphoric nature of Indian English is demonstrated in the elaborately embroidered phrases that Das, Coomaraswami, and the Rajah use, and in the "Hobson-Jobson" game that Das and Flora play. Yet this linguistic playfulness is perceived, at least by Flora, as frustrating and excessive indirection, even dishonesty; she tells him to "stop being so Indian": "You only do it with us. I don't believe that left to yourself you can't have an ordinary conversation without jumping backwards through hoops of delight, *with* whoops of delight" (*In the Native State*, p. 6; *Indian Ink*, p. 12).

This insecurity extends to Das's failure to command a European style of portrait painting in his first "official" portrait of Flora. Unlike the high modernists Brancusi and Modigliani, whose nude sculptures and portraits happily incorporate African-influenced "primitive" styles, Das cannot successfully appropriate European aesthetics; his first portrait remains unfinished. *Indian Ink* suggests that his second portrait of Flora is successful not because it blends European and Indian influences, but because its Indianness emerges as "authentic" in spite of his Eurocentric aspirations. The second portrait is "a composition in the old Rajasthani style" (*Indian Ink*, p. 58) as compared to his first attempt which, as Mrs. Swan tells Pike, "is fairly ghastly, like an Indian cinema poster" (*Indian Ink*, p. 10).

Both plays suggest that some version of the "authentic" Indian – backward, irrational, and disorderly – will expose itself as ultimately incompatible with British civilization, efficiency, progress, and health. Significantly, characters who do not speak English – such as Nazrul, engaging in the comic thefts of pâté and chickens, and Das's second wife, from a peasant background – remain at the background as testimony to an even more authentic, uncontaminated "native" state.

In the Native State and *Indian Ink* employ such stereotypes, evoking "India" as incomprehensible, erotic, irrational, unsophisticated, and childlike, and "England" as central, stable, and coherent.[15] Yet happily Stoppard's plays do not rely only on these problematic identifications. Acts of Indian rebellion, ranging from modest protests such as Das's "home-made banner at the Empire Day gymkhana" (*Indian Ink*, p. 61) to Gandhi's march to the sea, testify to an emergent national identity, one that allowed for the unification of groups distinct from one another in religion, culture, and caste into a movement for national unity and independence. As Lowe points out, "it was India's identification of itself as 'Indian,' and the power of this notion to unify diverse Indians – Hindus, Muslims, Sikhs, Jains, "representative" or not – which enabled the Indians to demand independence as a nation."[16] But what is "Indian" in Stoppard's plays is irrevocably tied up with what is "English"; even the reliance on a binary opposition between Indian and English cultural values does not fully imagine these categories to be mutually exclusive and essential. Ironically, as Das suggests, it is the institution of English as a common national language that helps formulate this Indian national identity.

> I have to thank Lord Macaulay for English. It was his idea when he was in the government of India that English should be taught to us all. He wanted to supply the East India Company with clerks, but he was sowing dragon's teeth. Instead of babus he produced lawyers, journalists, civil servants – he produced Gandhi! We have so many, many languages, you know, that English is the only language the nationalists can communicate in! That is a very good joke on Macaulay, don't you think?(*In the Native State*, pp. 11–12; *Indian Ink*, p. 19)

When Das is pushed by Flora to meet her expectations of rebellion ("If you don't start learning to *take* you'll never be shot of us"), to throw off the shackles of his Anglophilia, what he immediately reveals is not a heroic nationalist, the "thorn in the flesh of the British" (*In the Native State*, p. 8) that his son imagines him to be, but rather someone who is deeply attached to both traditional Indian and English culture, someone who is the product of this tension. When Das finally defends his love of English literature and European art, he does so on the basis of its parallels with traditions of Indian art; he argues that these complement, rather than displace, one another. Stoppard does no more than suggest that Flora and Das consummate their romantic interactions; as Mrs. Swan suggests, the question of "who does Flora sleep with" is not relevant: "It hardly matters, looking back. Men were not really important to Flora. If they had been, they would have been fewer. She used them like batteries. When things went flat, she'd put in a new one" (*In the Native State*, p. 76; *Indian Ink*, pp. 79–80). Yet their interracial relationship is central to the politics as well as the plot, not least because it presents the desire to bridge immense cultural differences.

Perhaps even the staging of *Indian Ink* through the conflation of English and Indian landscape, with its permeable boundaries between India and England as well as past and present, indicates the hope that English and Indian might merge into some newer sensibility. A developing Anglo–Indian identity is expressed when Francis (Eric in *Indian Ink*) announces proudly that "We're going to field a test team" in cricket; the "we" refers to "India" rather than England. Likewise, Mrs. Swan lapses into reminiscences of her beloved "fruit trees at home" (*In the Native State*, p. 81; *Indian Ink*, p. 80). Conversely, for Anish Das, "home" is London. In *Indian Ink*, this idea of an Anglo–Indian affinity is accentuated by the expanded role of Eldon Pike. Pike's many slips of decorum remind the audience that, despite his extensive knowledge of Flora's life, as an American he remains a cultural outsider. The final decision of Mrs. Swan and Anish Das to keep their discovery of the nude portrait and the affair between Flora and Das to themselves suggests that they share a "family" history in more ways than one. Their alliance suggests that both English and Indian are implicated in the larger space of empire; those twentieth century members of the former British Empire can define their commonalities against those much more removed from their colonial pasts.[17]

Stoppard creates characters who are not beings autonomous of culture but who are pointedly products of the real and imaginary spaces they inhabit. Flora is disappointed to be reminded that, despite her sympathies, she is still considered the "memsahib" (p. 43). In *Indian Ink*, Flora tells Das yet again to "Stop being Indian"; he finally replies angrily "And you stop being English!" (*Indian Ink*, p. 37). And yet, there is some flexibility in these positions. Even as Das rises to defend being "Indian," it is the nature of this Indianness that is in question. Both plays show the desire to move beyond the old divisive stereotypes of "Indianness" and "Britishness"; but what is to replace these divided spaces is unfortunately as yet not quite resolved. What emerges is only a gesture towards hybridity, the possibility of movement across what seems like an insurmountable divide.

NOTES

1 "Certainly the main one [starting point] was a rather generalized idea to write about the Empire and more particularly the ethics of empire And I'm not saying that *In the Native State* is *that*. In a way, I still want to do that. But this play is some sort of introduction to the subject for me." Interview with Paul Allen broadcast on *Third Ear*, BBC Radio Three, 16 April 1991, reprinted in *Stoppard in Conversation*, ed. Paul Delaney (Ann Arbor: University of Michigan Press, 1994): pp. 239–247, p. 240.

2 *In the Native State* (London: Faber and Faber, 1991), p. 10; *Indian Ink* (London: Faber and Faber, 1995), p. 17.

3 Allen interview; reprinted in Delaney, ed., *Stoppard in Conversation*, p. 243.

4 C. Phillips, H. C. Singh and B. N. Pandey, *Select Documents on the History of India and Pakistan*, Vol. IV, *The Evolution of India and Pakistan, 1858–1947* (London and Oxford: Oxford University Press, 1962), pp. 10–11, quoted in Gail

Ching-Liang Low, *White Skins/Black Masks: Representation and Colonialism* (London: Routledge, 1996), p. 105–106.

5 S. Gopal, *British Foreign Policy in India, 1858–1905* (Cambridge: Cambridge University Press, 1965), p. 11; Low, *White Skins*, pp. 105–106.

6 Kenneth Tynan, *Show People: profiles in entertainment* (New York: Simon and Schuster, 1979), p. 61.

7 "On the other hand, India is the only Empire country I would want to write about in any way I was there between the age of four and eight and the country has always fascinated me." Allen interview; reprinted in Delaney, ed., *Stoppard in Conversation*, p. 240.

8 Lisa Lowe, *Critical Terrains: French and British Orientalisms* (Ithaca, N.Y.: Cornell University Press, 1991), p. 118.

9 "I thought I was going to write a play simply about the portrait of a woman writing a poem and her poem is about being painted. Then I found the idea of her poetry so perversely enjoyable I went on writing her poetry for far longer than you'd believe." Interview with Gillian Reynolds, *Daily Telegraph*, 20 April 1991; reprinted in Delaney, ed., *Stoppard in Conversation*, p. 249.

10 Richard Dyer, *Heavenly Bodies: Film Stars and Society* (London: Macmillan, 1986), p. 56.

11 Low, *White Skins*, p. 30 and 29.

12 Renato Rosaldo, "Imperialist Nostalgia," *Representations* 26 (Spring 1989), pp. 107–122, at p. 108.

13 *Sources of Indian Tradition*, ed. William Theodore de Bary (New York: Columbia University Press, 1958), p. 49.

14 Homi Bhabha, "Of Mimicry and Man: the Ambivalence of Colonial Discourse," in *The Location of Culture* (London: Routledge, 1994), p. 86.

15 Lowe, *Critical Terrains*, p. 109.

16 Ibid., p. 118.

17 "I would like to write about Americanness and Englishness, probably in the same play which would be one good way of doing it . . . as you know I came here when I was eight and I don't know why, I don't particularly wish to understand why but I just seized England and it seized me. Within minutes it seems to me, I had no sense of being in an alien land and my feelings for, my empathy for English landscape, English architecture, English character, all that, has just somehow become stronger and stronger. And now on the other side I'm very interested by American character and how different it is from what's it's supposed to be." Allen interview; reprinted in Delaney, ed., *Stoppard in Conversation*, p. 246.

FURTHER READING

Ashcroft, Bill, Gareth Griffiths, and Helen Tiffin. *The Empire Writes Back: theory and practice in post-colonial literatures*. London: Routledge, 1989.

Bhabha, Homi Il, ed., *Nation and Narration*. New York: Routledge and Kegan Paul, 1990.

Chaudhuri, Una. *Staging Place: the geography of modern drama*. Ann Arbor: University of Michigan Press, 1995.

Fanon, Frantz. *The Wretched of the Earth*. Trans. Constance Farrington. New York: Grove Press, 1968.

Gilbert, Helen and Joanne Tompkins. *Post-Colonial Drama: theory, practice, and politics*. London: Routledge, 1996.

Rushdie, Salman. *Imaginary Homelands: essays and criticism, 1981–91*. Harmondsworth: Penguin, 1991.

Said, Edward. *Orientalism*. New York: Vintage, 1979.

Suleri, Sara. *The Rhetoric of English India*. Chicago: University of Chicago Press, 1992.

2
THE WORKS

3

PETER J. RABINOWITZ

Narrative difficulties in Tom Stoppard's
Lord Malquist and Mr Moon

Tom Stoppard's early *Lord Malquist and Mr Moon* leaves critics in an awkward situation. It is sufficiently substantial that no one tracing Stoppard's career can afford to ignore it. But since it is the only novel by a man universally classified and acclaimed as a "playwright," it is difficult to know precisely what to do with it. As a result, critics usually treat it as a dry run for the plays to come.[1]

Before discussing how they do so, let me provide a summary, since the novel is not widely known. Moon is a hapless historian aspiring to write a history of the world, one that articulates the "patterns" governing "all the things which have made things turn out the way they have today" (p. 128).[2] But in part because he has a phobia about the infinite (especially the infinite regress brought on by the search for first causes), he is unable to get down even the first sentence. As a stopgap, he takes a job as the Boswell to Lord Malquist – an aristocratic (and, we eventually learn, bankrupt) aesthete. These two provide the central contrast of the book. Moon, terrified by his inability to take a clear stand or draw clear boundaries, wanders around with a bomb in his pocket, in the hopes that he can explode reality into some kind of sense; Malquist, committed to style over substance, blithely buffers himself from reality, including the fact that his horse-drawn carriage has run down a Mrs. Cuttle who (we later learn) had apparently mistaken it for a similar-looking vehicle being used in a promotional campaign for toilet paper. Circling around these two are a bizarre set of ostentatiously cardboard characters including Moon's voluptuous wife Jane, whose beauty and flirtatiousness attract nearly all the men in the novel, but whose fear of consummation keeps her a virgin (at least until the final pages, when she may or may not be deflowered by Malquist); Malquist's alcoholic wife Laura, who eventually seduces Moon; Jasper Jones and Long John Slaughter, rival suitors for Jane's favors who appear to be cowboys but who turn out to be part of a publicity campaign for a pork and beans company; a man on a donkey who presents himself as the Risen Christ; O'Hara, Malquist's coachman, a Black Catholic

55

from Ireland whose Borscht-belt Jewish accent contradicts his abiding anti-Semitism; Marie, the Moons' maid, who appears to be selling kinky sex on the side; an unnamed general who is one of her clients; and Rollo, Malquist's pet lion. In the chaos of perverse comedy that erupts from their interactions, nearly half the characters get killed: Slaughter accidentally shoots Marie while trying to get rid of his rival; Moon kills the General in a rage while the General is trying to photograph Marie's corpse; Slaughter and Jones eliminate each other in an inept gunfight; and while Moon's own bomb turns out, to his surprise, to be a joke (it merely inflates a giant balloon with "a two-word message – familiar, unequivocal and obscene"; p. 154), on the final page he and O'Hara are blown up by a real bomb thrown in revenge by Mrs. Cuttle's anarchist husband, who mistakes Moon for Malquist.

Three qualities of the novel have allowed critics to mine it for insights into Stoppard's plays. First, because it is extravagantly allusive, it provides a window on the author's early influences: not only such Stoppard staples as Shakespeare's *Hamlet*, Joyce's *Ulysses*,[3] Beckett's *Waiting for Godot*, and Eliot's *The Love Song of J. Alfred Prufrock* but also (among others) the mare-beating dream from Dostoevsky's *Crime and Punishment*, Conrad's *The Secret Agent*, Hemingway's short stories, Wilder's *The Bridge of San Luis Rey*, Proust's *Remembrance of Things Past*, and countless others as well.

Second, the novel introduces the prototypes of many of Stoppard's favorite shticks and characters. The unnoticed corpse, for instance, which serves centrally in *Jumpers* and *The Real Inspector Hound*, turns up in this novel as well; the infinite regresses familiar from many later works are presaged in the picture on the cans of pork and beans ("a cowboy holding a tin with a picture of a cowboy holding a tin with . . ."; p. 38) and in the image of Moon looking at infinite reflections of himself in a hinged mirror (p. 81); the game of charades, which serves as a cover for erotic engagement in *Jumpers* (and its prototype *Another Moon Called Earth*), appears in the same way here, too. Moon is the first in a string of similar characters (for instance, the protagonist of *The Real Inspector Hound*, also named Moon); Jane (like Penelope in *Another Moon Called Earth*) can be seen as a first draft of Dorothy in *Jumpers*. Even some of the specific lines in the novel show up in different contexts in his plays: "*What good's a brick to a drowning man?*" Moon asks himself (p. 47; italics in original), a question asked by Rosencrantz as well.[4]

Third and most interestingly, it introduces a set of thematic concerns that would fuel Stoppard's work for years to come. True, different critics latch on to different strands of the novel's complex thematic fabric. Victor L. Cahn argues that the novel presents "a world as confusing and incomprehensible as the one which surrounds George Riley . . . and the court that surrounds Rosencrantz and Guildenstern."[5] According to C. W. E. Bigsby, the novel asserts the truth that "'substance is ephemeral but style is eternal.'"[6] For Paul Delaney, in contrast, Stoppard "writes of mankind as existing in a realm in which right and wrong are universal metaphysical absolutes."[7] But no matter how readers interpret the plays (at least the early plays), the chances are that they will see the novel as a thematic sibling.

Useful as these inquiries are, they sidestep two key facts about *Malquist and Moon*. First, as a narrative rather than a drama, it is formally unlike any of Stoppard's more popular works.[8] Second, although written more or less simultaneously with *Rosencrantz and Guildenstern*, it is – to filch Thomas R. Whitaker's tactful phrasing – "not his most powerful work."[9] More specifically, *Malquist and Moon* has not attracted a wide audience because it falls slightly short of its target both emotionally and philosophically. In this chapter, I would like to suggest that these two points are connected: that the novel's emotional and philosophical deficiencies stem from problems in Stoppard's handling of narrative.[10] Some things are easier to do in drama than in narrative; and while Stoppard's projects at this time in his career were not inherently impossible to carry off in narrative, they required a technical finesse that, as a fledgling novelist, he did not yet have.

To explain the technical challenges facing the author of *Malquist and Moon*, I need to take a theoretical detour to consider the acts of reception (who's listening?) and of presentation (who's speaking?). To begin with reception: I have loosely referred to "audience," but especially when dealing with fiction, the term is more complex than such offhand usage admits. That is because any fictional work (including both novels and dramas) is an "imitation" in the sense that it pretends to be something other than what it "really" is. In this case, an imaginary story is presented as if it were a true account of two people named Malquist and Moon. As a result of this duality, the act of reading operates on at least two levels simultaneously.

On the one hand, in order to make decisions about how to design his novel, Stoppard had to start with assumptions about what he could expect from his readers – for instance, that they would recognize allusions to Conrad and Eliot. Since he did not know who his actual readers would be, he could not be sure that these assumptions would turn out to be correct; all he could do was write for a hypothetical audience that I call the *authorial audience*.

In this regard, his novel resembles any other communication made by people who do not know their audiences personally: physicists and political candidates, too, write with a hypothetical authorial audience in mind. But fiction, because of its imitative nature, brings another audience into play. Since a novel generally imitates some nonfictional form, the narrator (explicit or implicit) generally imitates an author and writes for an imitation audience that I call the *narrative audience*: an audience that, in the case of *Malquist and Moon*, believes that Malquist really exists. To read the novel, we must not only join Stoppard's authorial audience (which reads the novel as what it is – a novel) but at the same time pretend to be members of his narrative audience (which reads the text as if it were what it pretends to be – a true account).[11]

Issues of presentation are, if anything, even more complex. To understand what is happening in *Malquist and Moon*, we need to consider in particular the complications added to our participation as narrative audience by the structural features often loosely grouped under the phrase "point of view" – or, in more technical narratological terminology, the elements clustering around such rubrics as "focalization" and "voice."[12] Point of view has vexed narrative theorists for some time, in part because it covers several quite different areas. For my purposes here, I need to stress the distinction between perspective and what I call source.

In its most literal meaning, perspective refers to the angle of perception from which something is considered: when the novel tells us that Moon, tapping on Marie's door, "heard the stealthy rattle of the safety-chain" and saw "cautious creature-eyes above the chain" (p. 23), we are sharing Moon's location, hearing what he hears and seeing what he sees. More broadly, perspective is taken metaphorically, too, so that it covers such areas as beliefs or understandings (as one might argue "from a Marxist perspective").[13] Even in this broad sense, though, perspective is different from source: the consciousness within the text – on the level of the narrative audience[14] – that makes the decisions about what to present and how to present it.[15]

This distinction is usually of trivial import when reading drama. Here, perspective and source generally coincide: we learn what a character sees, understands, or values according to the words that he or she has chosen to speak.[16] Thus, when Sophie, in *Artist Descending a Staircase*, says of the three artists "I was unable to describe you with enough individuality . . . You were all fair, and well built,"[17] she is not only describing what she saw but also determining how to express it: the word *fair* is Sophie's choice. As a consequence, any play with more than one character has more than one source, and true conversation, in the sense of dialogue among different sources, is almost inevitable. That is true even when, as Stoppard says of his own plays, all the characters speak the same way (in fact, the way that he does).[18]

But as narrative theorists warn us, in fiction the presence of a narrator fractures this easy unity, requiring more careful and self-conscious manipulation by the author.[19] Of particular concern here is the fact that once one gets beyond first-person narrative (or quoted dialogue), it is risky to draw conclusions about the source of an expression from the perspective it inhabits, even when, as in *style indirect libre*, the narrator attempts to represent a character's consciousness. To return to the phrase I quoted above: when Stoppard's narrator tells us that Marie's eyes are "cautious," we can be reasonably sure that we are getting a fair sense of the *sort* of perceptual experience that Moon has; the eyes he sees are not frank and candid. But from the perspective alone, we cannot be sure whether Moon really senses that they are "cautious" rather than "careful" – or whether the narrator chooses that term to communicate something more inchoate in Moon's mind.

This theoretical discussion helps us understand why *Malquist and Moon* has not shared the success of Stoppard's plays. In terms of audience dynamics, narrative is more complex than drama – and, I would argue, Stoppard was not always able to keep this complexity fully under control. In particular, his purposes in the text were occasionally thwarted by the challenges of balancing the authorial and narrative audience and of negotiating the complex interaction of perspective and source found in third-person narrative.

What exactly were those purposes? Stoppard described his early work as "seriousness compromised by my frivolity, or . . . frivolity redeemed by my seriousness"[20] – and beneath its slapstick surface, the novel is just as serious as *Rosencrantz and Guildenstern*, in terms both of its intended emotional effects and of its philosophical point. Let me take each of these in turn, showing how the novel's imperfect narrative structure gets in the way.

To begin with the novel's emotional flavor: loosely speaking, one can argue that most of the works in the western canon that we think of as "tragedies" put the audience in a superficially contradictory position. On the one hand, we hope that Othello will discover the truth of Iago's deception in time to be reconciled with Desdemona; on the other hand, were the play actually to end in that optimistic way, contemporary readers would feel cheated.[21] One way to treat that contradiction is to consider it as a conflict between the authorial and narrative audiences. That is, one structural root of this special tragic flavor is the incongruity between the authorial audience's detached intellectual desire for the formal closure of death and the narrative audience's sympathetic emotional desire for the character to survive.[22]

For this conflict to produce that special unsettled feeling, it is necessary to have strong engagement on both the authorial and narrative levels – anything that tips the balance one way or the other will stifle the effect. In a powerful performance of Puccini's *Madama Butterfly*, for instance, we may be so caught up as narrative audience that the heroine's death feels more like gratuitous sadism than tragic necessity. In contrast, Nabokov's *Invitation to a Beheading* so emphasizes the authorial level that it is almost impossible for the reader to get deeply involved in playing the role of narrative audience and to get caught up in the protagonist's suffering under totalitarianism. The novel therefore becomes an intellectual puzzle rather than the wrenching emotional experience its terrifying subject matter might lead one to expect. In *Rosencrantz and Guildenstern*, Stoppard managed brilliantly to balance our engagement on the authorial and narrative levels.[23] In *Malquist and Moon*, however, he produces (unwittingly, I believe) something closer to *Invitation*'s ingenious indifference.

In part, this is because of the self-conscious artsiness of *Malquist and Moon*, which regularly calls attention to its own style. Thus, the second section introduces the cowboys in a parody of dime-novel westerns: "Sitting easy in the saddle, L. J. (for Long John) Slaughter moseyed down the slope, hat low over his eyes" (p. 7). The third, which introduces Laura and Rollo, shifts ostentatiously into a nearly monosyllabic pastiche of the Hemingway of "The Short Happy Life of Francis Macomber": "From behind the scrub of thorn the lion watched her. He was not sure yet and the wind was wrong" (p. 8). In a drama or a first-person narrative, such stylistic display would not necessarily diminish involvement as narrative audience, because we could, on the narrative level, associate the cleverness with the characters. But in *Malquist and Moon*, we have an omniscient, undramatized narrator – someone who, on the surface, is difficult to distinguish from "the author." And that undramatized narrator serves as both perspective and source for both of these scenes. We are therefore invited to associate the stylistic acrobatics with Stoppard rather than with the world of the characters. Having been encouraged to read that way by the opening chapter, we are apt to assume that the undramatized author-identified narrator is similarly the source of stylistic virtuosity later in the book (at least, any stylistic virtuosity that does not come in the form of quoted speech by one of the characters), even in passages from a particular character's perspective. As a consequence, *Malquist and Moon*'s considerable verbal dazzle usually directs our attention to the authorial rather than the narrative level.

To compound the imbalance brought about by style, the novel incorporates a theme that further privileges the authorial level: it continually reminds us that the people we are reading about are characters in a novel. Of course, in *any* novel, all characters are read as "characters in a literary work" by the authorial audience. But in works like *Malquist and Moon* or Nabokov's *Invitation to a Beheading*, the image extends to the narrative level: the characters are literally "characters" subject to someone else's invention and control *even on the level of the narrative audience* – that is, even in the world of the novel.[24]

This theme is worked out in part through the persistent image of clockwork.[25] The cowboys' horses, for instance, appear to be mechanical animals: Slaughter may try to stop his horse by shouting "'Whoa, you bitch!,'" but it has no effect, and "he and the mare, like clock figures forever bound to the striking of the hours, passed on and out of sight" (p. 32). But the artificiality is signaled in other ways as well. When Slaughter shoots into Moon's house, the sounds are not properly synchronized (p. 30). Jane, coming down the stairs, "stop[s] the movie of her descent for a few frames" (p. 34). Moon often feels himself "acting out a move" (p. 53), and most of the characters seem to have no past, no existence prior to their appearance in the novel. It is thus telling that at one of the points where Moon thinks he is "within reach of a statement by which he could stand," in fact "the only thing that came into his head was a joke he had once heard about an actor" (p. 49) – a joke that, we later learn, centers on the actor's failure to distinguish the world of the stage from the world of the audience (pp. 163–164).

These devices combine to amplify an effect much like Brechtian alienation: they shift the balance of the reader's engagement, heightening intellectual awareness of the author's presence, and minimizing emotional involvement on the narrative level. None of the violence, for instance, really matters, because no one is any more a "real person" than the chess pieces in *Through the Looking Glass*. In the end, then, Moon's death – unlike the poignant deaths of Rosencrantz and Guildenstern – is liable to be experienced as simply a formal necessity in a way that saps the novel's emotional power.

Stoppard is, arguably, a playwright of ideas more than a standard tragedian. Indeed, one of the reasons he enjoys writing film scripts is that he does not have to "invent the story and character, parts I don't enjoy."[26] So it is perhaps no surprise that the strength of his early novel does not lie in its control of audience sympathies. What is surprising, though, is that it stumbles intellectually as well.

In his early works, Stoppard was trying to articulate a slippery epistemological stance, what might be called additive realization.[27] There are two competing strands to this position. One is an apparent relativism or skepticism growing out of his belief that intellectual inquiry leads to infinite regress, a belief that encourages him to reject privileged positions and the principal of noncontradiction. Indeed, Stoppard claims these rejections as the principal reason for being a playwright: "Writing dialogue is the only respectable way of contradicting yourself. I'm the kind of person who embarks on an endless leapfrog down the great moral issues. I put a position, rebut it, refute the rebuttal, and rebut the refutation. Forever."[28] "I don't write plays with heroes who express my point of view. I write argument plays."[29]

As for the second strand: Stoppard is committed to what he calls "a favourite thing of mine: the idea of an absolutely bizarre image which has a total rationale to it being seen by different people."[30] This "favourite thing" generates the basic action of *After Magritte* and *Artist Descending*, where shifts in viewpoint during the play bring into focus an image that appeared absurd at the beginning. We see the same principle endorsed in *Malquist and Moon* by the Risen Christ, who argues that changing one's point of view can increase understanding. When Moon suggests that it is "'odd'" for him to be "'going about on a donkey dressed like that,'" the Risen Christ replies, "'Not to me.'" Significantly, the phrase "Perhaps that was the answer" flashes through Moon's mind. But instead of considering it seriously, he "file[s] it away for the future" (p. 42).

At first glance, these two intellectual strands – the apparent skepticism and the belief that one can discover truths behind the superficially absurd by finding the right vantage points – seem incompatible, for the second seems to imply that some perspectives are, in fact, epistemologically superior to others. But while Stoppard's thinking is not entirely consistent, in his early plays these two arguments do, in fact, fit together. Granted, each perspective has its own special insights that may not be available to others (in this way, Stoppard is not really a relativist). But the "absolute truth" – the "ceiling view of a situation"[31] – can only be found by adding the partial views together. In this sense, the analog to early Stoppard in the visual arts is not dadaism but cubism.

This epistemological position leads Stoppard to certain literary techniques, in particular the play of multiple perspectives, each offering its own piece of wisdom, its own piece of a total truth which really exists out in the world (that is why many of his plays force us to reexamine the same material from different perspectives). True, it is often the audience, rather than the characters, that ultimately puts the puzzle together. But it is the narrative audience, not the authorial audience, that does so, having gotten those various pieces from the characters. Thus, while individual characters may remain in the dark, even at the end of the plays, that is because they have failed to attend carefully enough to one another (when Birdboot foolishly joins the stage action in *The Real Inspector Hound*, for instance, he has already been warned by Moon not to do it). The truth may be elusive. But it is, at least theoretically, accessible within the world of the narrative audience. Stoppard may despair, but he is not really a skeptic.

At least that is the philosophical position that emerges in the plays. Something subtly different happens in the novel, where there is an uncomfortable ambiguity, not only about ontology (about what is the case) but also about epistemology (about what it is possible to know). And I suspect that the ambiguity is not intentional, but that – like the emotional imbalance between the authorial and narrative audiences – it arises accidentally, as a consequence of Stoppard's inexperience in the nuances of narrative technique.

Of course, in many places the novel does represent the same kind of additive realization as the plays; indeed, the novel's pathos comes from Moon's failure to recognize, much less put together, the varying insights of the people around him. As we have seen, he does not take the Risen Christ's "Not to me" sufficiently seriously as a key to the universe he inhabits. Nor does he catch the premonition implicit in Malquist's twist on the familiar line when he says "'I am an island, Mr Moon, and when the bell tolls it tolls for thee'" (p. 4) – indeed, when he describes the moment later on, he misremembers it: "Lord Malquist also quoted from the poets, 'No man is an island etc.'" (p. 92). Nor does Moon take seriously Laura's observation that there is no difference between the random and the inevitable – that in either case, there is no "point" to the world, and you therefore "have to provide your own" (p. 129).

But there is something further going on. Moon frequently has glimpses of some even deeper truth about the world he lives in, something "he did not . . . have the words to formulate" (p. 18): "the edge of some old haunting" (p. 37) that flickers just out of sight, "the feeling that reality was just outside his perception" (p. 29), "a reality which for some reason had eluded him again" (p. 65). At his point of sharpest insight, Moon feels that "it was as if he were the victim of a breathtaking conspiracy instituted at his birth" (p. 140).

As I have already argued, the "haunting," the "breathtaking conspiracy" is that even on the level of the narrative audience, Moon is a character in a novel. His momentary flickerings of that truth often take the form of an image (perhaps taken from *Through the Looking Glass*) suggesting the existence of some truer world on the other side of a glass window.[32] There are many variants of this: the fake country prospect (of Malquist's former estate?) painted on Moon's kitchen window in order to hide the prosaic reality of his back yard; the mirrors that dot the text; the shards of broken glass that keep lacerating Moon. Even more striking, Moon's jumping from one neurosis to another is compared to "the way the glass in a train window, infinitesimally loose in its frame, would shiver with a tiny chattering noise against the steel while Moon sat next to it for hours, holding himself in, waiting for it to explode around him" (p. 59). His otherwise inexplicable murder of the General makes a perverse sense in the context of this half-articulated desire to break through this glass to get to reality: he hits the General over the head with a bottle, which "bursts as violently as plate glass shattering in a train window but it didn't help" (p. 81).[33] And the novel ends when Cuttle throws his bomb "which smashe[s] the glass in the coach window" and gives Moon a brief moment of recognition before he is blown up (p. 180).

My purpose is not to detail the novel's hints of the imitative nature of Moon's world and the existence of another, higher realm, but rather to point to the problem of their source. A few exceptions aside, the hints come not from dialogue by the characters, nor from Moon's own thoughts, but from the narrator's articulation of what lies behind those thoughts. Since, as we have seen, this narrator is an omniscient and strongly author-identified narrator who does not inhabit the world of the text, these observations are not even potentially accessible to Moon.[34] Thus, when Moon feels trapped like an actor "without a cue" (p. 53); when Jane throws a mirror at Moon that explodes, "violent as plate glass bursting out of a train window" (p. 59); when Moon sees his notebook burn into a "black replica of itself" (p. 82); when Moon stands "uncertainly against the bookcase like a stranded actor denied the release of an exit because it would be purely arbitrary" (p. 117): in such cases, the perspective and the source do not match. Our visual (or emotional) position is Moon's; we are seeing what he sees or feeling what he feels. But given that Moon so often does "not even have the words to formulate" his thoughts (p. 18), the choices of presentation (including the richly resonant comparison of the mirror and the train's plate glass) seem to be the narrator's, not inarticulate Moon's.

One can easily multiply the examples. And as they add up, we are increasingly left with a sense, not only that Moon does not know the truth but that he could *not possibly know* the truth, given the epistemological limitations of the world he inhabits. Through his treatment of perspective and source, Stoppard has substituted a growing skepticism for additive realization.

In the end, then, because of Stoppard's narrative technique, *Malquist and Moon*, ingenious as it is, creates a cold emotional effect unlike that found in any of his plays of the period – and it offers an almost cruel skepticism that is similarly at odds with the far more nuanced epistemology one can extract from his vastly more accomplished dramatic work. Perhaps this should be no surprise. After all, while one or two modern writers – Chekhov and Wilde come to mind – have managed to excel in both drama and narrative, each of these media requires substantially different literary techniques and hence different skills and aesthetic sympathies. Stoppard has not been able fully to master them both; but since he stands with Shaw and James in that regard, it is hardly a reason for shame.

NOTES

Thanks to Katheryn Doran, Elizabeth Jensen, Katherine Kelly, Sarah Knapp, and Nancy Sorkin Rabinowitz for their help and advice.

1 For example, Katherine E. Kelly entitles her chapter dealing with the novel "The Playwright Prepares." See *Tom Stoppard and the Craft of Comedy: medium and genre at play*, Ann Arbor: University of Michigan Press, 1991. Besides *Malquist and Moon*, Stoppard's narrative output consists of three early short stories. "Reunion," a recounting of a man's attempt to rekindle a relationship with a former lover, poignantly underscores the discrepancies between the banal surface conversation and his seething, but unexpressed, psychological anguish. "Life, Times: Fragments" offers disconnected snapshots from the bleak life of a failed writer who is only "discovered" after his death. "The Story," the longest and most conventionally realistic of the three, tells of a journalist whose casual decision to report on a minor indecency case leads to the offender's suicide. While the stories are promising, they are not particularly ambitious, rarely exhibiting the literary characteristics for which Stoppard is known.

2 Tom Stoppard, *Lord Malquist and Mr Moon* (New York: Grove Press/Black Cat, 1975). All further references to this edition will be made in the text.

3 See, in particular, Kelly, *Tom Stoppard*, p. 25.

4 Tom Stoppard, *Rosencrantz and Guildenstern Are Dead* (New York: Grove Press/Black Cat, 1967), p. 108.

5 Victor L Cahn, *Beyond Absurdity: the plays of Tom Stoppard* (Rutherford: Fairleigh Dickinson University Press, 1979), p. 67.

6 C. W. E. Bigsby, *Tom Stoppard*, British Council series on Writers and their Work, ed. Ian Scott-Kilvert (Harlow: Longman, 1976), p. 6.

7 Paul Delaney, *Tom Stoppard: the moral vision of the major plays* (New York: St. Martin's Press, 1990), p. 1.

8 Stoppard recognizes that writing plays differs from writing novels and that he prefers being a playwright: "I realized quite a long time ago that I was in it because of the theatre rather than because of the literature. I like theatre, I like showbiz, and that's what I'm true to" (quoted in Ronald Hayman, *Tom Stoppard*, London: Heinemann, 1977, p. 8).

9 Thomas R Whitaker, *Tom Stoppard* (New York: Grove Press, 1983), p. 28.

10 For a different approach to the way narrative suits Stoppard less well than drama, see ibid., esp. pp. 35–36 and 68.

11 For a fuller discussion, see my *Before Reading: narrative conventions and the politics of interpretation* (1987; reprinted Columbus: Ohio State University Press, 1998).

12 For a fuller discussion of these issues, see the works listed below.

13 See, for instance, Seymour Chatman, *Story and Discourse: narrative structure in fiction and film* (Ithaca, N.Y.: Cornell University Press, 1978), which distinguishes perceptual, conceptual, and interest points of view (p. 152).

14 Of course, from the perspective of the authorial audience, all choices are being made by the author.

15 I use the word *source* rather than the more familiar terms *voice* or *expression*, which tend to coalesce source (the consciousness making the decisions about what to present) and style (the characteristic language in which those decisions are couched). Style is not directly tied to perspective: had the novel used the word *secretive* rather than *stealthy*, we would have a difference in style but not in perspective. But style is not neatly tied to source, either. Authors sometimes shift

style to signal a difference in source; but, as will be clear, stylistic shifts do not *necessarily* entail shifts in either perspective or source.

16 Seeing a performance, of course, is often different, because gestures, staging, lighting, and other nontextual elements can influence viewers' reactions.

17 Tom Stoppard, *Artist Descending a Staircase, and Where Are They Now?* (London: Faber and Faber, 1973), p. 40. To complicate matters, blind Sophie is at that point seeing with the mind's eye; but that does not nullify the basic point.

18 See Mel Gussow, *Conversations with Stoppard* (New York: Limelight Editions, 1995), p. 35.

19 As Seymour Chatman puts it, using somewhat different vocabulary, "*The perspective and the expression need not be lodged in the same person*" (*Story and Discourse*, p. 153; italics in original).

20 Quoted in Gussow, *Conversations*, p. 14; ellipsis in original.

21 Of course, audiences at different historical moments react quite differently – and as the intermittent popularity of upbeat rewritings of Shakespeare demonstrate, the taste for bloody resolutions is not a constant.

22 For further discussion, see my "Pleasure in Conflict: Mahler's Sixth, tragedy, and musical form," *Comparative Literature Studies* 18. 3 (September 1981), pp. 306–313.

23 See my "What's Hecuba to Us? The audience's experience of literary borrowing," in *The Reader in the Text: Essays on Audience and Interpretation*, edited by Susan Suleiman and Inge Crosman (Princeton: Princeton University Press, 1980), pp. 241–263.

24 This theme is increasingly common in twentieth-century fiction, which often employs the crossing of narrative levels technically known as *metalepsis*. But the novel's connection to Nabokov is especially strong, albeit arcane. When Moon enters Marie's room, he unexpectedly finds a butterfly net (p. 80). Nabokov was an avid lepidopterist – and throughout his works, mentions of moths or butterflies are always a reference to the author's presence. Whatever sexual games Marie might be playing with the butterfly net, it also works here as a Nabokov reference.

25 For a fuller discussion of clockwork in Stoppard, see Richard Corballis, *Stoppard: the mystery and the clockwork* (New York: Methuen, 1984).

26 Quoted in Gussow, *Conversations*, p. 36.

27 I am taking some interpretive liberty here, on the assumption that I can read the novel in the way Stoppard reads plays by other writers: "I'm the world's best audience. I assume what I see is exactly what everybody meant me to see, and there's a reason for everything" (quoted in Gussow, *Conversations*, p. 50).

28 Quoted in Gussow, *Conversations*, p. 3.

29 Quoted ibid., p. 35. The "arguments" of his plays are not always intellectual; he also stages conflicts between his emotional and his intellectual commitments (see Gussow, *Conversations*, p. 14). In any case, Stoppard's work is a good example of Bakhtinian dialogism, and it is a sign of his success that critics who have attempted to specify his allegiances have been unable to reach consensus about where he stands. See, as but one example, the disagreement between Bigsby (who views early Stoppard as endorsing playful Wildean artifice) (Bigsby, *Tom Stoppard*, pp. 5–6) and Delaney (who sees him as holding stronger ethical commitments; *Tom Stoppard*, pp. 3–4 and elsewhere).

30 Quoted in Gussow, *Conversations*, p. 7.

31 Quoted ibid., p. 3.

32 For a fuller discussion of mirrors, see Neil Sammells, *Tom Stoppard: the artist as critic* (New York: St. Martin's Press, 1988), especially p. 50. Although it is not so explicitly concerned with mirrors, Wilder's *The Bridge of San Luis Rey* may fit in here as well. *Malquist and Moon* refers to Wilder's novel because it focuses on one of Stoppard's central questions: whether things happen by accident or by design. But among the other linkages between the two texts is the Marquesa de Montemayor's story about her ability to enter into paintings.

33 A similar bottle-smashing occurs in the protagonist's imagination in Stoppard's "Reunion." But in that earlier work, it is a reflection of a psychological state, not of any metaphysical truth.

34 As Anthony Jenkins puts it, "Moon's role in the novel makes consistent sense, but his voice becomes difficult to place since it frequently overlaps with that of the omniscient narrator, and this presents a major problem." *The Theatre of Tom Stoppard* (Cambridge: Cambridge University Press, 1987), p. 35.

FURTHER READING

For an excellent introduction to the problems of narrative poetics, see David Richter's anthology of classic texts, *Narrative/Theory* (White Plains, N.Y.: Longman, 1996). More specialized texts in narrative are listed as follows.

Bal, Mieke. *Narratology: introduction to the theory of narrative*. 2nd edn. Toronto: University of Toronto Press, 1997.

Banfield, Ann. *Unspeakable Sentences: narration and representation in the language of fiction*. Boston: Routledge and Kegan Paul, 1982.

Booth, Wayne C. *The Rhetoric of Fiction*. 2nd edn. Chicago: University of Chicago Press, 1983.

Cohn, Dorrit. *Transparent Minds: narrative modes for presenting consciousness in fiction*. Princeton: Princeton University Press, 1978.

Genette, Gérard. *Narrative Discourse: an essay in method*. Trans. Jane E. Lewin. Ithaca, N.Y.: Cornell University Press, 1980.

Herman, David, ed. *Narratologies: new perspectives on narrative analysis*. Columbus: Ohio State University Press, 1999.

Phelan, James. *Narrative as Rhetoric: technique, audiences, ethics, ideology*. Columbus: Ohio State University Press, 1996.

Prince, Gerald. *A Dictionary of Narratology*. Lincoln: University of Nebraska Press, 1987.

Rimmon-Kenan, Shlomith. *Narrative Fiction: contemporary poetics*. London: Methuen, 1983.

4

ELISSA S. GURALNICK

Stoppard's radio and television plays

If the "first duty of the artist," as Stoppard proposes in *Artist Descending a Staircase*, "is to capture the radio station,"[1] the second must be to capture television. Between them, these two domestic media command such giant audiences that they effectively shape modern taste. Playwrights cannot, in good conscience, let media so powerful escape them. Yet what constitutes their "capture" is not easy to say. Have radio and television been captured for drama when they broadcast a play that is suited to the stage; or have they merely been borrowed for alien purposes? Is radio, in particular, hospitable to drama; or does its invisible stage create impediments that playwrights may disguise, but not really transcend? Does television, for its part, have a nature of its own, with which drama may comport; or is it nothing but cinema at a double disadvantage: bright room, small screen? Vexing questions, every one, for a playwright like Stoppard, who has captured the theatre through impeccable stagecraft – that is, by treating the stage as the partner of words in making meaning in the theatre. Unless equivalent craft can be exercised in radio and television, Stoppard's "duty" to capture these behemoths of popular culture would seem wholly uninviting.

So it is that, in writing plays for broadcast, Stoppard probes the very nature of the domestic broadcast media. Seeking always to differentiate radio and television, not only from the theatre but also from each other, he attempts to discover what constitutes a stage on air and on screen, then induces each stage to speak in its own oblique language. The result is that Stoppard makes an elegant case on the radio for the medium's special expressivity in drama, while on television he pioneers in exploring the expressive dimensions of a medium that has yet to discover its idiom. Stoppard's work leaves no doubt that radio and television can be captured for drama just as he favors: they can both be enlisted to reflect a play's point, to enhance it, even sometimes to augment it. They function, in short, as

68

alternative theatres. Although underexploited and thus undervalued, they are articulate nevertheless.

In the mid-1960s, when Stoppard was emerging as a playwright, radio was the gateway to theatre in Britain. Budding playwrights apprenticed in the radio studios of BBC Broadcasting House, then graduated to the stage at the first opportunity – a career path that long remained viable, although cutbacks in BBC funding now endanger it. Clearly, theatre enjoyed pride of place in this arrangement. As Stoppard has observed, speaking of radio and television both, "in those early Osborne, Wesker and Pinter years, . . . bliss was it to be performed but to be *staged* was very heaven."[2] Even so, BBC Radio had considerable cachet. Through its Home and World Services, the BBC for decades had been radio-broadcasting all manner of literature from classical to contemporary: readings of poetry and fiction, radio adaptations of fiction and drama, original translations from numerous languages, and work commissioned specifically for radio. By the time Stoppard was seeking a production, BBC Radio had not only introduced drama into households worldwide; it had successfully promoted a new kind of drama entirely: namely, plays that depended for effect on their going unseen. Already there were masterpieces in the genre, among them Dylan Thomas's *Under Milk Wood* and Samuel Beckett's *All that Fall*. Stoppard was destined to add to the number.

In the first of his radio plays to be broadcast, *The Dissolution of Dominic Boot* (20 February 1964), Stoppard manages radio skillfully, if unadventurously, while introducing a motif – namely, time – that would eventually inspire immense ingenuity in his use of the medium. *Boot* builds on a simple conceit in which Dominic, dead broke, rushes about in a taxi, trying in vain to scare up the money to pay off his ever-mounting fare. The conceit has no necessary affinity to radio. It lends itself to sight gags as easily as verbal quips; and indeed, reconceived as *The Engagement*, the play was eventually filmed (more on which later). In the radio version, Stoppard exploits the medium's singular capacity for playing fast and loose with space – for accomplishing changes in scene with a single word or sound effect. Still, for twenty-some scene changes (conservatively tallied) to occur in a fifteen-minute play must be something of a record. We accompany Dominic in and out of his taxi as he seeks to make withdrawals from his overdrawn bank accounts, appeals to acquaintances both in person and by phone, demolishes his gas meter to confiscate its coins, then settles his fare by a barter arrangement in which he forfeits nearly all his possessions, including the suit on his back. The play thus takes spirited advantage of the insubstantiality of space on the radio: "here" becomes "there" becomes "anywhere" almost at whim. Meanwhile, time, that great abstraction, is reified in *Boot*. For the longer Dominic travels in his taxi, the more obsessively he calculates his fluctuating fare ("Seventy-one in all. Minus ten I gave him" [p. 9]). Let no one imagine that time is incorporeal: time in Boot's fable is transparently money.

Time figures again in Stoppard's second play for radio, *"M" Is For Moon Among Other Things* (4 April 1964). Hitchcock's *Dial M for Murder* (1954), heard briefly in the background, leaves no doubt about the thing that M is principally for; and murder – in particular, soul murder – is, in fact, what *Moon* depicts. A two-hander, *Moon* follows the pained internal musings and small conversation of a middle-aged couple who fail to connect. Alfred, the husband, studies a newspaper, attending to items that signify his sexual frustration: a girl's molestation, a car's engine thrust. Meanwhile Constance, his wife, inattentively flips through volume M of her encyclopedia, a birthday gift from Alfred, while pondering the date: "(*Thinks:*) August the fifth, nineteen sixty-two. (*Up*) Alfred, in half an hour I'll be exactly forty-two-and-a-half years old. That's a thought, isn't it? . . . Forty-two-and-a-half, and all I've got is a headache" (pp. 16–17). Alfred, however, is deaf to his wife's existential complaints. His sympathies awaken only when the late news on television reports the suicide of Marilyn Monroe. With Marilyn, Alfred is prepared to commiserate; with Constance, only to bicker. And so the evening passes, until the couple go to bed, having failed to touch each other with their longings and regrets.

Nothing, in other words, happens in *Moon*. Although turmoil abounds, it springs from the characters' psyches and never eventuates in action. Unlike *Boot*, which is virtually manic in its movements, *Moon* is a static piece of radio portraiture. Yet *Moon* otherwise mirrors *Boot*'s principal features: it makes poignant tragicomedy from the daily concerns of inconsequential people; it suits radio well, though a visible stage could also do it justice; and it worries aloud about the passage of time. As Dominic frantically calculates his fare, so Constance dizzily calculates the date ("The Friday before last must have been the twenty-seventh . . . [p. 16]). But dates in themselves are insignificant. They acquire importance, if any, from context. For Constance, 5 August 1962 marks precisely the moment when her life, if projected at a normal span of eighty-five years, is half over; while for Alfred, the very same date denotes Marilyn's death. Either way there is nothing to celebrate – a point driven home when Constance toasts herself ironically ("Happy anniversary, Millie" [p. 21]) as she downs her sleeping pills. If the tongue-in-cheek moral of *Boot* is that time is money, the straightforward moral of *Moon* is that time is loss.

To have dramatized so artfully these two propositions can have been no small feat for a fledgling playwright. Stoppard, however, soon proved capable of more. In his next plays for radio, he revisits time-as-loss and time-as-money, expressing these concepts through a radiocraft analogous to stagecraft. In *If You're Glad I'll Be Frank*, Stoppard actualizes time – the only physical dimension literally present in a radio broadcast – in order to convey the heartbreaking emptiness of its lonely expanses. Soon thereafter he raises a structure, Albert's bridge (*Albert's Bridge)*, whose upkeep over time requires sizable expenditures at odds with the bridge's ineffable nature – the very nature inherent in radio drama. While both plays are infused with Stoppard's usual whimsy, not to mention his usual angst, both exhibit as well a new apprehension of radio's special expressive possibilities.

If You're Glad (8 February 1966) issues from the teasing premise that Britain's Speaking Clock (reached by telephone) is actually Gladys Jenkins, missing wife to Frank, a bus driver. At the start of the play, Frank dials T-I-M, hears: "At the third stroke it will be eight fifty-nine precisely" (p. 26), identifies the voice as "my Gladys!" (p. 26), and sets about to rescue her. His efforts to penetrate the telephone bureaucracy, however, are hampered by his bus schedule. Still, by late afternoon, having gained on his schedule by a full four minutes, Frank bursts in on a meeting of the Telephone Board, demands his Gladys's whereabouts, and learns from Lord Coot that "we wouldn't trust your wife with the *time* – it's a machine, I thought everyone knew that" (p. 49). Yet through much of the play this so-called machine has expressed inner thoughts; and once Frank departs, she is heard to be sobbing hysterically, maintaining "I can't go on!" (p. 50). Lord Coot, though, successfully cajoles her, so that – whoever, or whatever, she is – she returns at the end of the play to dividing the minutes, while mentally mocking Lord Coot for "think[ing] he's God" (p. 50).

Here is a genuine radio play in that radio alone can produce it persuasively. Neither a machine nor a woman, Gladys is both simultaneously – a condition without any visible equivalent. Indubitably, Gladys must be a machine, since no person can track time in ten-second intervals, twenty-four hours a day, *ad infinitum*. Yet Gladys is also demonstrably human, moved by memories and longings, resentments and fears. Her intelligence is living, not artificial. But her life has been blasted, for she has reckoned with forbidden knowledge: the knowledge that time is not a clock

> And it doesn't go tick
> and it doesn't go tock
> and it doesn't go pip.
> It doesn't go anything.
> And it doesn't go anything for
>   ever
> It just goes   (p. 34)

This "inkling of infinity" (p. 33), as Gladys calls it, has made her what she is: half woman, half robot. Believing that figuratively she "counts for nothing" (p. 34), that she has no existential purpose, Gladys consents to "count for nothing" literally – that is, to mark time for its own sake. Unlike Frank, she adheres to no schedule; and unlike Lord Coot, she cares for no clock. She merely voices her consciousness of "the silence / in which [time] passes / impartial disinterested /godlike" (p. 34).

Now, for capturing the desolation implicit in the consciousness of time as infinity, as an "enormity" (p. 35) "rushing away, / reducing the life-size to nothing" (pp. 30–31), there is nothing like radio drama. A radio play, after all, fills no space whatsoever; it fills only time, and fills it only with images, shadows without any substance. In its insubstantiality, a radio play is a perfect imitation of life as Gladys understands it: an "illusion" of "scurrying insignificance," which Gladys aspires to "sabotage" (p. 36). Yet how? Gladys rightly anticipates that if she "coughed or / jumped a minute," the public would merely "correct their watches by my falter" (p. 36).

> And if I stopped to explain
> . . .
> they'd complain, to the Post Office.
> And if stopped altogether,
> just stopped, gave up the pretence,
> it would make no difference.
> Silence is the sound of time passing.   (p. 36)

The difference that Gladys proposes to make – namely, to shake people's "faith in / an uncomprehended clockwork" (p. 43) – eludes her, because people who call T-I-M are unprepared to hear silence as the voice of infinity.

By contrast, people who listen to radio drama may well be disposed to share Gladys's perspective. Radio audiences instinctively empathize with characters, like Gladys, who share their inner thoughts, since a confidential voice that emerges from nowhere, as if out of one's own head, is difficult to distance. Moreover, Gladys's compatriots are caricatured so broadly that they all appear laughably improbable, even inane, while Gladys herself, though in truth more improbable, acquires authority from the depth of her despair. There is particular resonance on radio, in fact, to Gladys's conviction of her own essential emptiness: "I'm empty anyway. / I was emptied long ago" (p. 31). For no matter how vividly the listener perceives her, Gladys is literally not there. Nor is *there*, on the radio, a concept that can ever be literally interpreted, unless it refers not to space, but to time, the only dimension that a radio broadcast can occupy. In reciting the seconds – and Stoppard intends that *"the actual time she announces should be related to the number of minutes or seconds that have passed (i.e. depending on the pace of the broadcast)*" (p. 25) – Gladys encourages listeners to ask whether time is not really, for them as for her, the only dimension that matters. Indeed, while the play is in progress, time must be supreme, since it governs the play's every action, its conceptual framework, even its conditions of performance.

Stoppard thus uses radio to fulfill the promise latent in the title of his play: the promise that he will be frank (that is, honest) if we will be Glad (that is, Gladys). By exploiting the radio's gift for encouraging audiences to identify with confessional characters, he makes us willing – even glad – to take Gladys's part. In addition, by frankly insisting that time holds us hostage while we listen to radio (if not also when we undertake other activities), he validates Gladys's contention that "the voice of the sun itself, / more accurate than Switzerland" is "definitive / divine" (p. 36). As for Gladys's impression that this divinity has all but annihilated her, who can deny it? The literal truth is that Gladys on radio, though not actually expunged, is certainly erased. And so, as Gladys argues, are all the other characters, if only they knew it. What Stoppard has achieved in *If You're Glad I'll Be Frank* is a subtle but pervasive mimesis, produced by his artful exploitation of radio's performance space – in other words, a consummate display of radiocraft.

Such craft marks the fundamental difference between *If You're Glad* and *"M" Is For Moon Among Other Things*. Though the plays share a darkly comedic apprehension that time entails loss, they diverge in their basic aesthetic identity. Whereas *Moon* is designed to be broadcast on radio, *Glad* is designed to be realized on radio – a major artistic advance. Thus *Glad* mirrors *Moon*, yet surpasses it, much as Stoppard's next radio play, *Albert's Bridge* (13 July 1967), both mirrors and surpasses his first play for the medium, *The Dissolution of Dominic Boot*. Like *Boot*, *Albert's Bridge* measures time indirectly, by the yardstick of money, with calamitous results. But where Dominic envisions no escape from his predicament – no release from his toing and froing in a taxi, at a ludicrous waste of money and time – Albert discovers what strikes him as a method of marking time and keeping it, even as he spends it. That there is madness in his method can hardly be doubted. Yet there is wisdom in it, too, of a sort that the radio validates.

What Albert has discovered is equanimity in painting – not painting as fine art, but as an aspect of the maintenance of Clufton Bay Bridge, the "fourth biggest single-span double-track shore-to-shore railway bridge in the world bar none" (p. 56). Painting this industrial giant captivates Albert as an enterprise free from any moral ambiguity. As he puts it, "there are no consequences to a coat of paint. That's more than you can say for a factory man; his bits and pieces scatter, grow wheels, disintegrate, change colour, join up in new forms, which he doesn't know anything about. In short, he doesn't know what he's done, to whom" (p. 55). Albert, by contrast, anticipates decades of self-contained activity, "keeping track of my life spent in painting in the colour of my track: / above it all" (p. 69). In essence, he expects that, at the end of fifty years, all that he has been and all that he has done – his entire past, in short – will be present in the paint. Time lost will be time kept, a most marvelous feat, though it comes at a price. For in painting his bridge in complete isolation, weekdays and weekends, even sleeping on the girders, Albert grows indifferent to the needs of other people. He neglects his wife and child, who eventually leave him; and he balks at sharing his bridge even with a man who plans to jump from it, but who changes his mind upon finding that the height yields "a vantage point [from which] the idea of society is just about tenable" (p. 78). Living "at a distance" when "life is all close up" (p. 69) makes Albert self-absorbed. So much so that, singing on the job, he comes to favor such lyrics as "I get a kick out of me" (p. 75), which Fraser, the would-be suicide, acidly calls the "egotist school of songwriting" (p. 75). Albert, however, is deaf to the insult. Whatever the cost of maintaining his bridge, he is willing to pay it unstintingly.

Unfortunately, the city's Bridge Subcommittee proves considerably less generous. Valuing the bridge as a symbol of Clufton's "prosperity" (p. 57), "quite apart from the money earned in railway dues" (p. 56), the committee embraces a plan for economizing on bridge maintenance. They upgrade from a paint that lasts two years to one that lasts eight, transfer three of the four individuals who have been painting the bridge in successive two-year cycles, and retain only Albert on a new eight-year plan. But the committee has miscalculated. At the end of two years' time, when Albert has painted but a quarter of the bridge, the remaining three-quarters has started to rust. Time has outwitted the committee, and it in turn seeks to get a jump on time. It sends a veritable army to finish the paint job in a single day's work. But when the army mounts the bridge without "breaking step" (p. 85), the laws of physics take their toll: overwhelmed by the force of feet tramping in unison, "the girders tens[e] and trembl[e] for the release of the energy being driven through them" (p. 86); the bridge shivers, pops some rivets, and collapses.

Now in a visual medium, the collapse of the Clufton Bay Bridge would be a shattering spectacle. Anything less would alienate audiences, accustomed as we are to special effects. But on radio, where visual events must be mediated – that is, transmitted to the eye of the mind by way of the ear – the collapse of the bridge is comparatively indistinct. Where the theatre or the cinema would turn every spotlight on involuting steel, radio closes in instead on Albert's pained incomprehension. "What did I have that they wanted?" (p. 86), he cries, as the bridge crashes down. And the cry, not the crash, arrests our attention. What, then, *did* he have that was worth someone's wanting? Literally, a gift for transforming the sweat of his brow into the life of his mind. Figuratively (for Albert, at university, studied philosophy) a priceless philosopher's stone – a magical means of transforming the base and corruptible metal of Clufton Bay Bridge into a golden abstraction, a pure and Platonic idea of a bridge: Albert's bridge. And for portraying this bridge, as distinguished from Clufton's, radio alone will suffice.

Radio, after all, strives by its nature to evoke mental images, Platonic or otherwise, whereas theatre and film rather seek to embody them – a distinction, to be sure, that only rarely makes a difference. Albert embodied on film, for example, is Albert no less than he is on the radio. But Albert's bridge, once embodied, is Clufton Bay Bridge, a structure entirely different from Albert's in quality and kind. Let the two appear together, as they do in Stoppard's play, and the medium chosen to exhibit them will determine the sort of impression they make. On film, Albert's bridge must appear a chimera, overshadowed by Clufton's, even absorbed by it. On radio, by contrast, Albert's bridge has authenticity – since mindmade images are what radio authenticates – while Clufton's is simply unable to materialize, except when we hear it collapse in a heap, at which point it is already scrap. As a radio play, *Albert's Bridge* thus endorses Albert's preference for mind over matter – an endorsement that a visual medium, in this case at least, is unsuited to duplicate.

Clearly, *If You're Glad* and *Albert's Bridge* mark Stoppard's mastery of radio – but not the limits of his talent for invention on an invisible stage. In three subsequent plays for the medium, Stoppard charts a new direction altogether, turning his attention from the facelessness of time (and the immateriality of ideas) to the faces of people who (though perfectly material) are hidden from each other, sometimes even from themselves. The new interest begins, as so often in Stoppard, ostensibly as a joke – one of two, as it happens, in *Where Are They Now?* (28 January 1970). In this play about an Old Boys' alumni reunion, the principal joke is that Jenkins, a graduate of Oakleigh, reminisces through an entire alumni dinner before finally discovering that the event he has attended is for graduates of Hove. The secondary joke is that, of three Old Hovians (Gale, Brindley, and Marks, nicknamed Groucho, Chico, and Harpo as schoolboys), the one who barely speaks until the end of the meal (Gale) turns out to have been Groucho, while the one known as Harpo for his disconcerting silence (Marks) now has Groucho's gift for gab. The confusions of identity central to the play would seem tailor-made for radio, as the radio listener's habitual predicament is to glean who is speaking from a host of aural clues. Still *Where Are They Now?* is not radio specific, since the confusions that it posits could be fully represented on a visible stage. Not until *Artist Descending a Staircase* (14 November 1972) does Stoppard contrive for three Old Boys (Martello, Beauchamp, and Donner), who again have boyhood nicknames (Banjo, Biscuit, and Mouse), to be realized nowhere better than on radio.

Dramatizing sixty years' worth of antics by the aging avant-gardists who have dabbled in art and electronic music, *Artist* renders their adventures as interlocking riddles, all originating in blindness, metaphorical or real. Donner's plunge down the stairs, for example, goes unwitnessed. The question thus arises: did he fall to his death, or was he pushed? A tape recorder that was running when he fell holds the answer; but Beauchamp and Martello misinterpret the recording. Each wrongly imagines that the other gave Donner an exasperated push in response to his bickering, which was rooted in his mourning for Sophie, a blind girl whom all of them loved in their youth. It was Beauchamp who eventually became Sophie's lover, Beauchamp who tired of her, and Beauchamp whose loss so appalled her that she leapt to her death from the window of his flat. But was it Beauchamp who had actually won her? In particular, was it Beauchamp whom Sophie had loved from a distance when, still dimly sighted, she had seen him standing next to his painting at an art show? Yes, if the painting, as she recalled it in her blindness, was black-on-white: "a border fence in the snow" (p. 142). No, if the painting was white-on-black: a "white fence . . . thick white posts . . . black in the gaps" (p. 154). For the man by *that* painting was Donner, Sophie's ardent admirer, who would never have left her, had he been her choice.

With Sophie long gone and with the paintings indistinguishable in retrospect, doubts about Sophie's affections persist, exacerbated by Donner's growing bitterness over the art that appears to have betrayed him – an art so abstract that, instead of yielding pictures, it yields riddles. Is such an art, which replaces "classical standards" (p. 125) with "mental acrobatics" (p. 116), fit to be considered art at all? No, according to Sophie, who deplored it. Yes, according to its chief exemplar, Marcel Duchamp, who is everywhere in *Artist*, yet nowhere: everywhere, since the play alludes to him continually, from its title (which puns on Duchamp's cubist painting *Nude Descending a Staircase*) to myriad quips throughout the dialogue; nowhere, since Duchamp never fully appears, being evident by implication only. Lucid, laughable, poignant, provoking, and, above all, impeccably constructed, *Artist* can work in any medium. Indeed, it has been staged to good effect. But as a play about knowledge offered and withheld, about people recognized and unrecognizable, about art conceived and misconceived, *Artist* rightly belongs on the radio, where the blindness of the medium complements, and even complicates, the blindness that the drama portrays.

The Dog It Was That Died (9 December 1982) similarly concentrates on questions of identity and art. Here identity is paramount, as Purvis, a British double agent connected to a Soviet safe house in Highgate, struggles to distinguish his primary employer from his secondary: "For years I've been feeding stuff in both directions [. . .] so the side I was actually working for became . . . well, a matter of opinion really . . . it got lost" (p. 181). Depressed by his predicament – which is wittily portrayed with Stoppard's trademark tragic lunacy – Purvis jumps off Chelsea Bridge, intending to drown himself. But his plan goes awry: he lands on a barge opportunely passing under him and ends up alive, though he crushes the dog that cushioned his fall. Alas, Purvis later drowns himself in any case. Sent to recuperate at a nursing home named Clifftops for its scenic situation on the coast, he contrives to plummet straight into the ocean in his wheelchair, rather than sustain an existence in which his two contradictory identities have become not one, but none. Though in name a double agent, Purvis is in truth no kind of agent whatsoever; he is lost to his employer no less than to himself. As the Chief of the British Secret Service explains, "Purvis was acting, in effect, as a genuine Russian spy in order to maintain his usefulness as a bogus Russian spy" (p. 192). In other words, while faithfully appearing for duty, Purvis was all the time missing in action – a paradox perfect for radio, where everything present is equally, irremediably, absent.

It is Purvis's predicament that gives *The Dog It Was That Died* its main affinity to radio. Jauntily, if tangentially, Stoppard broadens that affinity with radio hijinks related to art. He gives Purvis a boss, for example, who is building a huge architectural folly, crowned by a tower with an obelisk on top. Since the tower is octagonal, the "angles of the parapet throw the middle out," with the sorry result that the obelisk cannot "look centred from everywhere" (p. 167) – except, of course, on radio, where the eye of the mind can vanquish the laws of perspective. Is the mind's eye, then, omnipotent? Stoppard almost makes it seem so by contriving for *The Dog* to imitate his stage play, *After Magritte*, where the stage is arranged to resemble a surrealistic painting (*à la* Magritte), which the play then proceeds to explain with amusing banality. Surely, here is a conceit for which eyesight is necessary. Yet *The Dog* is a virtual radio equivalent, an audio play that explains – or explains away – a visually surrealistic scenario: the one painted by Purvis in his suicide note, with its visions of "an opium den in [the Chief's] house in Eaton Square," a "belly dancer [invited] to Buckingham Palace," an unidentified family heirloom that originally "belonged to a one-legged sea captain," and an unsavoury "savoury business" in Purvis's church (pp. 159–160). By the time that we encounter, shortly into the play, a donkey undergoing a surgical procedure in a drawing room chock full of clocks, it is abundantly clear that Magritte's sort of world can be painted on the radio as vividly as on stage or on canvas.

Between them, *Artist Descending a Staircase* and *The Dog It Was That Died* work such visual magic that Stoppard himself must have wondered how next to astonish his radio audience. The surprise up his sleeve was to abandon all surprises – to forgo a *tour de force* in favor of a memory play, *In the Native State* (21 April 1991), in which the son of an Indian artist discovers, in England, a secret romance from his father's distant past. As radio drama, *In the Native State* handsomely accommodates its medium of broadcast, just as the stage version, *Indian Ink*, aptly accommodates the theatre. But neither version actually invests in its venue: *Indian Ink* is not self-consciously a spectacle, and *In the Native State* is not self-consciously "radio," in that the meaning of the plays does not depend on their conditions of performance. Still, the care with which Stoppard has fine-tuned each version to the specific demands of its medium bespeaks his satisfaction, his craftsmanlike pleasure, at working in the theatre and in radio. Television would be a wholly different matter.

To hear Stoppard tell it, in comments recorded as filler for the NBC broadcast of *The Engagement* (1969) – a film shown on television, at least in the United States – theatre and radio spoiled him for film. Against backdrops designed, no doubt partly tongue-in-cheek, to suggest his aesthetic conservatism – a gracious country home (identified as his), croquet on the lawn, pool in the games room, and, naturally, a library – Stoppard speaks of a play as "something which happens behind closed doors between consenting adults," while "a film is a kind of three-ring circus, and the director's the elephant act and the writer's a sort of clown who comes on afterward and clears up the mess."[3] Proclaiming himself "definitely frightened of making this film," which transferred to the screen his radio play about Dominic Boot, Stoppard addresses the difficulty of "protect[ing] one's work." By his estimate, "given an optimum situation – the ideal director, the best possible casting, the best possible set-up – in the theater you will end up with something like 70% of what you meant . . . Now, with a film a writer hasn't even got . . . [a] casting vote. At least this is the fixed idea which I have about filmmaking." Whether *The Engagement* modified that idea, or merely reconciled Stoppard to working with a film crew, he proceeded thereafter to script numerous films, some of them for television, some for the cinema. Eventually, in *Squaring the Circle*, he would fashion that rarest of entities: a play so specifically imagined for television that the medium functions as part of the message. But the earlier plays do not foretell this accomplishment, nor do they suggest how difficult it would prove in the making.

Certainly, *The Engagement* is not specifically "TV," though it abounds with humor devised for the eye: Dominic, for instance, tumbling out of the taxi, or the taxi engaging in a preposterous police chase. There is even an inspired sequence in which a sight gag acquires metaphorical significance: when Dominic, desperate to pay off his fare, tries to earn enough cash by repeatedly donating blood at a blood bank till he farcically goes rubber-legged, we are given to know that the driver is guilty of bloodsucking. But the work's overall "filmness," as Stoppard calls it in the filler, is apparently the work of the director Paul Joyce, not of Stoppard himself. By Stoppard's own admission, "the actual style of the [film] I feel completely detached from. When one writes the dialogue, one has a vision of the whole composition, the people, the environment. And it was shocking to see through a close-up lens simply an ear when I thought that one would see a man on a street corner." Evidently, in translating *Dominic Boot* into *The Engagement*, Stoppard visualized a screenplay (as the credits aptly indicate) more nearly than a film script.

The same can be said, only moreso, about three of Stoppard's four plays for television preceding *The Engagement*. That Stoppard himself regarded *The Engagement* as the first of his films – "I've never made a film before," he says in the filler, "and I'm not terribly keen on being involved in one now" – would suggest that television struck him initially as a species of theatre. So, at any rate, he treats it in *A Separate Peace* (August 1966), where a certain John Brown, although fully in health, takes up residence in a hospital to escape from the world. Without the slightest alteration to the television script, *A Separate Peace* could transfer to the stage. Similarly, *Teeth* (February 1967) is essentially a stage play, requiring a camera for the closing shot alone: namely, a close-up of George's thin smile after Henry, the dentist whom George has been cuckolding, has revenged himself on George during a routine dental check-up by removing a middle front tooth from George's dazzling choppers. As for *Another Moon Called Earth* (June 1967), in its prefiguration of *Jumpers* the play is theatrical, not cinematic. Only in his television spy thriller, *Neutral Ground* (December 1968), does Stoppard fashion a script that depends on the camera for its realization.

Here Philo, an Eastern European who had worked as a British secret agent in Russia, has absconded to a neutral village, disgusted by the Cold War and its betrayals within betrayals. His cover blown, the Russians are seeking to kill him. Meanwhile, the British, who had dropped him on suspicion of his having switched sides, now recognize his loyalty, not to mention his usefulness, and are seeking him, too – for their part, to reenlist him, despite his contempt for them. The reenlistment, of course, must be accomplished by guile and persuasion, which Stoppard achieves by means of dialogue – shrewd, supple talk that is fiercely attentive to the moral contradictions inherent in Cold War gamesmanship. Narration, however, is left to the camera predominantly. It is the camera that relates how Philo escapes his would-be assassins at Russia's frontier, by the chance interaction of a fur hat and a pet monkey; the camera that reveals nearly all the behavior of the boy who acts as Philo's scout in the village where Philo is eventually found; and the camera that shows how a British secret agent bests Russia's assassins in their second attempt to gun Philo down. Like *The Engagement*, *Neutral Ground* is inherently "film," not a stage play entrusted to celluloid. But is it film that belongs on television, as distinct from the cinema? Not really. Whatever television drama might be, and the question is open, *Neutral Ground* gives no hint of defining the genre.

By contrast, television is the medium of choice for *Professional Foul* (September 1977), a film in which linguistic analysis, ethics, and catastrophe theory – all subjects of papers to be read at the Colloquium Philosophicum Prague 77 – meet challenges on the soccer field and in the Czech police state. A "professional foul" is a footballer's term for a deliberate infraction to prevent one's opponent from scoring. When just such a foul is committed by an English team playing in Prague the weekend of the colloquium, a philosopher takes the occasion to discourse insultingly, back at the hotel, on "yob ethics" (p. 175) until a member of the team knocks him down. The punch may be taken as proof of the position enunciated by another philosopher, Anderson, "that language is not the only level of human communication, and perhaps not the most important level" (p. 154). But though action initially speaks louder than words, it is words that have the final say, twice over. After Anderson discovers the Czech police searching the apartment of Pavel Hollar, his former graduate student and a Czech national who has been arrested for crimes against the state, Anderson commits two professional fouls of his own, both essentially verbal: he delivers an impromptu paper on a subject that the Czech government had not (and never would have) approved, "namely the conflict between the rights of individuals and the rights of the community" (p. 177); and he smuggles Hollar's politically volatile thesis out of Czechoslovakia by hiding it, without permission, in a fellow philosopher's briefcase. Although in doing so Anderson errs (commits fouls) against his ethical principles, his behavior conforms to catastrophe theory, which posits that a moral "principle reverses itself at the point where a rational man would abandon it," lest the principle become an "excuse for acting against a moral interest" (p. 169).

Intriguingly, the dramatic shape of *Professional Foul* reverses itself at precisely the same point as Anderson's ethics. For where dialogue and action are evenly balanced before Anderson rises to address the Colloquium, his provocative paper makes dialogue – indeed, monologue – paramount. Although the camera may cut, as Anderson speaks, to the policemen who rush to search his room, or to the backstage officials who silence him by sounding a fire alarm, these actions are merely *re*actions to Anderson's words: words that dominate the screen to an extent impermissible in cinema. As for Anderson's method of slipping a prohibited manuscript past the security check at the airport, the action is related in retrospect, not shown in itself. Thus does Stoppard subordinate camera work to speech in *Professional Foul*, with the consequence that television emerges less as a species of cinema than as a hybrid of cinema and radio – an approach to the medium entirely consistent with its unimposing screen, large enough to convey information, yet finally too small to make much of a visual impact.

A similar approach to the medium marks *Squaring the Circle* (May 1984), the last of Stoppard's television programs to date, and a work that treats television gingerly, in light of Stoppard's goal: to dramatize the birth of Solidarity in Poland. Such a dramatization is inherently problematic, because filmed reconstructions of actual events carry documentary force, though in fact they are fictional. To dissipate this force, Stoppard summons a Narrator – a role that he would have performed as the Author, had he not been overruled by Metromedia, which had rights to the program in America.[4] Still, even as an anonymous third party, the Narrator underscores television's artifice, by warning the audience that "everything is true except the words and the pictures" (pp. 191–192, also p. 258), by repeatedly changing his assessment of events under modest provocation from a ubiquitous Witness, and by permitting the Witness to "ruin" (p. 223), through mockery, any literary devices to which the film may resort – a chess game, for instance, or the "cheap trick" (p. 251) of looking to children for wisdom. The Narrator thereby makes television equivalent to radio, denying the medium its conventional eyewitness status, which has, after all, no analog in *ear*witnessing.

In its very construction, then, *Squaring the Circle* fosters skepticism about television's relation to truth. So, too, in its content, since television figures equivocally in the rise of Solidarity. When shipyard workers strike to form a union, for example, eyes turn to Gdansk, which is a media "circus," rather than to the equally radical Szczecin, where there are "no journalists, no cameras" (p. 209). Such is the power of television. But what validates this power? Surely not the medium's authenticity. Not when it enables First Secretary Gierek to address the nation from what seems to be his office, at what seems to be his desk, before what seems to be his bookcase, but is just "*a fake flat*" (p. 203) in a studio. Even Stoppard's revelation – or is it just a surmise? – that the actual bookcase is itself a sort of fake, being really a wall in which a *"door"* is *"concealed"* (p. 205), does not rescue television from the charge of purveying illusions. Solidarity's leaders are not the "saboteurs" that they "look like" (p. 260) on Polish television, any more than Lech Walesa is the "anti-Russian carnival" (p. 255) that the American media would make of him. Nor do televised events necessarily mean more than others, such as Cardinal Wyszynski's political sermons. Television may, in fact, mean the most when its meaning is most unintended, as when Szczepanski, Chairman of the State Committee for Radio and TV, wrests irony from the screen by idly switching channels from Gierek *"mouthing"* a speech to what serves as wry commentary, *"a mildly pornographic film"* (p. 210). Nonetheless, there is nothing ironic in Solidarity's threat to "close down TV and radio if we don't get the access we were promised" (p. 244). Although Deputy Prime Minister Rakowski may retort, "Are we here to talk about bread or TV?" the distinction rings false. Television establishes access to bread.

Television, in short, is a political tool, which Stoppard employs to make a political argument: namely, that the western idea of freedom cannot be reconciled with the Soviet idea of socialism because the two are incompatible. To join them is "impossible, in the same sense as it is impossible in geometry to turn a circle into a square with the same area – not because no one has found out how to do it, but because there is no way in which it can be done" (p. 193). Implicitly, though coincidentally, *Squaring the Circle* makes a similar point about the relationship of television to drama. In production, as Stoppard reveals in his original preface to the play, *Squaring the Circle* was subjected to intense commercial pressures, which had aesthetic implications. Through Herculean effort, Stoppard rescued the project, but not without injurious compromise. We are therefore left to wonder if reconciling commerce with aesthetics in television is not rather like squaring the circle – as good as impossible, given current modes of funding. Let us hope not. The evidence of *Squaring the Circle* suggests that Stoppard, so eminent in radio-craft, can produce craft in television, too. But what delights he might devise, were he given *carte blanche*, can only for now be supposed.

NOTES

1 *Stoppard: the plays for radio, 1964–1991* (London and Boston: Faber and Faber, 1994), p. 121. All further quotations from the radio plays will be cited in the text, with reference to this collection.

2 "Introduction," *Stoppard: the television plays, 1965–1984* (London and Boston: Faber and Faber, 1993), p vii. All quotations from the television plays will be cited in the text, with reference to this collection.

3 Transcribed from a tape of *The Engagement* as filmed by Memorial Films in 1969 and broadcast on NBC *Experiment in Theater* in 1970. The tape is available for

viewing at the Museum of Television and Radio in New York City. All subsequent quotations from Stoppard bearing on *The Engagement* come from this broadcast.

4 See Stoppard's "Introduction" to the first published edition of *Squaring the Circle* (London and Boston: Faber and Faber, 1984) for a full discussion of the problems he encountered in the production of this play.

FURTHER READING

Although much praised for their elegance and often studied for their thematic implications, Stoppard's radio and television plays have rarely been considered in light of the media for which they were written. Since television is largely a director's (and a producer's) medium, the dearth of attention to the television plays as "television" is probably justified. The radio plays, by contrast, deserve more scrutiny as "radio" than scholars have tended to give them. For a fine consideration of Stoppard's radio plays in general, see Katherine E. Kelly, "Tom Stoppard Radioactive: a sounding of the radio plays," *Modern Drama* 32.3 (September 1989), pp. 440–452. For *Artist Descending a Staircase* in particular, see: Katherine E. Kelly, "Tom Stoppard's *Artist Descending A Staircase*: outdoing the 'Dada' Duchamp," *Comparative Drama* 20.3 (fall 1986), pp. 191–200; and Elissa S. Guralnick, "*Artist Descending a Staircase*: Stoppard captures the radio station – and Duchamp," *PMLA* 105.2 (March 1990): pp. 286–300, republished with additions and revisions in her book *Sight Unseen: Beckett, Pinter, Stoppard, and other contemporary dramatists on radio* (Athens: Ohio University Press, 1996), pp. 29–52.

5

IRA B. NADEL

Stoppard and film

At the age of eleven Tom Stoppard met Hamlet – on the screen in Laurence Olivier's 1948 film. Six years later, at the beginning of his career as a journalist, Stoppard formalized his relationship with the cinema. The presence of a movie theatre next to one of the Bristol newspapers where he worked – and where he and other reporters spent numerous hours on "assignment" – was one source; another was his appointment as film critic on the *Bristol Evening World*, soon to be supplemented by work as a film columnist for the *Western Daily Press*. Such exposure enhanced his sense of the visual as well as his fascination with the creative possibilities of action, point of view, and dramatic dialogue. Mixed with his admiration for movie culture – he interviewed such stars as Diana Dors and Albert Finney – it is no surprise that as his career developed, he would have his own work optioned by the studios and be asked to adapt the work of writers he admired for the screen. The job paid well and he was able to graft his talent for dialogue on to the plots of others.

Adaptations, rather than original screenplays, became Stoppard's *métier*; through adaptation, he developed a lucrative secondary talent as a "script doctor." From Nabokov's *Despair* to Graham Greene's *The Human Factor* and John le Carré's *The Russia House* (and most recently, *Enigma*, a script based on the Robert Harris novel dealing with espionage and the Bletchley Park decoding project during World War Two), Stoppard showed himself to work best in film with the work of others. While finding the money terrific, he welcomed the work as a break from searching for original play ideas. His career, in fact, has alternated between writing stage plays and screenplays, a pattern that parodied itself when he wrote his only original screenplay: a rewrite and adaptation of his *own* work, *Rosencrantz and Guildenstern Are Dead*. As he explained in a 1991 interview, only *he* would have the courage to cut scenes without fear of criticism or complaint from the author.[1]

I

Stoppard's assignment as the film critic for the *Bristol Evening World* initiated the youthful journalist's fledging interest in what was, in 1958 England,
a new fascination with film, then trapped between Pinewood studio dramas,
Boulton comedies, Hollywood blockbusters and the intellectual efforts of
European *cinématistes* embodied in the French *nouvelle vague*. His early film
reviews were of standard fare, ranging from *Jet Storm* (a group of British
filmstars competing for screen time with a bomb) to *Don't Give up the Ship*
with Jerry Lewis and *I'm All Right Jack* starring Peter Sellers. The writing in
these pieces is descriptive and straightforward without the puns, *double
entendres* or witticisms that would soon mark his later film criticism.
Stoppard opts for summaries of the plot, perfunctory comments on the stars
and a brief judgment. Of the thriller *Blind Date*, for example, he ironically
notes that because it has "no ambitious pretensions . . . it registers heavily
as an enterprising and entertaining thriller."[2]

Stoppard clearly enjoys and parodies film culture, particularly that of the
stars; one of his funniest pieces is a critique of the supposed hardships of
film stars on location and their struggles to remain fashionable while in the
jungle or the desert. The cause for his complaint is publicity for the Walt
Disney-produced *Swiss Family Robinson* shooting in Tobago. Stoppard
plays up a hurricane, sharks and injuries to the stars as overwritten and mis-
leading; the injury to the star, for example, occurred on the diving board of
the Bluehaven Hotel, not clambering about the steep and rugged granite of
a waterfall. What prompts film people, he asks, "to play up this side of their
well-upholstered existence to the extent of implying that *we* are the lucky
ones?" In the same column, he then comments, in a wonderful deadpan
manner, on the careers of various actresses noting that Sylvia Syms "turns
from being a striptease girl in 'Expresso Bongo' to a novice nun in
'Conspiracy of Hearts,'" adding her insightful remark, "'I suppose variety
is the spice of life.'" He ends the piece by admitting that he is probably "the
only man in England who walked out of [South Pacific] in the interval – the
stereo sound, the sickly effusions of colour and Rosanno Brazzi drove me
into the street."[3]

By September 1959, Stoppard had a column headed "Films," alternating
with his more gossipy "Camera Call," the title of pieces featuring movie
news or publicity. Gradually, however, his critical and comic voice became
clearer: ending a review of *Evil Eden*, he writes, "Simone Signoret cannot
make up for the loose direction, in spite of her own talents, and furthermore
the whole piece, posters and X-certificate notwithstanding, is as sexy as a

currant bun."[4] And he is not beyond offering cultural quips: on the return of Olivier's *Richard III* to a Bristol screen, he remarks that it is a "crying shame and commercial fact that the word Shakespeare keeps more people out of the cinema than a hot day"; or that the ABC Theatre in Bristol "offers the best combination that a double-X programme can give. One for horror and one for sex"; or that "the cinema public will have grown up the day it realises that the director is more important than the star."[5] A quick turn of phrase also appears in his writing: of *Goliath and the Barbarians*, he snaps a "saga of biceps and busts"; *Crack in the Mirror* "has an idea which is so ingenious that it is defeated by its own ingenuity"; "the fact that Mr. [Jerry] Lewis and I don't get on made it no easier to enjoy a script which is more chronic than comic."[6]

When Stoppard began to write for the arts page of the *Western Daily Press* in 1961, edited by his friend Anthony Smith, he contributed a regular film column that was more wide-ranging than those in the *Bristol Evening World*. One week he would offer a critique of *la nouvelle vague* and the next of *Spartacus*. The reviews were witty, insightful, and informative: epics, comedies, foreign films buttressed by ideas on film and principles of criticism all came under his scrutiny.

Not surprisingly, his reviews became a testing ground for an aesthetic. In a piece dated 5 January 1961 entitled "Critic and his Credo," Stoppard argues for the inseparable link between aesthetics and commitment. You cannot divorce art from politics, he argues in a defense of film as art, not entertainment.[7] Other reviews refine his aesthetic: reviewing *Shadows* by John Cassavettes, Stoppard writes that the disjointed film is like life with a reality that is not stylish but unfinished. Human speech, he adds, "is hesitant, often thoughtless, almost always unoriginal. Never a script." His complaint is that film presents an ordered world unlike life, which is often "muddled, aimless, imprecise, inactive" with blurred visions and incoherent voices: "in technical terms, life is very bad cinema."[8] Another review opens with the remark – prescient in that it foreshadows his own later work as a screenwriter – that "for all its intrinsic art, the cinema largely depends on other media for material. Original film scripts are not uncommon, but the chief progenitors are the novelist and the playwright." In this review of four films, *Lucky Jim*, *Room at the Top*, *The Entertainer*, and *Saturday Night and Sunday Morning*, Stoppard celebrates a new realism in English cinema.[9] His review of *Spartacus*, published in the newspaper under the pseudonym of Tomik Sträussler (the same page has an article by Tom Stoppard on Arnold Wesker), celebrates the spectacle of the film, the directing of Stanley Kubrick and the script by Dalton Trumbell (1 March 1968: p. 8); his comments on *Ben Hur* two weeks later are even more laudatory and ironic: "the falsity of the prevalent distinction between Art and Commerce in cinema is shown up as never before." The chariot race between Charleton Heston and Stephen Boyd was, he writes, thrilling, leaving "one gasping and incredulous" (15 March 1961: p. 8).

Stoppard, however, understood film as a register of English social change, commenting on *No Love For Johnny,* starring Peter Finch as an antihero who ascends to the Establishment and chooses power over love, that he was "riveted by the sight of the anti-hero making the social grade" (5 April 1961: p. 8). In his column on *La Dolce Vita* by Fellini, Stoppard criticizes the boredom that emerges in a society pursuing only pleasure, although he celebrates the film's originality, adding, however, that "the present cut has been dubbed with a technical expertise and a depressing banality" (28 June 1961: p. 8).

Stoppard's *mea culpa* as a film critic appeared in a long 1961 essay/review of *Breakfast at Tiffany's* approached through a critique of Richard Hoggart's *The Uses of Literacy* and the moral evasions of mass entertainment which the unreality of cinematic life confirmed. The alternative to Hoggart is Salinger's *Catcher in the Rye* because there the hero sees through the phoniness of life. Film creates a world that is too tidy and, hence, unreal.

In a paragraph, Stoppard summarizes the overall, dismal situation:

> For six darkened months I was a film critic, and on the absurd grounds that I was being paid for it, I had to sit through hours of predictable tailored crises presented with little art but a great deal of artfulness. Patterns, interlaced but distinguishable, are superimposed on the medium like a frieze or more aptly a giant comprehensive stencil offering a rigid variety of situations . . . the Errant Maiden Condoned would be a generic tale for a host of sad tales. . . . [so is] Money is the root of all happiness.

He next exposes the changes to the original Truman Capote story as he vents his displeasure at sanitizing the heroine from a woman of eleven lovers to none and the shift of the ending from a flight to Brazil to marriage with the hero. He hates the slicked up sugary changes to the story and ends with a manifesto of sorts on film:

> Why is all this nonsense thought necessary? The unwritten code of film-makers decries that people don't like to be reminded that (a) even nice people are cuckolded (b) some enchanting bitches really are bitches, not just wild young things waiting for love to conquer all (c) people with ugly little flats are worth attention, (d) our side was not always glorious in the big war daddy, (e) boy does not always marry girl (f) especially if she gets pregnant, (g) and produces an uncute baby. Complete up to z.
>
> As an escape from the business of living, the cinema is at worst an invidious therapy. But if anyone takes it as a complete guide to life, he'd better pin his faith on waking up one morning a duke.[10]

A postscript softens some of Stoppard's criticism. He claims that there are enough good films to get him into a cinema and that his article has ignored the best "but the dichotomy of minority art and popular rubbish is slowly making way for popular art – *Saturday Night and Sunday Morning* has been one of the biggest money makers this year" (p. 8).

Films, however, would provide Stoppard with ideas and even names for his characters. The ubiquitous "Moon" is a case in point, appearing in *The Real Inspector Hound, Lord Malquist and Mr Moon, Another Moon Called Earth* and *"M" is For Moon*. The origin of this obsession began with Paul Newman in *Left Handed Gun*. Viewing the movie in Bristol, Stoppard noted that at one point in the film the moon is reflected in a horse trough. Drunken cowboys suddenly shoot the reflection, while Newman shouts the word Moon which is also the name of one of the characters in the movie. Stoppard at the time was working on an early draft of *Real Inspector Hound* and needed the name of a critic. Moon, he explained, seemed right.[11]

Through Anthony Smith, journalist, novelist, dramatist, and editor of the arts page of the *Western Daily Press*, Stoppard met John Boorman, a television producer/director with BBC Bristol who first suggested that Stoppard and Smith prepare some scripts for television. Boorman then had the idea to make a six-part documentary for the new BBC 2 tracing the life of a young couple in Bristol. Originally called *The Smiths*, it became *The Newcomers* starring Anthony Smith, his wife Alison and – occasionally – Stoppard. The title referred to newcomers to Bristol and also the new generation, the first to benefit from the Welfare State. Smith was to script it but when Boorman decided that Smith would be featured, Boorman wrote the script; or rather, he gave Smith, Alison, and Stoppard the subject and angle he wanted them to talk about and left it to them to improvise the actual dialogue. The six-part documentary shot in Bristol was shown on BBC2 and then recut to three parts and shown on BBC1. Stoppard, not identified by name but playing himself, appears in a restaurant scene and then a disco, dancing and chatting up a woman.

Boorman wanted Smith and Stoppard to start writing scripts and, through meetings and instructions, he told them how to fashion a screenplay and television scripts, even offering Stoppard what he (Stoppard) later called the best definition of filmmaking he knew: "'the business of turning money into light and then back into money again.'"[12] But Smith and Stoppard were unsuccessful with such alchemy despite trying various scripts about numerous subjects, none of which were ever approved.

Nevertheless, Bristol became the study in which Stoppard, through his filmgoing, film criticism and early efforts at television, learned the visual grammar of film. The importance of dialogue in defining character as well as situation, plus the economy of structure necessary in a film that began to define his work, most notably in his successful radio play *Albert's Bridge,* emerged through his exposure to the movies. In *Albert's Bridge,* for example, Stoppard conveys both the domestic intensity of Albert and his wife and the visual breadth of painting the bridge. With Cecil B. de Mille like flair, he ends the play with an army of painters marching across the span which causes it to collapse. Stoppard's early and constant wish to transform his radio and stage work into film – from almost the beginning of his career, he encouraged his agent Kenneth Ewing to explore the cinematic possibilities of his work – originated in his attempts at film in Bristol.

Such an exposure to film continued in London, where he moved in 1962. Although he wrote principally drama criticism for *Scene,* he also kept current with the new cinema, while his efforts at radio and television drama refined his sense of cinematic structure which expanded when he went to Berlin for five months in 1964 on a Ford Foundation grant. Stoppard used the time not only to write *Rosencrantz and Guildenstern Meet King Lear,* the prototype of his 1966 Edinburgh and 1967 London hit, but hung out with a number of filmmakers, at one point actually playing the part of a cowboy in a Danish experimental filmmaker's attempt at a western shot in front of the Brandenberg Gate. His two English friends at the symposium, Piers Paul Read and Derek Marlowe, were also equally interested in film, Marlowe going on to a career as a screenwriter, and Read later adapting his own work for the screen. Again, the visual grammar of this alternate medium aided Stoppard in the conception and treatment of his work, notably the use of rapid fire exchanges of dialogue, cuts in structure and sudden shifts in scenes, all elements that appear in his first dramatic success, *Rosencrantz and Guildenstern Are Dead.* His introduction to film and his attempts to write television scripts in Bristol, soon to become his source of income in London, formed the basis of his later screenwriting.

Although Stoppard hardly needed encouragement, it was Boorman again who, in December 1967 through his connections with MGM, suggested that Stoppard write a screenplay of *Rosencrantz and Guildenstern.* Stoppard immediately got to work and prepared a lengthy screenplay with sixty-eight scenes (the 1989 filmscript which became the shooting script for the 1990 release had 54; a 1987 first draft had only 38). But Stoppard's sense of the play's limitations as a film was clear: "I can't see it working as a sort of time/space layercake with actors playing actors playing R, switching from reality to roleplaying, from 1968 to some indefinable Elizabethan age, and so on," he explained to Boorman. Perhaps the main reason for the play's effectiveness, he added, "is that it doesn't attempt to break down or analyze or explain; it simply pitches you into its ambiguities." The narrative is seen from the limited angle of Rosencrantz and Guildenstern instead of the wide angle of *Hamlet*. "Personally, I think that this difference of angles can be used much more and to better effect in the film than in the play." Furthermore, the play was written to be funny and must be produced that way; if it isn't, "it just becomes rather pretentious and boring . . . I think the film ought to be made in Europe and on location anywhere between Yugoslavia and Finland; America doesn't smell right for it. I swear the light is different."[13]

MGM believed that Boorman might direct the work (he had a recent hit with *Deliverance*), took an option on the play and provided an advance, but the studio was quick to express disappointment when they reviewed Stoppard's first effort. Studio criticism stressed his failure to give an adequate sense of the events occurring in *Hamlet* at the same time as the adventures of Rosencrantz and Guildenstern. Difficulties with the introductory passages and too little embellishment of the visual were further objections. Stick closer to the dramatic thread of *Hamlet* and establish a background that will involve the audience more was the studio's comment, adding somewhat obtusely that "the very real vacuity of R&G is a handicap in terms of screen-projected drama . . . neither R or G is interesting nor sympathetic nor iden-tifiable" (HRC 112.4). Stoppard had added much to the play, commenting in 1993 that there were "yards of new wonderful stuff . . . MGM paid for it because the play was on Broadway then, and the script I wrote was really awful in the sense that it wasn't a movie."[14] The project was dropped until 1987 when Stoppard attempted another version which reached final form in 1989.

Stoppard was rapidly learning a basic lesson of screenwriting which Boorman outlined in 1974 when commenting on Stoppard's effort to write a screenplay of David Hare's *Knuckle*. "A script," Boorman explained,

> [And therefore the writer] must be subject to alteration, development, evolu-tion at various stages – to some extent the writing process is indivisible from the making of the film. Casting alters it, locations often demand or suggest developments, rehearsal reveals problems and shooting itself exerts constant pressures on the script. I like – planned – to allow the script and the film to grow . . . A script is never really finished. I often find that during editing new lines are needed to replace ones that have suffered excision, for instance in *Deliverance* we altered 30 or 40 lines during post-synching to assist the flow of the film.[15]

Stoppard soon absorbed and understood the professional treatment of the script, learning to distance himself from the text once it was completed.

II

A Walk on the Water, broadcast on Independent Television in November 1963, followed by a series of radio plays for the BBC in February and April 1964, marked Stoppard's breakthrough in getting his work seen and heard. And while Ewing sent various scripts of the television plays to directors and producers suggesting short films when television pilots failed, Stoppard explored other possibilities: short stories, drama, and fiction. The sudden success of *Rosencrantz and Guildenstern* in London and then New York – 421 performances and a Tony Award for best play – led to the MGM offer, as well as other possibilities: Anthony Blond, the publisher of Stoppard's only novel, suddenly suggested a film treatment of the work which Stoppard drafted; and in the summer and early fall of 1969, Al Brodax, who produced *Yellow Submarine* for the Beatles, asked Stoppard and Anthony Smith to prepare a film version of the award-winning *Albert's Bridge*, radically departing from the radio play by introducing two Alberts, one an executive, the other a painter.[16] About this time, Stoppard even discussed a film version of *Enter a Free Man* with Richard Attenborough.

By February 1969, Stoppard felt he could speak out in *Today's Cinema* under the heading "Confessions of a Screenwriter." He disarmingly began by admitting he was not a screenwriter – but that the title was important and that he had written two screenplays (*Rosencrantz* and *Albert's Bridge*) and that the work involved was always daunting. However, he questions the "nobility" of screen writing, complaining that "cinema still lacks plausibility as the patron and repository of a writer's best work."[17] In drama, the playwright's position is unequivocal: no changes can occur to the script without his consent. Not so with film where the whim of the star, the director, the producer, or the studio can impose revisions. In such circumstances, "a script becomes just another variable, to be changed as easily and as often as an actor's costume. The enormous sums of money at risk make scripts much too important to be left to writers," he remarks (p. 5). The screenwriter Warren Leight recently summarized the situation: "'Film is good money but there's a reason: they pay you to go away.'"[18]

"Symbolically, perhaps no one ever speaks of talkies any more. They are all movies," Stoppard adds, noting the diminished status of the screenwriter whose script is appropriately and ironically called "a property." Occasionally, the cynical Stoppard of 1969 comments, "when we write a film we are putting ourselves into the hands of gangsters and poltroons" (p. 5). He cites various examples of such enforced changes and concludes by reasserting that when he has a real idea to write, "it has never occurred to me to write it as a film." But with a Stoppardian twist, he optimistically concludes that by year's end "my first film will have been made and I might feel very differently" (p. 5). But it was not: the MGM project to film *Rosencrantz* collapsed, although Stoppard received a handsome fee. In 1970, however, he prepared a script entitled *The Engagement*, a fifty-minute film for television shown on NBC based on *The Dissolution of Dominic Boot*. Critics did not like it.

Stoppard's success on the stage led to various movie offers while, conversely, he began to offer his own projects to Hollywood. In 1971 he had a contract with Paramount for a production of *Galileo*, an adaptation of Brecht's play related to a more extravagant production he envisioned involving the London Planetarium which did not come off. The work appealed to Stoppard because of its dramatization of science and conflict of principle and ideas; he again prepared a filmscript, but it remained unproduced. However, four years later he worked on his first feature-length film, *The Romantic Englishwoman*, which starred Glenda Jackson, Helmut Berger and Michael Caine, from the novel by Thomas Wiseman. It turned out only to be about three weeks of work for director Joseph Losey and did not have Stoppard's interest: "I was doing it for Losey personally, not because I wanted to; he had a script which he had to shoot in a hurry and didn't like much." Nonetheless, Stoppard's name, as cowriter along with Wiseman, appeared on screen and he was praised in reviews as adding most of the humor, "allowing Losey to ricochet apprehension off sly social comedy."[19]

Stoppard next undertook the screenplay for Nabokov's 1966 novel *Despair*, directed by Rainer Werner Fassbinder. As correspondence with the star Dirk Bogarde makes clear, the finished product was a disaster. Stoppard admired Nabokov and wanted the film, especially its dialogue, to be treated with lightness and speed. The opposite happened: it became ponderous and introspective, resulting in an overly long and boring film. Stoppard in fact walked out of the screening. Its secondary virtues, he later explained to one of the producers, of decor, composition, and camera were ruined by its primary faults of pretentiousness, poor sound, labored explications, and slow pace. Cuts also meant a lack of shape and structure. Stoppard was infuriated since he had pointed out many of these lapses in an April 1977 memo when he had read Fassbinder's reworking of his script. Stoppard objected to a betrayal of the spirit of the work rather than to changes of his words. To Bogarde, he wrote that the film is "a turkey which I believe is American for lemon." "The crux of it," he continued, is that "I wanted to write the script because it was Nabokov's book and Fassbinder wanted to film the story *despite* its being Nabokov's book" (10 December 1977). Nevertheless, he called the script "the only film which I wrote on my own."[20] All the others, with the exception of *Rosencrantz and Guildenstern*, involved coming in to rework existing material.

Graham Greene's *The Human Factor*, a 1978 bestseller, was next. Approached by Otto Preminger after Greene himself turned down the chance to write the screenplay and Peter Shaffer was unavailable, Stoppard was thrilled. "To be honest," he told an interviewer, "if Otto had said I can't pay you but you'll get one or two lunches with Graham Greene, I might have done the job. I was much more nervous of displeasing Graham Greene than I was of displeasing Otto." Stoppard and Greene spoke by phone while Stoppard worked on the script, which he approached carefully: "I began *The Human Factor* by taking it down into its structural components. To get the overall balance right you have to have a notion as to how much screen time each scene is worth. There's no point in writing a brilliant 12 minute scene that should be 4 minutes."[21] When Greene finally saw the movie in 1980, he expressed surprise. To Stoppard he said, "You needn't have stuck so closely to my original."[22]

The film was highly praised for the acting as well as the script, with Vincent Canby applauding Stoppard's talent for adaptation. "It is so carefully done that I don't think one could be sure of Mr. Stoppard's ellipses and transpositions without putting the screenplay alongside the novel," he concluded.[23] Not the least appeal of the work for Stoppard, in addition to working with a writer as celebrated as Greene, was the chance to deal with the subject of espionage, a theme he would enlarge in *Hapgood* (1988), as well as in his 1990 screenplay for John le Carré's *The Russia House* and the 1998 screenplay, *Enigma*. The complexity of motive – Castle, Greene's hero, commits treason as a debt of honor paid to the Communist underground which rescued his black wife from a South African jail – strongly appealed to Stoppard. The timing was also superb since three months before the movie's release, Civil Service spies had become a public worry with the revelations of Sir Anthony Blunt as a mole in the British Secret Service. Equal to praise of the script was Stoppard's praise of Preminger, a notoriously difficult director. "Say what you will about Otto, he would never make a change in the script without consulting the writer first."[24] Following hard on Nabokov's *Despair*, *The Human Factor* extended Stoppard's engagement with writers he admired, bringing him direct exposure to their methods and styles. Their books also gave him something to work with and eliminated the need to be original, something – at least with plot – he has never claimed to be.

What followed, however, contradicts his disclaimer of originality: the triumphant *Brazil* (1985), Stoppard's first script nominated for an Oscar and winner of the LA Critic's Award. Surprisingly, it lost to the now forgotten *Witness*, a mystery about the Amish starring Harrison Ford. Although there were disputes over the shaping of the story and the nature of certain scenes, especially the opening, the final screenplay displays a surrealistic power and visual creativity that incorporates Stoppard's sense of the absurd as much as the Monty Python background of director Terry Gilliam. Stoppard, for example, wanted to begin the movie with a dream so that "it seems that the landscape of England has been lifted up and placed on top of a building which stretches as far as the eye can see . . . I got rather taken with the idea of an English landscape which turns out to be a gigantic roof garden." And exhibiting his sense of the dramatic and the visual, Stoppard added that "with all the rereading of the script, I find that the only bits I began to hate were the editorials about Society. I think we have to let all that be implied."[25]

But controversy erupted when Gilliam brought in another writer, Charles McKeown. Stoppard found the new work troublesome and critiqued individual moments that struck him as unsuccessful: "Scene 72 – this scene's been written so many times and it now seems to be longer than ever and flatter than ever" (24 October 1983). A follow-up from Gilliam to Stoppard notes their different working styles, pinpointing the dilemma for the writer turned screenwriter: "I like working in collaboration with the window open & you like working alone – possibly with the window closed" (19 November 1983). The process, as Gilliam outlines it, means that every film has a long "pregnancy with constant changes & continual rewriting – it doesn't necessarily make a better film but it seems to be a necessary process" (19 November 1983). Gilliam's need to work continuously on the script and on a far more informal basis required another hand which "certainly altered the attitude of the Hollywood money men." Stoppard was generous in his reply acknowledging that producing and directing a movie is a gigantic and complicated job and that he was satisfied that the largest changes, those to the narrative, occurred after his reworking of the first draft. He will not offer any more line changes, however, since he believes his concern with lines is "at a tangent with your concern about *film*" (28 November 1983). Assuming a professional attitude, Stoppard has little formal objection to bringing in McKeown. The final credits read "screenplay by Mr. Gilliam, Tom Stoppard and Charles McKeown."

The satire, wit, and accomplishment of the film, however, was celebrated by critics in Britain and America. And Stoppard's hand was apparent in names like Tuttle and Buttle (the confusion between the two is the catalyst of the plot, echoing *Rosencrantz* or Moon and Boot in *The Real Inspector Hound*) and in phrases like "Suspicion Breeds Confidence," as well as the intense parody of conformism that runs throughout the film. Again, the theme of oppression breeding revolt, or totalitarianism prompting freedom reflects Stoppardian concerns that are equally political and artistic. But two years after its release, Stoppard played down his role, saying that Gilliam "had the script, I only put in a few jokes. The resulting film was a bit bleak, a bit relentless for my taste." He actually thought the film was "too black and about 50 minutes too long." When he made those remarks before students, however, he was nearly hissed off the stage, as he told one interviewer.[26] Nevertheless, for critics, the movie was more than fancy; it was sinister and parodic and, in its process and outcome, Kafkaesque.

Empire of the Sun (1987), the first of J. G. Ballard's works to be filmed, was a different experience, partly because the plot of the novel was close to Stoppard's own experiences of living in Singapore from 1939 until it was overrun in 1942 when he, his brother, and mother were evacuated to India. His father, a physician, stayed behind and was killed in a bombing raid on the harbor. Stoppard's being hired to write the script was purely coincidental, he explained, since it was Kenneth Ewing who first brought the novel to his attention after a visit to Los Angeles. An anecdote concerning the script related by Stephen Frears, the British director, reveals much about Stoppard's humor and priorities. According to Frears, Stoppard's version of the script was written before Steven Spielberg took over the project. Spielberg brought in his own writers to beef up Stoppard's version and then showed it to David Lean who politely told Spielberg that it was not very good and that he should get Stoppard back on the project. After the studio failed to lure him back, Spielberg himself reportedly called to ask him to return. Stoppard said no, he could not make it because he was "doing something for BBC." "But that's just television," Spielberg insisted. "This is Hollywood." "No" replied Stoppard. "Radio." Stoppard has admitted that something like that did happen, "but I don't think it was Steven Spielberg."[27]

From Spielberg, however, Stoppard learned much about filmmaking. While interfering with the editing at Spielberg's elbow in post-production, Stoppard realized that

on the page you feel you must have a certain line, but when you see the film you want to cut all over the place. Even now I'd take out the odd phrase here and there from the 'Empire' screenplay if I could . . . the genius of filmmaking I so much admire is to capture the same feeling I get from words by showing. It's awfully seductive. Another great thing about film is its fixedness, where the great thing about plays is they can be changed. That fixedness of film is a relief and a luxury for a playwright, but most deceptive.

The writer, he admits, is no more than "a privileged tourist on a set while the film is being made."[28] Nevertheless, Stoppard's screenplay which streamlined the novel is crisp, although some sections of the film are so visually expressive they barely require dialogue. Despite the project's visual splendor and heroic adventurousness, it gave rise to a controversy over screen credit which Stoppard won, but only after taking the matter to the Writers Guild of America.

The Russia House (1990) meant working again from an accomplished novel, this time by John le Carré. Sean Connery, as well as Michelle Pfeiffer, and Klaus Maria Brandauer, headed the cast. The subject suited Stoppard, not only in content – the secret removal of a manuscript relating to Russian military strength to the West by a slightly seedy, maverick British publisher recruited by British intelligence (in some ways duplicating the situation in his television drama *Professional Foul*) – but in style. Cross-cutting, dislocated conversations unattached to images, and a rapid pace reflect the method of both the director, Fred Schepisi, and Stoppard, the sole screenwriter. Critics were moderately enthusiastic, one noting the evidence of Stoppard's hand through the wit in the dialogue, "but the lines are not easily spoken, which is not to say that they are unspeakable . . . sometimes they are even over-ripe."[29] The authentic Soviet settings, however, won praise as did the acting of both Sean Connery and Michelle Pfeiffer; so, too, did the Stoppardian juggling of time and place – Lisbon one moment, Moscow and London the next.

Rosencrantz and Guildenstern are Dead, the movie, followed, the first work Stoppard directed as well as adapted from his own material, joining a list of distinguished playwright/novelists who became occasional film directors: André Malraux, Jean Cocteau, David Mamet, and even Norman Mailer. Impetus to make the movie came from the Hollywood producer, Michael Brandman, who had made a series of television movies of stage plays. Brandman first contacted Stoppard in late 1986. Unsure of how to actually make a movie but eager to learn, Stoppard had, some ten years earlier, taken David Puttnam to lunch, where he discovered that all a director needed to know was what he wanted the picture to look like, that is, its color tones and atmosphere. Once that was established, all you needed was to rely on the expertise of a team of creative technicians rather than on one's ambition; bluffing was out.

Stoppard soon reworked the script of *Rosencrantz*, editing, extending, and compressing scenes. When an important six-line speech brought the film to a halt, he ruthlessly cut. He also added a number of visual delights: the verbal tennis match between Rosencrantz and Guildenstern near the end of Act 1 occurs on an empty, Felliniesque court; a paper airplane effortlessly flies through various scenes; a double-decker sandwich makes its silent debut in Elizabethan drama. Sean Connery, instrumental in securing the backing to finance the movie, was to star. This led to last-minute problems, when, a month or so before shooting was to begin in February 1989, Connery told Stoppard that throat problems might mean his absence from the film. Stoppard flew to Los Angeles to tell Connery that he and the production would wait for him to improve. Connery, communicating through his wife on the phone to Stoppard, declined to participate in the film. Stoppard suggested there was a commitment; Connery took umbrage. Producers then sued and the matter was settled out of court. In turn, Connery said that but for his throat, "I would have sued Stoppard out of the country," to which Stoppard replied in a letter to the *Times:* "He is confusing different parts of his anatomy. Connery paid up because he didn't have a leg to stand on."[30]

Despite the contretemps, the movie went ahead with Richard Dreyfuss as the Player, which necessitated a younger cast for the film: Gary Oldman took the role of Rosencrantz and Tim Roth that of Guildenstern. Stoppard, who favors westerns, borrowed that motif for the film, which intentionally confuses locale – a nondescript but dramatic landscape of sheer cliffs and verdant woods plus a rough castle, actually all shot in Yugoslavia. To set the mood, the movie opens with country and western music as two figures carefully ride along a sensational cliff, Rosencrantz stopping to pick up a coin on the ground and then becoming engrossed in tossing coins. The western theme runs throughout the movie through evocative costumes and haunting but stylized music. The motif even appeared in the promotion of the film, the British posters showing only "two boots and a noose" and with copy that boasted the "original buddy movie."[31]

As a director, Stoppard was, of course, inexperienced. "After a few days of shooting," he recalled, "the producer came up to me and said 'The camera isn't moving very much.' It was at that point that I realised that it wasn't moving at all. I was doing seaside photography." Thanks to his cameraman and cinematographer, however, motion and point of view shifted throughout the film – "but only because I had the sense not to pretend that I knew how to do something that I couldn't do."[32]

Preceding its general release, the film won the prestigious Golden Lion award at the Venice Film Festival, beating Martin Scorsese's *Goodfellas* and Jane Campion's *An Angel at My Table.* But Gore Vidal's announcement of the winner brought whistles, shouts, and general distress at the closing press conference. Italian journalists were dismayed that Marco Risi's *Boys on the Outside* was passed over; English-speaking journalists were upset that Jane Campion's movie was dismissed to second place. Insiders reported that Vidal, chair of the judges, pushed a divided jury to accept his favorite, *Rosencrantz.* The audience poll actually favored Scorsese's tale of American gangsters. Yet, Vidal prevailed, and when he presented the award, he began by saying "in every country, democratic or totalitarian, language has been so debased in this century that it is very difficult to communicate anything complex at all in life, or in art. The prize I am about to give is a tribute to the force of the mind, of wit and of logic in human affairs."[33] Stoppard's film was the first British entry since Olivier's *Hamlet* of 1948 to win the Golden Lion, a work which ironically cut out the parts of Rosencrantz and Guildenstern. The American release of the film in the winter of 1991, however, did not turn it into a popular success. One critic complained that "the words have the effect of absorbing all thought. The realism of the settings. . . also doesn't help. Rather, it calls attention to the abstract nature of the play without supporting it."[34] English critics were equally unreceptive, commenting on fatigue from the language and, in the absence of a stage, the pointlessness of the film's Shakespearean tradition as well as its slapstick humor. Nevertheless, the film imaginatively treats the original stage play.

In the nineties, Stoppard continued to work as a scriptwriter, adapting E. L. Doctorow's *Billy Bathgate* (1991), starring Dustin Hoffman, Nicole Kidman, and Bruce Willis, and reworking an earlier script of Raymond Chandler's last novel, *Poodle Springs*, shown on pay-for-view television in July 1998. Bob Rafelson directed and James Caan starred as Philip Marlowe. Stoppard's latest script, *Shakespeare in Love*, a reworking of a Marc Norman effort, was released to great critical and popular praise in December 1998, winning three Golden Globe awards in January 1999 for best script and best comedy, and seven Academy Awards, including Best Original Screenplay and Best Picture. Directed by John Madden, this romantic comedy of Shakespeare overcoming writer's block, is played for humor as much as romance, with Gwyneth Paltrow as the courtly woman who opens the heart of the youthful playwright struggling with a new work entitled *Romeo and Ethel, the Pirate's Daughter*. The film appealed to many in part because of the trademark Stoppardian repartee and comic exposé of the pitfalls of theatrical life. For example, when asked by the distraught Elizabethan theatre owner Henslowe if he has started his new play, Shakespeare poetically responds with "Doubt that the stars are fire, / doubt that the earth doth move?" Henslow cuts in with "Talk prose. Where is my play?" The poetic Will Shakespeare – first seen in the film practicing his signature – and the prosaic Henslowe get the film off to a quick start. Near the end, a nervous Henslowe pauses after uttering the phrase, "the show must . . ." An anxious Will Shakespeare implores him, "Go on!" Stoppard cannot resist newly minting some of the oldest theatrical clichés. His latest screenplay, *Vatel* (Roland Jaffee directing), originates in France with Gerard Depardieu as a famous chef attempting to regain the favor of Louis XIV.

III

A survey of Stoppard's screenplays identifies what he has contributed to film – but what has film contributed to his dramatic writing? If Stoppard has introduced a precise sense of *dialogue* to film, has the structure and precise sense of scene required in film enhanced his plays? The answer, of course, is yes. Awareness of what will work dramatically and what will not has been sharpened by the rigors of time and structure in film. Pace, rhythm, and action in his dramas have absorbed what he has witnessed in the shooting and editing of his work. The visual and dramatic effect of layered time in *Arcadia*, or the intertextual treatment of scene in *The Invention of Love*, to cite his two most recent plays, illustrate how the elements of screenwriting, from the inciting incident to the development of story as structure, shape his work. In his plays, dramatic impact partly derives from cinemagraphic effect, as in the opening scene of *The Invention of Love* when the elder A. E. Housman confronts Charon as he arrives to carry him across the river Styx. The *mise-en-scène* echoes the rhetorical surprise of the play's first words: "I'm dead, then. Good." Onstage, a visual grammar establishes dramatic significance with a moving boat in a misty landscape. In Stoppard's early radio play, *Albert's Bridge*, a character exclaims "I'm a victim of perspective,"[35] a condition experienced by many in his audience.

Film is as much a fantasy for the writer as for the filmgoer. Unproduced Stoppard scripts include *Galileo*, *Knuckle*, *Hopeful Monsters*, and *Cats*. Others, like the new work *Enigma*, or *Vatel*, proceded slowly. But his facility with language has meant constant requests to revise, rewrite, or doctor material (he did some revising on *Indiana Jones and the Last Crusade,* as well as *Schindler's List*, for example). In 1972 alone, he was approached by Hal Prince to consider a screenplay based on Alvin Toffler's *Future Shock*; by David Merrick for a film based on the short stories of Scott Fitzgerald; by Otto Preminger, who asked him to consider a mystery; and by Harry Saltzman for a film about Nijinsky. But many projects never materialize: in 1984, after the film rights for *The Real Thing* had been sold, a director came to his home and spent three hours discussing the development of the movie. After he left, Stoppard never heard from him again. Yet, the appeal of film beckons. He has expressed a wish to adapt *Arcadia*, although he knows it poses new problems. In an interview in 1998, he explained that "I've never found a way to compensate for the problem of its first theatrical plank, which is: a person alive in 1809 leaves a room and someone who's alive in 1998 enters the room and nothing else is different."[36]

Ironically, Stoppard claims that screenwriting is easier than writing for radio or stage. In a script, "you can just describe something which doesn't require words in film – a sort of rest." Yet, he admits a certain inability "to see a film in my mind, to experience the way it moves and its dynamics . . . the best parts of my film scripts are scenes which might be in a play – that is, linked together."[37] But Stoppard also knows that the writer will lose control over the work and be disappointed with the final result. What you write you almost never see on the screen since screenwriting by definition invites interference by others: "the writer serves the director, and you kind of give it over to him" but in the theatre "the director is there to serve the writer. It's more or less the opposite of the movies where there is a directorial vision and the writer comes in to serve that vision."[38] But Stoppard remains remarkably positive about the process, despite occasional disagreements over screen credits and payment for rewrites always in question.

In a 1994 interview, Stoppard displayed greater acceptance of the director's control than in 1969 when he wrote "Confessions of a Screenwriter." Acknowledging that "the Hollywood studio system distorts the point of view of who the artists are," he nevertheless accepts the need "to serve the director."[39] Working at 3 a.m. with Fred Schepisi, the director of *The Russia House*, Stoppard recalled that Schepisi *was* going to get the script the way he wanted to shoot it despite Stoppard's best protestations: "I wasn't even going to be there when the film was shot" he admits, which contrasts with his practice of attending rehearsals of the first productions of his work and cooperating with the director until first night. A film, Stoppard concedes, is the director's work: "a writer and a director don't have exactly the same vision; they're not standing in quite the same place" (p. 9). But despite the interferences, rewrites, cuts, and frustrations for the writer, Stoppard remains positive on film: "It's worth being good at movies. I mean, I love movies, and a lot of them are at least as good as works of art as most plays – much better, in many cases. It always feels a bit of luck that they somehow made it through the system" (pp. 9–10). This accommodating view differs strongly from Ian McEwan's perception. Of Hollywood and its writers, he has quipped, "it's an opportunity to fly first-class, be treated like a celebrity, sit around the pool and be betrayed."[40]

Of course, Stoppard has had his problems with the system. A dispute over screen credit for *Empire of the Sun* had to be settled via the Writers Guild of America; the script of *Cats* went through numerous rewrites and has yet to be made. The script of Nicholas Mosely's *Hopeful Monsters* remains unproduced, as does his scripts for his novel *Lord Malquist and Mr. Moon* and David Hare's *Knuckle*. But the production of *Poodle Springs*, Raymond Chandler's last novel and the successful release of *Shakespeare in Love*, plus his screenplay for newly released *Enigma* (Mick Jagger is financing), and work on the new French production, *Vatel*, attest to Stoppard's continued commitment to film as he reaches audiences in larger numbers than could ever fill a theatre – while willingly accepting catastrophe theory as a natural explanation of the filmmaker's experience.

"Le project d'un film arrive à un point critique" he explained to a French film critic, "et ensuite il n'y a plus qu'une possibilité."[41] Yet the freedom of film is irresistible, the energy of action unstoppable – or is that unstoppardable?

NOTES

1   Tom Stoppard in John Stanley, "Move Over, Hamlet," *San Francisco Chronicle* (Sunday Edition), 24 February 1991, p. 14.
2   Tom Stoppard, "A Hard-Hitting Thriller," *Bristol Evening World*, 29 September 1959, p. 11.
3   Tom Stoppard, "They're Having a 'Terrible' Time Again, all the same I'm prepared to join the film stars," *Bristol Evening World*, 3 October 1959, p. 3.
4   Stoppard, "Hard-Hitting Thriller," p. 9.
5   Tom Stoppard, "But it's a pity it had to sag," *Bristol Evening World*, 20 October 1959, p. 11; "'On the Beach' a superb piece of film-making," *Bristol Evening World*, 9 March 1960, p. 12.
6   Tom Stoppard, "The Lovers," *Bristol Evening World*, 17 May 1960, p. 11; "The 'Before' and 'After' of a Course of Lifemanship," *Bristol Evening World*, 12 July 1960, p. 11.
7   Tom Stoppard, "Critic and his Credo," *Western Daily Press & Times Mirror*, 5 January 1961, p. 8.
8   Tom Stoppard, "The Wrong Door," *Western Daily Press*, 18 January 1961, p. 8.
9   Tom Stoppard, "New Hero is Spinning Money," *Western Daily Press*, 8 February 1961, p. 8. Additional reviews will be cited by date in the essay.
10   Tom Stoppard, "Sugar at Tiffany's," *Western Daily Press*, 18 December 1961, p. 8.
11   Tom Stoppard, "Ambushes for the Audience," *Theatre Quarterly*, 4 (May 1974), reprinted in *Stoppard in Conversation*, ed. Paul Delaney (Ann Arbor: University of Michigan Press, 1994), pp. 70–71.
12   John Boorman to Tom Stoppard in "Stoppard in Greeneland," *Sunday Times*, 20 January 1980, p. 32.
13   Tom Stoppard to John Boorman, ? April 1968, Harry Ransom Humanities Center, University of Texas at Austin: Stoppard Collection 1124.
14   Tom Stoppard as recorded in a "Platform," National Theatre, London, 14 April 1993.
15   John Boorman to Tom Stoppard, 24 September 1974, HRC 9.2.
16   In a letter to A. C. H. Smith, Stoppard objects to some developments with the play, telling Smith we "need a hard story-line that gets through the film with a *plot* which an audience wd be interested in following. Please comment. / On this topic: the radio play gets along with such a hard-driving 'plot' because it lasts less than an idea and is more unashamedly a play of ideas. I think a 100 minute film of ideas wd not work. Let's think about our denouement and see what we can find to lead up to it" (HRC 17.2). The final film treatment was forty-seven pages in length, formally typed by a script service and sent to Kenneth Ewing. It opens with a naked woman, quickly understood to be a model posing in an art class.

17 Tom Stoppard, "Confessions of a Screenwriter: 'Strange I find I'm in the property business,'" *Today's Cinema*, 3 February 1969, p. 5 Hereafter cited in the text.

18 Warren Leight, "Screenwriting," *New York Times*, 21 June 1998, C12.

19 Tom Stoppard, in Nancy Shields Hardin, "Interview," *Contemporary Literature* 22 (1981), p. 163. See Penelope Houston, "The Romantic Englishwoman," *The Times*, 17 October 1975, p. 11; Vincent Canby, "The Romantic Englishwoman," *New York Times*, 27 November 1975, p. sect. 1, p. 46.

20 Tom Stoppard to Dirk Bogarde, 10 December 1977, HRC 1012; Stoppard in Shields Hardin, "Interview," p. 163.

21 Tom Stoppard in Tom Buckley, "Stoppard Adapting Graham Greene's *The Human Factor*," "At the Movies," *New York Times*, 14 July 1978, C6.

22 Graham Greene, "Greene and *The Human Factor*," *New York Times*, 3 February 1980, p. 15.

23 Vincent Canby, "The Human Factor," *New York Times*, 8 February 1980, C8, p. 5.

24 Tom Stoppard in Richard Freedman, "Author Stoppard's Wartime Experiences Nearly Mirrored Those of 'Empire's' Hero," *Star Ledger* (Newark, N.J.) 24 January 1988, p. 12.

25 Tom Stoppard to Terry Gilliam, 21 June 1982, HRC 37. Further references and dates are to HRC 3.7.

26 Tom Stoppard in Peter Buckley, "Tom Stoppard: boy genius grows up," *New York Daily News*, 17 May 1987, p. 3, also the source of the quotations here.

27 Stephen Frears in Rob Baker, "A Few Words from Tom Stoppard," *Women's Wear Daily*, 18 May 1987, p. 16; the same story appears with slightly different wording in Robert Chesshyre, "Tom Stoppard, Putting on the Ritz," *Daily Telegraph Weekend Magazine*, 16 February 1991, pp. 19–20.

28 Stoppard in Freedman, *Star Ledger*, p. 12.

29 Vincent Canby, "The Russia House," *New York Times*, 19 December 1990, C15.

30 Tom Stoppard, "Connery Dispute," *Times of London*, 13 October 1990, p. 15.

31 Geoff Brown, "Tell the Truth, Face the Consequences," *The Times*, 23 May 1991, p. 21.

32 Tom Stoppard in Lyn Gardner, "The Heart in the Closet," *Guardian Weekend*, 16 January 1999, p. 18.

33 Gore Vidal in "Gored," *Economist*, 22 September 1990, p. 173.

34 Vincent Canby, "Rosencrantz and Guildenstern are Dead," *New York Times*, 8 February 1991, C14.

35 Tom Stoppard, *Albert's Bridge*, in *Plays for Radio, 1964–1991* (London and Boston: Faber and Faber, 1994), pp. 81–82.

36 Tom Stoppard in Paula Span, "Living on Bard Time," *Washington Post*, 26 December 1998, C1.

37 Stoppard in Shields Hardin, "Interview," pp. 163–164. An interview in 1998 expresses the same attitude. Playwriting, he explains, "is slow and painstaking . . . but you can manipulate the bits in a screenplay . . . You're involved with something that's not in love with its own mystery. It's pragmatic." Stoppard in Span, "Living on Bard Time."

38 Tom Stoppard in William Stevenson, "For Some, Screenplays Aren't Just Writes of Passage," *New York Magazine*, 11 February 1991, p. 127.

39 Tom Stoppard in Katherine E. Kelly and William W. Demastes, "The Playwright and the Professors: an interview with Tom Stoppard," *South Central Review* (winter 1994), p. 8. All further references are from this source.

40 Ian McEwan in Natasha Walter, "Interview: looks like a teacher, writes like a demon," *Observer Review*, 24 August 1997, p. 3.

41 Tom Stoppard in Michel Ciment, "Ecrivain mercenaire, écrivain exigeant: entretien avec Tom Stoppard," *Positif*, 361 (1991), p. 25.

6

NEIL SAMMELLS

The early stage plays

All fine imaginative work is self-conscious and deliberate.

Oscar Wilde, *The Critic as Artist*

When *Rosencrantz and Guildenstern Are Dead* (*R&GAD*) opened in New York, an interviewer asked Stoppard what it was about. "It's about to make me very rich," came the Wildean (Malquistian?) response.[1] The play had already made Stoppard's name: Harold Hobson, in the *Sunday Times*, described the 1967 National Theatre production as "the most important event in the British professional theatre" since the opening of Pinter's *The Birthday Party* in 1958.[2] One of the springs of the play is probably Oscar Wilde's observation in his prison letter *De Profundis* that the two deracinated courtiers are "little cups that can hold so much and no more," who, in their dealings with the machiavellian Danish court, find themselves "merely out of their sphere": a state of terminal bewilderment which, Wilde says, means that genuine tragic status "is really not for such as they."[3] However, the Wildean influence on Stoppard's early work goes beyond this specific instance, and is demonstrably at work before *Travesties*. When the young Stoppard – then a journalist on the *Bristol Evening World* – had declared himself "a confirmed addict and admirer (literary)" of Wilde,[4] he was acknowledging an affinity we can trace in Stoppard's emerging aesthetic ideas and dramatic practice. Indeed, the way that Stoppard appropriates Wilde is central to our understanding of his characteristic strengths and weaknesses as a dramatist.

Between September 1962 and April 1963, Stoppard reviewed the London theatre for the short-lived magazine *Scene*.[5] The most substantial and interesting of these reviews reveals his emphasis on the necessary discipline of writing for the stage – the construction of what Wilde (ironically lamenting his own fading ability to muster the discipline) called the "architecture" of art.[6] Stoppard is dismissive, for instance, of the apprentice work of novelists-turned-playwrights Muriel Spark and Edna O'Brien. Like Spark's

Doctors of Philosophy, O'Brien's *A Cheap Bunch of Nice Flowers* "is the first stage-play of a young novelist, and it can hardly be a coincidence that the two share the same virtues and faults: the final effect is of a worthwhile literary achievement which barely survives its own assault on the technical canons of stagecraft."[7] In describing his own work, Stoppard has echoed these sentiments throughout his career. "There's a kind of play that I don't write and Rattigan doesn't either," he has said, declaring an apparently unlikely similarity, "a play where one says all these outmoded forms of drama are such a bore and I'm going to free the whole thing from these fetters . . . and the result is an absolute boring mess."[8] *Jumpers*, despite its acrobats, striptease, and dreamlike coda, he has described – a little disingenuously – as an "absolutely traditional straight" play about "people who don't know very much about what's going on."[9] Indeed, Stoppard's desire to locate himself within an artistic tradition, to declare a degree of aesthetic conservatism, means that he has little interest in that relative newcomer: theatrical naturalism, or what he describes in *Scene* as "the plot-riddled uproar of domestic crisis."[10] "I think that sort of truth-telling writing," he told Ken Tynan, "is as big a lie as the deliberate fantasies I construct. It's based on the fallacy of naturalism. There's a direct line of descent which leads you down to the dregs of bad theatre, bad thinking and bad feeling."[11] The phrase "deliberate fantasies" is artfully chosen and revealing: it signals Stoppard's Wildean dismissal of the pretensions of naturalism (neatly encapsulated in Wilde's dictum that Life imitates Art more than Art imitates Life) and his willed, deliberate, self-conscious construction of theatrical alternatives. For Wilde, "there is no fine art without self-consciousness, and self-consciousness and the critical spirit are one."[12]

Stoppard's own awareness of the relationship between "self-consciousness and the critical spirit" can be seen at work in his review of Hugh Wheeler's *Big Fish, Little Fish* which opened in London in the autumn of 1962; his comments are doubly interesting because of the light they shed on his own *A Walk on the Water*, the play he had completed some two years previously and which, after rewriting and several changes of title, became *Enter a Free Man*. Wheeler's play, claims Stoppard, lays itself open to the suspicion of having been assembled from a tried and tested theatrical cookbook. Much of contemporary American drama, he notes, is a celebration of the failed tightrope walker. We discover him firmly established on one secure platform, warily eyeing the other: ideals, opportunity, individuality, moral uplift. The influence of Arthur Miller is clear but Stoppard points out that lately lesser men have been "giving frustration a whirl in an alien context: drawing-room comedy spiked with newly acceptable neuroses, guaranteed to flatter the intellect, painlessly." *Big Fish, Little Fish* unfolds with a sense of "deep, detached familiarity." Wheeler simply replicates form without examining it critically: his Millerian model dictates the play's shape so that *Big Fish, Little Fish* is "merely complete, tidy."[13]

Enter a Free Man is Stoppard's own version of the failed tightrope walker: the inept dreamer hoping to assert his individuality against the collective ethic by means of his inventions. Stoppard says of it that he feels a great deal of gratitude and affection, and a certain amount of embarrassment: "It works pretty well as a play, but it's actually phoney because it's a play written about other people's characters."[14] Acknowledging the debt to Miller and Robert Bolt, he has referred to it as "Death of a Flowering Salesman." Its theatrical ancestry does not, of course, end there: Riley's self-proclaimed status as inventor, and the fostering of his illusions by his family, recall Ibsen's *The Wild Duck*, for instance. Stoppard's embarrassment is caused, I suspect, less by his borrowing from other writers (ubiquitous in his later work, of course) than by the fact that the play tries to have it both ways. George's habitual self-dramatization – his theatrical entrances and stagey rhetoric – promises a self-conscious, critical engagement with genre; but the play ends up as a triumph of the tidy mind, an affirmation of genre. When *Enter a Free Man* opened in London in 1968 – some five years after being broadcast as a television play – it was poorly received. J. W. Lambert felt that, tactically, Stoppard had made a mistake in refurbishing it for the stage: "It will certainly release damaging waves of reaction against the enormous success of 'Rosencrantz and Guildenstern.'" The most revealing objections came from Irving Wardle in *The Times*. He felt its main virtues were its theatrical neatness and the chance it gave Michael Hordern to steal the show as George. It did not, however, suggest to him a strong theatrical talent: "What this proves, I think, is the power of theatrical convention to take over from the playwright." In other words, Wardle criticizes Stoppard in much the same terms as the latter had criticized Hugh Wheeler. *Enter a Free Man* was a professional job producing "a depressing sense of facility,"[15] an accusation which recalls Stoppard's "deep, detached familiarity" with *Big Fish, Little Fish*.

Wilde's career as a writer might be mapped in terms of his engagement with the power of literary and theatrical convention; his was a struggle to reinvent genre. Such reinvention of genre – what he tried to do with Gothic fiction in *The Picture of Dorian Gray* and with Victorian melodrama and the French "well-made" play in his society comedies, but only fully achieved with *The Importance of Being Earnest* – cannot be attained with a simple, dismissive attitude to the models that are being redeployed. Susan Sontag says of stylization that it "reflects an ambivalence (affection contradicted by contempt, obsession contradicted by irony) toward the subject matter. This ambivalence is handled by maintaining, through the rhetorical overlay that is stylisation, a special distance from the subject."[16] This "special distance from the subject" is entirely characteristic of Wilde, and of Stoppard at his most Wildean. That "rhetorical overlay" is what *Enter a Free Man* maintains only superficially and fitfully – but which characterizes Stoppard's arch redeployment of Shakespearian tragedy, absurdist theatre, existentialist fable, West End farce, whodunnit, and Shavian debate in the more substantial of his early stage plays: *R&GAD* and *Jumpers*. What the reviews in *Scene* show is that, for Stoppard, such stylization is hard-won: it amounts to a critical, self-conscious, deliberate, and skilled subversion of genre from within, not an assault on it from without.

By way of explaining that *Hapgood* used to be in three acts but was now in two because managements prefer only one interval, Stoppard claimed in 1988 that theatre "is perhaps the most pragmatic art form, apart from advertising."[17] While working for *Scene*, he clearly used his experience of the London stage to clarify in his own mind what he believed was pragmatically possible in the theatre. His *Scene* reviews of Beckett are especially revealing in this respect, helping us to understand the exact nature of Beckett's influence on him in general and, of course, on *R&GAD* in particular. Critics, naturally, were quick to point out the similarities. Reviewing the original student production at the Edinburgh Festival in 1966, Ronald Bryden described the play as unabashedly dedicated to Beckett, "but as witty and vaulting as Beckett's original is despairing." Others were less complimentary, seeing it as an extended "undergraduate joke." Robert Brustein, writing in the *New Republic*, was particularly damning: Stoppard, he claimed, was not fighting hard enough for the insights which came to him, prefabricated, from other plays. Derivative, familiar, and prosaic in execution, *R&GAD* is described as a theatrical parasite, as "Beckett without tears."[18] I want to suggest that the *Scene* reviews help us to see that what Stoppard is actually giving us is not Beckett without tears, but stylized Beckett: Beckett with "Style."

Stoppard's first article on Beckett is his review of *End of Day*, a one-man show at the New Arts Theatre presented by Beckett's friend Jack MacGowran in October 1962. MacGowran captured, for Stoppard, "the comic essence of the Beckett refugee" who – like his own Rosencrantz and Guildenstern – could be seen "rebounding back and forth from lifeless capitulation to a short-lived sense of purpose, caught between memory and desire." Of MacGowran's series of speeches and scenes hung around the skeletal frame of Beckett's *Act Without Words*, Stoppard declared: "Nothing happens. Nobody comes. Nobody goes. It's awful. It's so awful you have to laugh. When I saw it, hardly anyone did – they had come for punishment, as a misguided tribute to Beckett. He would not thank them for it."[19]

Stoppard's insistence on Beckett's humor (he would later say "I find Beckett deliciously funny in the way that he qualifies everything as he goes along, reduces, refines and dismantles"[20]) is important: it helps to define the "rhetorical overlay," that "special distance from the subject" characteristic of *R&GAD* in its playful stylisation of *Waiting for Godot*. Of course, the specific bent of that humor – the process of self-examination and self-criticism inherent in the way Beckett reduces, refines, and dismantles as he goes along – is for Stoppard another example of the self-consciousness which binds the artist and the critic. What *Scene* also demonstrates is that Stoppard's admiration for Beckett is not boundless. In reviewing *Happy Days* at the Royal Court, he says that *Waiting for Godot* "liberated something for anybody writing plays. It redefined the minima of theatrical validity." However, he now sees *Happy Days* as the testing-point for Beckett's independence of stage conventions. The problem as he sees it is that the contraction of Beckett's drama has produced a uniform shrinking of enterprise among the young playwrights he has influenced. There is no very good reason, he feels, why *Happy Days* should be acted rather than read: "From the little of 'Godot' and the less of *Endgame*, we have reached the least of *Happy Days* and dramatically it is not enough."[21]

Stoppard is here demonstrating his acute sense of audience: like Wilde, he sees himself as a commercial playwright trying to both meet, satisfy, and ambush the expectations of a specific theatregoing public. Christopher Bigsby has said of Joe Orton – the "Oscar Wilde of the Welfare State" whose brief and brilliant career as a playwright both coincided with and outshone that of the early Stoppard – that his work is "as much a critique of theatre (though especially of bad theatre) as it is upon the substantialities of a world at whose hands he suffered" and that Orton's ideal target was an audience "not fully adjusted to the experimentalism of the art theatre but rather the middle-brow adherents of the West End."[22] Stoppard's ideal target is the same audience: one literate enough to recognize that in *R&GAD* he is redeploying not just a Shakespearian pretext but a modern "classic" too, and, of course, to be flattered to be asked to recognize these and other allusions. His dramatic strategy is to lure that audience into a series of more or less challenging ambushes; one of his principal tactics is to constantly dislocate the audience's perspective by means of a critical engagement with their knowledge of the conventions and limitations of dramatic genre. This, at its most stimulating, is a potentially radical project – Wilde's parodic strategies and subversion of naturalism amount to a refusal of "oppressive normativity" in political, ethical, cultural, and sexual terms.[23] The same is true of Orton: another Stylist as Subversive. In Stoppard's drama, however, the effect is significantly different.

In this context, Stoppard's treatment and understanding of individualism is important. Two reviews for the *Bristol Evening World*, written in 1960 when *A Walk on the Water* was undergoing gestation, are useful here because they show us Stoppard commenting on reflections of his own pre-occupations. In the first, he argues that Richard Attenborough's film *The Angry Silence* – the story of a factory worker's refusal to buckle under union pressure – is "a cry from the dock on behalf of every stubborn, proud, infuriating little man who has ever committed the crime of preferring to do his own thinking for himself." This emphasizes, obliquely, the positive side to George Riley's refusal to conform, and closes the gap between the comic, peripheral figures of the early plays and the political dissidents of the later. However, a further dimension to Stoppard's presentation of George is suggested by a second film review – of Peter Sellers' *The Battle of the Sexes* – which chronicles the fortunes of a Dickensian firm of Scottish tweed weavers resisting the intrusion of the twentieth century in the form of an American efficiency expert. Sellers, the little man, rebels "and this is like a rabbit showing its teeth: no matter how ferocious the effect is meant to be, the result is merely comic."[24] These remarks help to give a sense of historical specificity to Stoppard's interest in individualism: for him, it is defined by resistance to the collective ethic, and is characteristic of a nostalgic rejection of a new "leftist" collectivism in postwar British politics and culture. In this respect, Stoppard's "little men" and the politics they obliquely represent have the same coloration as their fictional siblings in the world of the Ealing comedies. (There is a kind of double-bluff at work here: the comic deflation of Stoppard's dissenters allows him to establish a political position while simultaneously distancing himself from it.) Indeed, the difference between Wilde's understanding of individualism – in which, as he argues in *The Soul of Man Under Socialism*, it can be paradoxically associated, through the agency of art, with a collective politics – and Stoppard's is crucial to an understanding of why Stoppard's drama operates in the way it does.

In *R&GAD*, the pressures of collectivism are stylized in the dilemma faced by the courtiers – whether to resist or accede to the momentum of the action that threatens to sweep them away. Guildenstern is repeatedly ambushed by his terrified sense of the sheer inevitability of what is happening around him. He advises Rosencrantz to relax and let the logic of the action unfold: "If we start being arbitrary it'll just be a shambles: at least, let us hope so. Because if we happened, just happened to discover, or even suspect, that our spontaneity was part of their order, we'd know that we'd be lost."[25] Deprived of the power to disrupt events, the two attendant lords would disappear as completely as cause detached from effect: indeed, Guildenstern can be seen trying to keep at bay what Stoppard, in a review of James Saunders's *Next*

Time I'll Sing To You, had called the repressed fury of schizophrenia: "the knowledge that his spontaneity is part of a nightly repeated plan."[26] The Player, on the other hand, willingly relinquishes control. "We have no control," he announces proudly, "Tonight we play to the court. Or the night after. Or not" (p. 25). "Don't you see," he asks, "We're *actors* – we're the opposite of people" (p. 63). Rosencrantz and Guildenstern fight to preserve the distinction between actor and agent, to hang on to the short-lived sense of purpose that will give their actions meaning. "This is all getting rather undisciplined," murmurs Guildenstern as he looks for the letter to the English King, "We must not lose control" (p. 107). Of course, these increasingly desperate attempts to wrest control simply bring the pair face-to-face with their own uncertainty. "We don't know what's going on, or what to do with ourselves," cries Guildenstern, "We don't know how to *act*." "Act natural" (p. 66) counsels the Player, with a line borrowed directly from Saunders – one which wilfully confuses action with acting, and the agent with the actor. The pun leaves the central question unanswered: is there any possibility of a spontaneous act, or is the agent's sense of purpose – and hence identity – just capitulation to a logic unstoppable and absurd? Are we all just actors in someone else's script – defined not by individual, authentic essence, but by the pressures of collectivism?

By posing these questions, *R&GAD* explores the usefulness of theatre as a metaphor for life. In this sense, it is, I suspect, influenced by Lionel Abel's *Metatheatre*, published in 1963, which Stoppard may have read while working on *R&GAD*. For Abel (himself a playwright), the self-referentiality of *Hamlet* expresses itself not just in the explicit commentary on actors and acting, but in the way the play is constructed as a continuing conflict between different dramatists – each jostling the other in an attempt to control the script, the action, and the other actors; in effect to shape the kind of play in which they are appearing. The Ghost, for instance, is – according to Abel– a writer of Revenge Tragedies who, by asking him to kill his uncle and not his mother as well, denies to Hamlet the tragic stature for which he believes himself ready; Claudius is a writer of crude melodrama, advocating sensationalism from start to finish; Rosencrantz and Guildenstern are two vain and very minor playwrights; and Hamlet is the first character in world drama who really knows the form of the plot in which he is acting. Abel divides Shakespeare's *dramatis personae* into those who are dramatists (attempting a measure of control by trying to dictate the nature of the play and distributing roles to those around them) and those who are dramatized. Stoppard's courtiers, of course, move uneasily between these two categories, chafing at restriction yet yearning for the apparent security enjoyed by those who are dramatized. Abel describes his willingness to be dramatized, to relinquish control, as something of a regression to childhood. "Is not any son," he asks, "forced to be an actor in his parents' script. They chide him, spank him, coddle him, order him around: to be a child means to take direction." Actors, he adds parenthetically, "in general, are childish."[27] Stoppard echoes this analogy, strengthening the suspicion that *Metatheatre* may have played a part in crystallizing his own play as well as in his thinking about *Hamlet*: "To be taken in hand and led," says Guildenstern, counselling his partner to relax and let events take over, "like being a child again, even without the innocence, a child – it's like being given a prize, an extra slice of childhood when you least expect it" (p. 29).

Abel's somewhat slapdash, if fertile, insights into the self-consciousness of *Hamlet* can be contrasted with the full-blown debate about the nature of art that Stoppard frames in *R&GAD* – a debate also clearly and more heavily influenced by Wilde, who observed that Hamlet's insistence on the naturalistic basis to drama, that it should hold a mirror up to nature, was an attempt to convince bystanders of his absolute insanity in all art matters.[28] Guildenstern and the audience are ambushed by the histrionic skill of the Player, mistaking his feigned death for the "real thing": a demonstration of Wilde's notion that what we recognize as "natural" is, in fact, artifice. This disavowal of naturalism allows Stoppard to work his stylistic tricks, particularly as he constructs the play's dramatic language from a diversity of materials from Shakespearian blank verse to subphilosophical disquisition and Beckettian stichomythia. In this respect, *R&GAD* is a celebration of theatre – of the styles in which we can present our world, and present ourselves to it.

Roger Sales has argued that by reinventing (we might say, in restyling) *Hamlet* as self-referential and self-conscious metadrama, Stoppard depoliticizes it, because his attendant lords "stand outside the web of political intrigue and corruption."[29] This, whatever Stoppard's intention, does the play less than justice. The choices faced by the two courtiers, and the pressures that envelop them, are clearly political pressures: the pressures of individuals trying to assert themselves against collectivism. *R&GAD* is as political a play as its exact contemporary, Stoppard's adaptation of Slawomir Mrozek's *Tango*, first performed by the Royal Shakespeare Company in 1966. According to Martin Esslin, the original Polish audience of *Tango*, in the Warsaw of 1964, would have seen the play as a bitter and sardonic comment on Stalinism and its totalitarian structure of terror.[30] The peculiar power of *Tango* lies precisely in its political exploitation of absurdist theatrical devices – designed to reflect a society in which traditional values and order have been overturned – in a stylistic maneuver identical to the dramatic strategy at the center of *R&GAD*. The two courtiers never make the choice that could have saved them: to disentangle themselves from murderous court politics, and thus to make a stand. By dramatizing their failure to make a choice, however, the play insists that such a choice was possible. Stoppard, of course, would later write directly about Eastern Europe and the iniquities of Communism; in so doing, he seemed to be taking a new direction – certainly for those critics who believed that the early plays were all about withdrawing with style from the chaos (to use a Malquistian formulation). In fact, Stoppard's dramatic investigation of individualism has always had a political coloration, though one which, in his early career, was necessarily and ideologically self-denying – and it has always involved a somewhat simplistic opposition between the individual and the collective.

There is a telling paradox at work here. Stoppard succeeds where Rosencrantz and Guildenstern fail: he manages to *act upon* Shakespeare's original, restyling it with Beckett's help. In effect, an act of criticism – that is both interpretive and transformational – becomes, in a way that is simultaneously Wildean and characteristically postmodern, an act of creation. In *The Soul of Man Under Socialism*, Wilde had claimed "the theatre-going public like the obvious, it is true, but they do not like the tedious; and burlesque and farcical comedy, the two most popular forms, are distinct forms of art. Delightful work may be produced under burlesque and farcical conditions, and in work of this kind the artist in England is allowed a very great freedom."[31] This provides a template for what Wilde himself would later achieve with *The Importance of Being Earnest*: a radical redeployment of the popular form of the West End farce; a stylization of "low" culture, of the subliterary, which Russian Formalism has termed "the canonization of the junior branch." It is also, of course, precisely what Stoppard achieves in his next full-length stage play, *Jumpers*, a work which engages self-consciously and playfully with the conventions of farce and whodunnit (rather than with "classic" and "avant garde" theatre as does its predecessor) and which, in the way it handles questions of politics, morality, and ethics, struggles to maintain the balance implied in Wilde's claim that "an ethical sympathy in an artist is an unpardonable mannerism of style."[32]

George Moore, refusing to bend his knees in *Jumpers*, declares it his intention to set British philosophy back forty years, "which is roughly when it went off the rails."[33] The paper he hopes to deliver to the philosophical symposium is structured accordingly around a protracted critique of A. J. Ayer's *Language, Truth and Logic* (1936). Jonathan Bennett argues that there is no structural relationship between such academic philosophical material and the rest of the play: compared to the philosophical content of *Rosencrantz and Guildenstern Are Dead*, which is "solid, serious and functional," George's academic struggles serve *Jumpers* in only a marginal and decorative way.[34] Stoppard himself would readily admit that the philosophical content is hardly cutting edge: he knows that Logical Positivism was as dead as a dodo before he started writing the play.[35] However, George's pained confrontation with the central tenets of Logical Positivism demonstrates Stoppard's continued exploration of the nature of criticism, and his treatment of the political implications of the individualist, dissenting voice which, actively denied the means to talk sense, will, nevertheless, not be silenced.

In championing absolute values against the brutal new pragmatism he sees dominating modern political and social life, George runs flat up against that bulwark of Logical Positivism: the Verification Principle. Dotty provides the best introduction to the problem when she recites the Gospel according to the Malquistian Sir Archibald Jumper. "Things and actions, you understand," she intones, "can have any number of real and verifiable properties. But good and bad, better and worse, these are not real properties of things, they are just expressions of our feelings about them." George's response is characteristically skeptical: "Archie says" (p. 41). According to Ayer, the outcome of this supposition is that we can only make significant statements about those properties which we can verify. A statement can only be meaningful if we know what empirical observations would prove its truth or falsehood. If we cannot think of a method to prove or disprove a statement then it is of no significance, has no meaning, is literally, nonsense. The consequence of Ayer's argument with regard to both moral and aesthetic value judgments is to deny that there can be any debate about them, that in speaking of them we can talk anything but nonsense. Despising the leap to religious faith, George's search for the philosopher's God is rendered futile before it has begun: he simply cannot bend the discourse of philosophy to his purposes. At the very moment when he stands up most volubly against the Verification Principle, George is glaringly wrong. "There are many things I know," he insists, "which are not verifiable but nobody can tell me I don't know them, and I think that I know that something happened to poor Dotty and she somehow killed McFee, as sure as she killed my poor Thumper" (p. 78). What the audience knows is that Dotty did not kill McFee: George did, accidentally impaling the hare on an arrow unleashed to prove the absurdity of Zeno's paradox and the necessity of a First Cause.

These, and other, dramatic ironies ensure that George is far from an unproblematic spokesman for traditional values, but Stoppard's political double-bluff is at work here. George sees himself as a philosopher first and a citizen second. He recalls, for instance, trying to discuss the Theory of Descriptions with Bertrand Russell: "I was simply trying to bring his mind back to matters of universal import, and away from the day-to-day parochialism of international politics"; a response which elicits Dotty's exasperated, "*Universal import!* You're living in dreamland!" (p. 31). George's

2 A scene from the National Theatre 1972 production of *Jumpers* – Michael Hordern (George) and Diana Rigg (Dotty).

eccentricity, his semiheroic comic failure to recognize what is happening around him – and to act against it – is identified, nevertheless, with the individualistic and the authentic as against the collectivist Radical Liberal pragmatism in both public and private life. This identification is cemented by a thread of literary allusion that runs throughout the play: Dotty refers to Keats, Milton, and Shelley in trying to articulate the frightening new perspective brought about by the moon-landing; she wails from the bedroom in fragmented lines from *Macbeth* as George has God typed out in the study; in the coda Archie quotes from *Richard III*, suggesting that the dreaming George now sees him as the murderous Gloucester. If George sees Archie as Gloucester, he casts himself in the role of Hamlet: "Now might I do it, Pat" (p. 43), he whispers to his tortoise, marching to the door, confident that Archie is the caller. Earlier he has compared himself to Prufrock, dramatizing himself as Eliot's "attendant lord" (p. 33). The point is clear: literature provides a stable point of reference in a world in which things appear to be falling apart. It provides the bedrock for the play's formal exuberance. It also operates as a token of cultural continuity for the audience that recognizes the allusions; Stoppard flatters, adroitly. Indeed, the deliberate artifice of the play's construction is – just as with Henry's cricket bat in *The Real Thing* – its own point: a demonstration of pattern, order, certainty, skill, in a world which seems to want to do without them, qualities emblematized so dramatically in the climactic "dance to the music of time" in *Arcadia*.

Years before, in *Scene*, Stoppard had described Muriel Spark as a writer who believed that "we are so conditioned to life's accepted norm that we reject a multitude of aberrations which, did we not blink at those precise moments, would reveal human absurdity and, perhaps, a supernatural power." This, he acknowledges, is not an original thought, but – crucially – Spark "has more fun with it than most, mainly because she does not treat it as a thesis, but as a premise. She does not attempt to prove it or promulgate it; she simply accepts it. And toys with it."[36] This emphasis on ideas in performance is, again, characteristically Wildean, recalling his dandy Lord Henry in *The Picture of Dorian Gray*: "He played with the idea, and grew wilful; tossed it into the air and transformed it; let it escape and recaptured it; made it iridescent with fancy, and winged it with paradox." The notion of "play" is interesting here, suggesting not only the idea of having fun – perhaps stylizing – an idea but also that the theatre can function as a paradoxical and hence critical medium: "To test Reality we must see it on the tight-rope. When the Verities become acrobats, we can judge them."[37] Stoppard said in a letter to Ken Tynan, in which he recalled discussing Logical Positivism with him during the period he was working on *Jumpers*, that "a sense of renewed endeavour prevails – more concerned with the dramatic possibilities than with the ideas, for it is wrong to assume that plays are the end-products of ideas (which would be limiting): the ideas are the end-products of the plays."[38] This suggests that, like Spark, he is deploying – performing with – an intellectual premise (a critique of Logical Positivism and associated collectivist attitudes) rather than trying to promulgate a thesis. However, he told *Gambit* in 1981 that his early writing career could best be seen in terms of his sense of alienation from the Osbornian school of angry young men writing socially engaged drama: "I took on a sort of 'travelling pose' which accentuated my insecurity about not being able to fit into this scheme, and I tended to overcorrect." However, he had felt the need to change and had done so in *Jumpers*: "There the play was the end-product of an idea as much as the converse."[39] To return to the cricket bat analogy: *Jumpers* has been artfully fashioned in order to *score*.

When *The Invention of Love* transferred to the West End in 1998, Stoppard admitted that "I had an argument with Ken Tynan about Wilde in the Seventies. He tried to present Wilde as a socialist before his time. I didn't buy that. My route to Wilde left out the politics; what I valued was style raised to genius." For Stoppard, Wilde is a paradoxical martyr to the individualism he has explored throughout his career as a playwright: "He sacrifices himself to self-fulfilment, if that's an intelligible statement."[40] Stoppard's Wilde – as in other contemporary fictional versions of him, such as Brian Gilbert's 1997 film starring Stephen Fry and David Hare's 1998 play *The Judas Kiss* – is a kind of all-purpose enemy of a vaguely conceived Victorianism which, in its tolerance and bigotry, is inimical to the individual, "authentic" personality.[41] In *The Invention of Love*, A. E. Housman's inability to face up to and to act upon his "true" sexual nature brands him as indelibly Victorian, while Wilde makes his salutary appearance as an example of modern sexual assertiveness and fidelity to self. ("Better a fallen rocket than never a burst of light," says Wilde's ghost.[42])

In his early stage plays, Stoppard develops a Wildean aesthetic with an inverted politics, based on a refusal to acknowledge the material politics shoring up Wilde's apparently romantic individualism. Deliberately fashioning theatrical alternatives from a diversity of materials, Stoppard can be seen as refusing the collectivist pressures of convention. However, the radical potential of this self-conscious engagement with dramatic form and his audience's expectations, as well as his stylized redeployment of genre – the "camp" qualities identified so clearly by Sontag as characteristic of Wilde[43] – is effectively and continually canceled by an insistent construction of individualism in conservative political terms. The ambushes Stoppard sets for his audiences affirm the "normativity" that Wilde undermines. There is, then, a direct line of descent from his early, comic (quintessentially English?) dissenters to his later "heroic" dissidents who deliberately and successfully subvert the communist authoritarianism satirized in *Professional Foul*, *Every Good Boy Deserves Favour*, *Dogg's Hamlet Cahoot's Macbeth*, and *Squaring the Circle*.

James Saunders has said of his former friend's politics: "He's basically a displaced person. Therefore, he doesn't want to stick his neck out. He feels grateful to Britain, because he sees himself as a guest here, and that makes it hard for him to criticize Britain. Probably the most damaging thing that could be said about him is that he's made no enemies."[44] Stoppard himself is explicit in his admiration for British society, which he characterizes as a "Western liberal democracy favouring an intellectual elite and a progressive middle class dedicated to the pursuit of Christian moral values."[45] "I don't lose any sleep if a policeman in Durham beats somebody up," he declared to Tynan,

> because I know it's an exceptional case. It's a sheer perversion of speech to describe the society I live in as one that inflicts violence on the underprivileged. What worries me is not the bourgeois exception but the totalitarian norm. Of all the systems that are on offer, the one I don't want is one that denies freedom of expression – no matter what its allegedly redeeming virtues may be. The only thing that would make me leave England would be control over free speech.[46]

Night & Day, of course, dramatizes Stoppard's defense of the "free" British press and is founded on the premise that a free market is the necessary index of a free society. His argument is simply an extrapolation of the political choice between a society which measures freedom in terms of the individual's putative economic liberties and that which promises economic equality at the expense of other fundamental rights. In this respect, Stoppard can be seen as suffering from a case of what radical historian E. P. Thompson called in 1981, "Cold War Calvinism," which "commences within the premises of the Cold War and assumes that no other premises are possible. It is predicated on that facile division of the world into binary antinomies which has so often tricked the human mind: good/bad, the damned and the saved."[47] The personal force of Stoppard's damning of the totalitarian norm no doubt derives from the knowledge that his family's flight from Czechoslovakia saved him from the horrors of Nazism, and the suppression of individual liberties under Communism personified in the years of persecution suffered by his friend and fellow playwright, Vaclav Havel.

In the end, we can draw a constructive comparison between two "strangers": Wilde and Stoppard, the Irish Englishman (English Irishman?) and the

English East European (East European Englishman?). For one, Englishness becomes a target for subversion, for the other a deliberate fantasy of the eccentric, the authentic, the individualist and the traditional. Stoppard's early plays, in the way they champion the quirkiness of the "little man" and seek to demonstrate the "real thing" (the elaborated disciplines of artistic production), inch toward the militant conservatism that characterizes the political and aesthetic project of his later work. In so doing, they show the extent to which Stoppard strays from the example of his Wildean mentor, who did not so much offer "style raised to genius," as use style to undermine the certainties Stoppard takes on trust.

NOTES

1 Stephen Schiff, "Full Stoppard," *Vanity Fair*, 52.5 (May 1989), reprinted in Paul Delaney, ed., *Stoppard in Conversation* (Ann Arbor: University of Michigan Press, 1994), p. 219.
2 Harold Hobson, "A fearful Summons," *Sunday Times*, 16 April 1967, p. 49.
3 *The Complete Works of Oscar Wilde* (London: Collins, new edn, 1966), p. 950.
4 *Bristol Evening World*, 23 April 1960, p. 3.
5 For a much fuller discussion of Stoppard's work as a drama critic, see Neil Sammells, *Tom Stoppard: the Artist as Critic* (Basingstoke: Macmillan, 1988), pp. 16–39.
6 Letter to Ernest Dowson, October 1897, quoted in Ian Small, *Oscar Wilde Revalued: an essay on new materials and methods of research* (Greensboro: ELT Press, 1993), p. 63.
7 *Scene*, 12, 29 November 1962, p. 19.
8 Interview with Janet Watts, *Guardian*, 21 March 1973, p. 12.
9 In Mel Gussow, *Conversations with Tom Stoppard* (London: Nick Hern, 1995), p. 4.
10 *Scene*, 14, 12 December, 1962, p. 44.
11 Quoted by Kenneth Tynan in *Show People: profiles in entertainment* (New York: Simon and Schuster, 1979), p. 64.
12 *Complete Works of Wilde*, p. 1020.
13 *Scene*, 3, 28 September 1962, p. 22.
14 Interview with *Theatre Quarterly* 4.14 (1975), p. 5.
15 J. W. Lambert, *Sunday Times*, 31 March 1968, p. 14; Irving Wardle, *The Times*, 29 March 1968, p. 13.
16 Susan Sontag, *A Sontag Reader* (Harmondsworth: Penguin, 1983), p. 141.
17 Shusha Guppy, "Tom Stoppard: the art of theater VII," reprinted in Delaney, ed., *Stoppard in Conversation*, p. 185.
18 Ronald Bryden, *Observer*, 28 August 1966, p. 15; Robert Brustein, *New Republic*, 4 November 1967, p. 26.
19 *Scene* 7, 25 October 1962, p. 19.
20 Interview with Giles Gordon, *Transatlantic Review*, 29 (1968), p. 23.
21 *Scene*, 10, 15 November 1962, p. 19.
22 Christopher Bigsby, *Joe Orton* (London: Methuen, 1982), pp. 17, 32.

23 See Terry Eagleton, *Heathcliff and the Great Hunger: studies in Irish culture* (London: Verso, 1995), p. 334.

24 *Bristol Evening World*, 15 March 1960, p. 11; 5 April 1960, p. 11.

25 *Rosencrantz and Guildenstern Are Dead* (New York: Grove Press, 1967), p. 60. All further references are included parenthetically within the text.

26 *Scene*, 18, 9 February 1963, pp. 46–47. For an extended comparison between Stoppard's play and *Next Time I'll Sing To You* which suggests the importance of Saunders as an early influence, see Sammells, *Stoppard: artist as critic*, pp. 32–39.

27 Lionel Abel, *Metatheatre* (New York: Hill and Wang, 1963), p. 47.

28 *Complete Works of Wilde*, p. 981.

29 Roger Sales, *Rosencrantz and Guildenstern Are Dead* (Hardmondsworth: Penguin, 1988), p. 66.

30 Martin Esslin, *Three East European Plays* (Harmondsworth: Penguin, 1970), p. 15.

31 *Complete Works of Wilde*, p. 1091.

32 Ibid., p. 17.

33 *Jumpers* (New York: Grove Press, 1972), p. 46. All further references to this edition are included parenthetically within the text.

34 Jonathan Bennett, "Philosophy and Mr. Stoppard," *Philosophy*, 50 (1975), p. 5.

35 Interview with Shusha Guppy, "Stoppard: art of theater VII," p. 187.

36 *Scene*, 5, 12 December 1962, p. 30.

37 *Complete Works of Wilde*, p. 43.

38 Quoted Tynan, *Show People*, p. 91.

39 Interview with Gollob and Roper, *Gambit*, 10 (1981), p. 6.

40 Peter Conrad, "Thomas the Think Engine," *Observer Review*, 1 November 1998, p. 5.

41 For a fuller discussion of how Wilde has been remade by contemporary writers and filmmakers, see the chapter, "From Baudeliare to Bowie," in Sammells, *Wilde Style: the plays and prose of Oscar Wilde* (London: Longman, 2000), pp. 117–129. The chapter, as its title suggests, also looks at the influence of Wilde's dandyism on contemporary pop culture and his conversion into a multi-form signifier of youth, rebelliousness, sexual nonconformity, and modernity.

42 Tom Stoppard, *The Invention of Love* (London and Boston: Faber and Faber, 1997), p. 96.

43 Sontag, *Sontag Reader*, pp. 105–120.

44 Quoted in Tynan, *Show People*, p. 71.

45 Tom Stoppard, "But for the Middle Classes," *Times Literary Supplement*, 3 June 1977, p. 677.

46 Quoted in Tynan, *Show People*, p. 71.

47 E P. Thompson, "Cold War Calvinism," *Guardian*, 31 August 1981, p. 10.

7

TOBY ZINMAN

Travesties, Night and Day,
The Real Thing

Stoppard thinks of himself as "quite an eclectic writer. I . . . finish a piece of work and by the time I'm talking about it I'm already fascinated with something none of you knows about."[1] The plays to be discussed in this chapter, *Travesties* (1975), *Night and Day* (1978), and *The Real Thing* (1982), form a surprising trio to readers and audiences who expect the similarity of tone and theme that you find in, say, Arthur Miller or in Samuel Beckett. But Stoppard's plays seem to be as unlike each other as like, taking up now *Hamlet,* now philosophy, now chaos mathematics, now Eastern European politics, now India, now journalism, now visual art, now poetry, now nineteenth-century Russia.[2] He writes about heterosexual love and homosexual love; he writes brilliant roles for both male and female actors, for old men and young boys, for old women and girls, and for actors of many races. "Eclectic" puts it mildly.

But surely we do mean something when we talk about "Stoppardian" qualities in a play, and these three plays offer the best evidence of those qualities because they are least like each other in both content and spirit. At the most obvious level, these plays share word-intoxicated characters ("I tend to put most of my money on a clarity of utterance . . . I don't understand the speech structures of people who are inarticulate or ungrammatical"[3]). Stoppard's immense vocabulary and complex sentence structure shape his characters as well as their dialogue. (As he told Michael Billington, referring to *Night and Day,* "When I write an African president into a play I have to contrive to make him the only African President who speaks like me."[4]) So that there is a quality of high Englishness about his work, his characters are almost inevitably well-educated, ironical and quick-witted, and when they are not, like the loutish Brodie in *The Real Thing,* they are despicable. The wit, the wordplay, the linguistic razzle-dazzle, the delight in talking, not only identify his characters but his kind of drama: intellectual as opposed to psychological, fast-tempoed as opposed to leisurely, crammed full as opposed to spare, dialectical as opposed to linear. It is, therefore, interesting that he feels struc-

120

ture is more important than dialogue. In an interview with Stoppard when he was in Philadelphia to advise on a revival of *On the Razzle*, he said that writing dialogue was the enjoyable part of playwriting for him, that his gift for it made it easy: "I don't take any credit for it, that's what a 'gift' means – something you're given. I look up and I've written two pages of dialogue. I don't know how. In some strange way, nothing crucial depends upon it, while everything crucial depends on getting the structure right." And working on the structure of a play is, for him, the hard part, a "dogged endeavor, trial and error" effort.[5] And so it is dramatic structure that I would like to address in this chapter – not just the construction but the vision that informs it, the meaning of the structure, of a dramatic architecture.

Stoppard's vision is not merely that of the mystery-solver, the sort based on a Holmesian clue that yields the pleasurable "ah-hah!" (although from plays as minor as *Artist Descending a Staircase* to plays as major as *Arcadia* there is such a clue). Stoppard refuses to oversimplify the universe, a refusal made gorgeous in the image of the moth in the cathedral in *Hapgood*. He can solve the mystery of the twin spies in that play, but he cannot solve the mystery of the wave/particle controversy in the theory of light. Stoppard equally refuses to reduce to rationality the irrationality of romantic love (the motivating idea of *The Invention of Love*), or to exclude the difficulties of morality and the enigmas of honor that make his politics so hard to label (the problem of *Professional Foul*). That morality and honor so deeply concern him suggests a contemporary author who is distinctly not a post-modern one.

The first of the three identifying structural characteristics, one noted by many critics as they write about individual plays, is that a Stoppard play begins with a false front, a scene the audience takes to be "real" but later discovers to have been a "*trompe-l'audience*" ploy.

Second, the structure always doubles (or trebles or quadruples) itself within the play; this is quite separate from, but certainly connected to, his predilection for doubling, mirroring, or twinning characters which is, in turn, quite separate from but certainly connected to his predilection for all the devices of linguistic twinning: puns, foreign languages (translated and not), invented language (translated and not), *double entendres*, and mala-propisms.[6]

And third, the set design, including sound and lighting, is always an integral part of the script rather than the interpretive decoration frequently left by dramatists to their directors. Stoppard's set directions echo – another form of twinning – the largest meaning of the play. Perhaps the best example of this is the table in *Arcadia* which accumulates "props" from both centuries, providing the objective correlative to the play's central idea, expressed

3 A scene from the Royal Shakespeare Company 1974 production of *Travesties* –
John Wood (Henry Carr) and Tom Bell (James Joyce).

in Septimus' beautiful consolation to Thomasina: "We shed as we pick up, like travelers who must carry everything in their arms, and what we let fall will be picked up by those behind. The procession is very long and life is very short. We die on the march. But there is nothing outside the march so nothing can be lost to it."[7]

The following discussion of three plays will be based on these three characteristics.

Travesties[8]

"I want to marry the play of ideas to farce. Now that may be like eating steak tartare with chocolate sauce, but that's the way it comes out. Everyone will have to decide for himself whether the seriousness is doomed or redeemed by the frivolity."[9]

Since much of *Travesties* depends on Stoppard's complicated travestying of *The Importance of Being Earnest*, the problem Stoppard delineates springs of course from Wilde's declaration that he had written "a trivial play for serious people." If this debate about seriousness or flippancy is the central critical question *about Travesties*, it is not, however, the central question *of Travesties*. Taking as its historical premise that in 1917, Lenin, James Joyce, and Tristan Tzara were working on their various revolutions while living in neutral Zurich, what follows that premise is a wildly hilarious, blindingly articulate debate about the relationship between art and politics, with Joyce as the high priest of art ("What did you do in the Great War?" "I wrote *Ulysses*"; p. 44) and Lenin as the high priest of politics (What did you do in the Great War? I created the Russian Revolution) and Tzara as the high priest of meaninglessness (What did you do in the Great War? Nothing!).

Arguing the crucial fourth position in the debate is Henry Carr, the high priest of the bourgeoisie. Whitaker calls Carr "a philistine narcissist who can produce neither art, nor anti-art, nor revolution. But . . . he is also a travesty of ourselves."[10] This idea is interestingly augmented by Simard's assertion that "Structurally, Carr is at the center of the play, just as Switzerland is at 'the still center of the wheel of war.'"[11] This is an apt analogy, especially if one views Switzerland as the emblem of bourgeois Europe. This is enormously complicated in that Carr not only speaks for the middlebrow, middle-class position – sometimes with great credibility – but since *Travesties* is a memory play, Carr's senile, self-aggrandizing mind theoretically contains the play. This is particularly interesting given the play's false front: *Travesties* begins in the Library with Joyce, Tzara, Lenin and Gwendolyn, but we will discover later that we are really in Henry Carr's memory, and that the scene has been 'imagined' by a now old Carr as opposed to experienced in the 'real' locale of the Room.

The prologue is not only *trompe-l'œil* – this is, we are not in the Library but in Carr's mind – but *trompe-l'oreille* as well, making this first scene aurally as well as visually deceptive. The first lines we hear are apparently dadaist poetry ("Eel ate enormous appletartza"; p. 2) which makes funny English semi-nonsense, but on closer audition and phonetic transliteration, actually compose a French limerick introducing us to the character speaking.[12] We move from apparently meaningless English on scraps of paper to meaningful French, which can be translated into meaningful English in Tzara's limerick. This is followed by another version of *tromp-l'orielle*, as Joyce dictates the opening of chapter 14 of *Ulysses*, a chapter that parallels the birth of English with the birth of a baby, so that now we move from Joycean English to Old English to modern English in the space of a third of a page of dialogue. This is followed by the Lenins' Russian conversation (which is translated in the text but which the non-Russian speaking audience would hear as unintelligible), followed by Joycean paper scraps in English and German, followed by Joyce's picking up Lenin's scrap of paper which he reads in English, and then the five-language exchange of politenesses between Lenin and Joyce as they exchange their scraps of paper – anticipating the twin scene later on when their folders containing portions of their manuscripts are mixed up and then returned. All these dialogue scraps, which seem so random and nonsensical, yield intelligible meaning, thereby establishing both the groundwork of the play's method and the angle of Stoppard's vision.

All of this also speaks to Stoppard's inclination to doubling and twinning, linguistically and structurally, an inclination more intensely rendered in this play than in any other, in that the impulse to travesty is itself an impulse to double, to twin the original. Thus, Stoppard may be doing to Wilde what Joyce was doing to Homer, although just as Joyce started with a work as monumental as the *Odyssey* and seemed to diminish it by the quotidian, yet finally exalted the quotidian by the "travesty" of the Homeric source ("It is a theme so overwhelming that I am almost afraid to treat it. And yet I with my Dublin Odyssey will double that immortality"; p. 42), so Stoppard works apparently in reverse, beginning with the apparent triviality of *The Importance of Being Earnest* and exalting it through his travesty. Of course, the Wordsworthian travesty ("Bliss was it to see the dawn!"; p. 10) suggests both a travesty of the passion of the French Revolution with Carr's relief at having lived through a battle and a travesty of the neutrality of Switzerland during World War One. The Duchampian travesties – if it is possible to trump the jokester ("The difference between being a man and being a coffee mill is art"; p. 29), and the Eliotic travesties (Carr as Prufrock, "asserting" his cravat "by a simple pin"; p. 10) all suggest that *Travesties* is the spectacular (and auricular) homage/burlesque of western culture's most dazzling era, from Romanticism through High Modernism.

Not only does Carr double as his younger/older selves but this doubling impulse is felt on every level, from the repeated formula of Carr's memoirs ("To those of us who knew him") to the linguistically/politically doubled name of the artist Hans/Jean Arp ("In what way is the first name of your friend singular? In that it is duplicate"), which also travesties Joyce's own pseudo-scientific travesty of the catechistical method in the penultimate chapter of *Ulysses*.

Stoppard splits the play's two acts between two locations, the Room and the Library, with the Room doubling as the Room then and the Room now. Stoppard tells us in the stage directions that "It is to be supposed that Old Carr has lived in the same apartment since that time" (p. 1), but while the first scene begins fictionally in the Library, it begins dramatically in the Room, since that is where Carr himself is located as he remembers the past.

Thus the two locations are actually one – which may be singling rather than doubling.

Carr's dips into memory are marked by lighting changes: the lights dim incrementally as a scene in memory draws to a conclusion, with "Low light on the motionless Carr" to signify a return to the "present." These time slips arrest the play briefly, resuming at Carr's "Well, let us resume," a lighting cue which restores "Normal light." This is Stoppard's ingenious demarcation not only of chronological shifts but of the shift from interior to exterior; the portions of the play in which we see Old Carr attempting to remember rather than seeing what he remembers, when we are looking at him rather than at his memories through the distorted lens of his mind, are the "reality" of *Travesties*. And thus his memory does not structurally encompass the entire play, nor does it stylistically encompass the travestying. Just as Zeifman suggests that the sheer exuberance and prodigality of the punning shifts our sympathies toward Joyce,[13] so Stoppard's travestying is Joycean in its celebration of the source works, thereby subtly and structurally (as well as linguistically) privileging the debate in favor of "the fabulous artificer."

Stoppard told Jon Bradshaw in an interview, "I tend to see everything through a comic prism."[14] It strikes me as significant that almost anyone else would have said 'comic lens.' It is worth noting that Wilde's Miss Prism is the only character without a twin/equivalent in Stoppard's play; we know from Peter Wood, the play's original director, that Stoppard originally considered titling this play "Prism."[15] It is tempting to think that she, the author of the manuscript exchanged for the baby, and the unwitting author and solver of the plot's mystery, finds her twin/equivalent in Stoppard himself, the author of the whole, the prismatic mind in which all these travesties dance.

Night and Day[16]

As Stoppard's first full-length play after *Travesties*, *Night and Day* was viewed askance when it opened in London in 1978. It was damned by many as a "descent into naturalism,"[17] and by Harold Hobson as "straightforward,"[18] while Walter Kerr questioned Stoppard's being "a true dramatist at all."[19] But nearly everybody seems to have agreed on the word *Shavian* as a shorthand description of its debate about the difficulties of freedom – although both Jim Hunter and Katherine Kelly see the play as "Chekhovian" rather than Shavian. That the play is a radical departure from the style of *Travesties* is obvious.

Night and Day opens with the signature false front: an opening scene which seems to be the "real world" of the play, but is actually a dream, which we, the audience/readers, take to be reality. It is as if we were the dreamer; we do not see a man on stage asleep, but we see his dream, briefly revisiting the memory device of *Travesties*. The sleeping man projects his anxiety about his work, dreaming his own death. Guthrie is a photojournalist specializing in "hot spots." The play begins cinematically with rapid nightfall and the sound of a distant helicopter growing closer. A jeep appears. Guthrie jumps out, shouting "Press! Press!" and when the helicopter's sweeping spotlight finds him, there are machine-gun bursts and he is killed. When Ruth enters, sees Guthrie asleep in her garden, wakes him, and thus reveals scene 1 to have been a dream, the play proper then seems to begin. But of course the play begins when the play begins, and it has already begun.

The significance of the several illusionary elements here exists on different levels of importance. For example, some are ironic, like the sound of the telex machine which Guthrie incorporates into his dream as machine-gun fire (it is ironic since this machine – the only possibility of getting news out of Kambawe – will also be, as the plot develops, the machine keeping the news from getting out). And of course the telex machine's noise is merely a theatrical sound effect. But most important is the structural significance of that first scene, a significance that cannot register until Act 2 when the dream of the prologue becomes reality and the jeep carrying Guthrie and Milne, driven by Francis, is attacked and Milne is shot and killed. It is worth noting that in Act 2 we only hear about the murder in the jeep, those events having already been seen at the beginning of the play, a difference in delivery that not only underscores the two basic vehicles of theatre – the visual and the verbal – but also underscores the two different kinds of journalists in the play – photographer and reporter.

The second act also begins with a false front: Ruth fantasizes Milne's return and the start of their love affair; this is complicated by the fact that not only do we not know that Ruth is imagining, nor that Milne is already dead, but Ruth's fantasy incorporates her inner self, the character "Ruth" who often speaks aloud, making her thoughts audible. Thus the first scene of Act 2 actually presents three layers of Ruth. In production, we should have a clue to the scene's unreality by Milne's clothing: the first act closes on Guthrie's exasperation with Milne's khaki shirt with epaulettes and his camouflage bush hat: "Oh, bloody hell, he's dressed up like Action Man!" (p. 68). If in her fantasy Milne is wearing the shirt Ruth last saw him in – not the khaki shirt nor the tennis shirt we are told he has in his bag – and if we are watching with a Holmesian eye, we will catch, if not yet understand, the discrepancy. But although this structural device of the false front is important to the theatricality of the play, the real structure of the play is political, not metadramatic, a fact most commentators do not mention. And in being political, it underscores the very subject of the play, which is freedom, not drama.

The most obvious issue of freedom lies in the fictitious African country of Kambawe, which has recently freed itself from British rule. It is now ruled by President Mageeba, a dictator who is, significantly, a product of the London School of Economics, and who is still dependent on the expertise of colonialists like Geoffrey Carson to manage the copper mines. And although Carson and his wife Ruth still live a highly privileged life, it is at the pleasure of Mageeba, whose presence – and unpredictable violence – is clearly terrifying to Carson. Thus, the two characters who embody the issue of political freedom in its largest sense reveal the vexed complexity of the question of symbiotic dependence as a bald version of the truth of the modern world. This issue is further complicated in the plot by the revolution staged by Colonel Shimbu, leader of the liberation front, who has seized the mines – placing the nation's wealth in yet another set of hands. If Shimbu seems superficially to be the power of the people, we are quickly reminded that he is dependent on a Russian-built airstrip and Cuban pilots.

The vile shenanigans in the public/military arena are subtly echoed by the jockeying for power in the sexual arena, and it is here that the play's structure becomes truly Stoppardian as we see that every set of circumstances is likely to be doubled and trebled. In the sexual arena, there is a lopsided triangle which is really a square: Wagner and Ruth have had a one-night fling in London, and although he is powerfully present both as a professional as well as sexual authority, she is now drawn to Milne, the young idealistic freelance reporter who has scooped everybody by lucking into an interview with Colonel Shimbu. Ruth's husband, Carson, the fourth corner of this uneasy flirtation, seems the least defined of the male characters, although his power over Ruth – matrimonially and economically and socially – is so great that his mere existence ensures the inevitability of his sexual triumph despite Ruth's philanderings.

If sexual politics double military politics, then Carson surely doubles England itself, and thus becomes a figure defined more by wealth, title, power, and attitude than actual personality. As England is to Africa, so Carson is to the marriage: displaced but not replaced, still very much present. If we pursue these equations, Wagner, who is arrogant and dictatorial, and whose colonialism (remember, he is Australian) generates aggressive defensiveness, parallels President Mageeba: both are opportunists who talk a good game but abandon morality for self-interest without a moment's worry. His rival, Milne, is therefore the double of Colonel Shimbu, the apparently idealistic rebel, refusing to kowtow to the dictates of the Establishment – whether that Establishment is defined as Mageeba's government or the journalists' union. Just as Milne and Wagner are rivals for Ruth's sexual interest (with Carson's assumed sexual "rights" forming the tense backdrop for their contest), so Ruth, then, is Kambawe itself, represented in the play by the servant Francis, who is submissive and obedient but who runs to Shimbu's side as soon as the opportunity presents itself. Ruth, like Francis, like the population of Kambawe, is not a contender in the fight but rather that which is fought over. Consider Debbie's dismissive line about marital fidelity in *The Real Thing*: "Exclusive rights isn't love, it's colonization." If colonialism is merely a metaphor in that play, it is literalized in *Night and Day*.

If Wagner has brief prior claim to Ruth, Milne certainly wins her affection, a metaphoric vote for what we gather to be Shimbu's populist cause. Shimbu has captured Kambawe's mines, formerly owned by Carson and about to be bombed by Mageeba, at which point (just after the play ends, presumably) he will destroy the Nationalist Front. Then, Carson predicts, "the Russians will be interfering the stuffing out of Mageeba's army, until Kambawe is about as independent as Lithuania" (pp. 82–83). Just as Shimbu cannot win in his arena, so Milne cannot in his; Milne's death represents the triumph of the cynical alliance of the repressive forces of Carson and Mageeba, England and militarized dictatorship, aided by the opportunism of Wagner. Ruth will clearly spend the night with him again, at the cost of self-disgust and pessimism, allowing herself to become Wagner's "tart" – a tiny cynical definition of emergent nations – until her husband returns, reasserting marital rule. Stoppard does not seem to have much hope for freedom.

And mirroring all this is the overt subject of the play: freedom of the press. In an interview for British television, Stoppard spoke with uncharacteristic intensity on this subject, both as a former journalist and as a citizen:

> I had always felt that no matter how dangerously closed a society looked like it was getting, as long as any newspaper was free to employ anybody it liked to say what it wished within the law, then any situation was correctable. And without that any situation was concealable. I felt that very strongly; I feel it strongly now. I am passionate about this. It's the one thing that makes a free society different from an unfree one. It's the crucial thing. It's the last thing to go. While you've got it, you're in a situation where you can get better. Once you've lost it, it can only get worse.[20]

But despite this vigorous belief, Stoppard characteristically debates the subject rather than preaches about it. Every position is given a voice. Wagner, like Mageeba, uses the press for his own advantage ("what Dick wants is a right-thinking press – one that thinks like him"; p. 64). Wagner, however, is hoist on his own petard (his pro-union whistle-blowing shuts down the newspaper with a strike, thereby preventing Wagner's own scoop from being published). After much talk about "solidarity," the telex slogan, WOTWU ("workers of the world unite") becomes heavily ironical, in that Wagner, the union man, has united with none of his fellow workers, and has self-interestedly, albeit inadvertently, sent Milne to his death. If Ruth is the ironic (and ironical) representative of Africa – the pampered upper-class woman who symbolically represents her servant Francis – her position on the power of the press perfectly expresses this class irony: "The populace and the popular press. What a grubby symbiosis it is. Which came first? The rhinoceros or the rhinoceros bird?" (p. 48). *Night and Day* seems to have grown more rather than less relevant with time, as tabloid journalism becomes a favorite subject of mainstream journalism and as hard news turns soft and sensational. Guthrie, the play's least political and least articulate character (a photographer for whom a picture is worth a thousand words, etc., etc.) gets the last word on the debate about freedom of the press: "I've been around a lot of places. People do awful things to each other. But it's worse in places where everybody is kept in the dark. It really is. Information is light. Information, in itself, about anything, is light" (pp. 108–109).

If light, metaphorically, is the key, this is a dark play: it begins at sunset and ends in darkness, and its grimly mirthless final scene is visually telling in its parodic noirishness: As "Ruth" sings "The Lady is a Tramp" to herself, Wagner sends Milne's obituary to England on the telex and the play concludes:

> RUTH. Is that it?
> WAGNER. That's it.
> BLACKOUT. (p. 113)

This is Stoppard's most pessimistic conclusion, which is, perhaps, a way of explaining why this is not among his best plays, working as it does against the optimism inherent in the comedic vision.

The Real Thing[21]

Optimism and happy endings abound in *The Real Thing*. Like *Travesties*, *The Real Thing* is about art and politics. Like *Night and Day*, *The Real Thing* is about sex and politics. Unlike both earlier plays, this play takes an unprecedented leap on to the minefield of romantic love, and, likewise unprecedented, does not base its structure on debate but merely seems to.

Many critics have found *The Real Thing* less satisfying than his earlier work.[22] No doubt anticipating this, Stoppard has his character, Henry, a playwright, tell his daughter, "I suppose that's the fate of all us artists . . . People saying they preferred the early stuff" (p. 61). The play is generally viewed as a step toward humanizing Stoppard's wit, and much of the critical debate about the play, whether *The Real Thing* proves that Tom Stoppard has a heart after all, is undercut by his own declaration that it is not an auto-biographical confession but rather a structural game he was playing right from the start. His comment to Mel Gussow is instructive:

> I'm not talking about that. I'm talking about my scheme, my idiotic game, a play where it turns out a woman is married to the man who wrote the first scene. If the writer's wife has got to be in both situations, she's got to be an actress. It's determined by the playful idea of having people repeat their situation in fiction.[23]

Yet in another conversation with Gussow, only a short time after, Stoppard said, "For better or worse, that's it – the love play! I've been aware of the process that's lasted 25 years, of shedding inhibitions about self-revelation. I wouldn't have dreamed of writing about it 10 years ago, but as you get older, you think, who cares?"[24] Regardless of whether *The Real Thing* is lesser or greater Stoppard, whether it is an intricate game or a soul-baring, it shares the same three structural characteristics with the previously discussed plays.

It begins with a false front, a scene that tricks us into thinking it is "real" when it is "merely" the performance of a scene from a play the main character has written. This has been addressed thoroughly and brilliantly by Hersh Zeifman in "Comedy of Ambush," as he points out not only that the scene from "House of Cards" tricks us but that part of Stoppard's use of this "structural dislocation" shows us "how difficult [it is] to know precisely what is 'real,'"[25] which is both the problem of life and the pleasure of the theatre.

This first false scene ends as the snow in the souvenir paperweight engulfs the stage, creating a magical and Shakespearean image of the theatre as globe. This device of a play within a play shows us art imitating and thus twinning life since the plot will later turn and turn again on adultery, and will then reverse itself as life imitates art, when Henry the playwright plays the role he had written for the jealous husband in his own play.

Dialogue is twinned by theatrical dialogue slyly quoted within theatrical dialogue by theatre people who may or may not "get" it and to audiences who may or may not "get" it. The allusions include scraps from *Romeo and Juliet* and from Noël Coward's *Private Lives*. The scene from Strindberg's *Miss Julie* subtly revisits the class struggle inherent in the sexual flirtation between Brodie and Annie, while Ford's *'Tis Pity She's a Whore*, another play about sexual betrayal and jealousy, is put to multiple uses. Stoppard doubles the zing of this allusion by having Annie, now living with Henry, cast in a production as Annabella and beginning an adulterous affair with her leading man. Annabella is a role Henry's former wife Charlotte played years before, losing her virginity to her leading man. Zeifman points out that these allusions to cultural artifacts (one of Stoppard's favorite forms of twinning) actually begins with the door slam as Charlotte enters in Act 1, scene 1, a slam that echoes (more aural twinning) the door Nora slams behind her at the end of Ibsen's *A Doll's House*, modern drama's most famous sound effect. The slamming door collapses the literal house of cards Max has been building, as well as the figurative house of cards that is their marriage,[26] and the structural house of cards that scene 1 is in relation to the actual play we are watching.

This twinning permeates every aspect of the play, in props, costumes, and sets as well. For instance, there is the crucial telltale handkerchief (Henry's found by Max which ends Annie and Max's marriage) suggesting *Othello*, although most of the props in this play (the cricket bat, the coffee mug, the phonograph records, the vegetable dip) all strike me as tediously illustrative, lacking the sparkle of witty obliquity that marks Stoppard's uses of props in his earlier works (say the scraps of paper in *Travesties*) or the splendid philosophic resonance of the props in his later works (say the accumulation of objects on the table in *Arcadia*). There is costume twinning: "Charlotte enters barefoot, wearing Henry's dressing gown which is too big for her" (1, 2) and "Annie enters from the bedroom door, barefoot and wearing Henry's robe, which is too big for her" (1, 4).

There is a Chinese box-like succession of sets as the play moves from one living room to another, first the false one, a set within the set, next the true one, the set, and then each of those two living room sets reappears throughout the twelve scenes as the couples are reconfigured. The other twinned set is the train, one false and one true, while the pivotal scene, scene 8, takes place in "An empty space" during the rehearsal of a play. This not only provides the event (Annie begins an affair with Billy) that will move the plot forward, but gives us the Stoppardian theme most vividly as it reveals the interpenetration of art and life. The theatrical metaphor, made literal so many times in this play, coalesces at this moment. It is significant that this central, crucial scene is almost entirely in Ford's dialogue, not Stoppard's, and does not involve Henry, the central character. Thus, structurally, *The Real Thing* is hinged in the middle; twinning suggests this pat structure, as does Debbie's indictment of bourgeois morality: "They think all relationships hinge in the middle. Sex or no sex. What a fantastic range of possibilities" (p. 61).

Most obviously, we see "House of Cards" double the plot of *The Real Thing* – even to the detail of Charlotte's most recent lover having been an architect – and Act 2 twins Act 1, thus suggesting both that Henry's two marriages twin each other and that one wife is much like another. We hear the dialogue twinned in ways that create intriguing gender similarities: for example, Henry is considering joining the Justice for Brodie Committee as a way of being near Annie; when Charlotte protests his lack of proper motivation, he replies, "What does he care if we're motivated by the wrong reasons" (p. 32) and later, when Billy expresses his willingness to act in Brodie's awful play as a way of being near Annie, she replies, "You shouldn't do it for the wrong reasons"; Billy replies, "Why not? Does he care?" (p. 57), suggesting that all men think alike. The dialogue duplications resonate in various ways: when Billy launches into their love scene from 'Tis Pity on the train as a way of declaring himself to Annie, "Oh, Annabella, I am quite undone!" she replies, "Billy!" in amused protest. Later, during a "real" rehearsal in Glasgow, Billy, in his role as Giovanni, says, "Thou wilt chide me, then. / Kiss me: – " [He kisses her lightly.] and Annie says, "[quietly] Billy . . . [she returns his kiss in earnest] (p. 67).

Stoppard twins the dialogue not only as a structural device and not only as intertextual allusion but also realistically, the way people repeat what others have said to them. Debbie tells her father, in her indictment of marital fidelity as the cornerstone of conventional morality: "Exclusive rights isn't love, it's colonization" (p. 63), a line Henry finds appalling, another piece of T-shirt philosophy, an "ersatz masterpiece. Like Michelangelo working in polystyrene" (in other words, not the real thing). Later (see p. 75) we hear Henry speak Debbie's line to Annie, along with her allusion to the Latin for harlot, *meretrix*. What are we to make of this repetition and influence? It seems to function as a thread to hold scenes together and move the play along linearly, but it seems to me it only seems to mean. The play shows us that Henry was wrong and Debbie was right: "the real thing" is not gauged by "did she have it off or didn't she" (p. 61), just as love can be recognized, as Annie says, by one's willingness to hurt and be hurt by the loved one and through it all sustaining belief (thus the concluding music, the Monkees' anthem "I'm a Believer"). This debate about love and sexual fidelity, about caring and not caring, which progresses through Henry and Charlotte, Henry and Debbie, Henry and Annie, remains, to me, unconvincing and sophistic, a toney version of some bumper-sticker theory like "Love means never having to say you're sorry." The plot resolves the debate peculiarly: Charlotte gets what Stoppard apparently thinks she deserves – a series of affairs – while Henry and Annie are still together, their alliance reinforced when Annie finally sees what a goon Brodie is; even Max has found love, thus absolving Annie and Henry of residual guilt.

Never before has Stoppard weakened a play by quashing the dialectic with the structure, suggesting that there is, after all, something autobiographical in Henry's lament: "I don't know how to write love. I try to write it properly, and it just comes out embarrassing . . . Loving and being loved is unliterary. It's happiness expressed in banality and lust . . . I mean, I talk better than this" (p. 39). What, then, is "the real thing" *The Real Thing* claims exists? The debate about "real thing"-ness seems finally resolved by Annie's grabbing the phone from Henry and telling her director who is badgering her for being late, "Keep your knickers on, it's only a bloody play" (p. 76), apparently validating the middle-brow, middle-class prejudices against taking art too seriously. But it is important to remember that what Annie is late for is not a stage play but the shooting of Brodie's play Henry has rewritten for television, dreadful hack work not unlike the science fiction screenplay he is writing for alimony money, and thus not the real thing at all. But surely Stoppard is not saying that only writing for the stage confers authenticity, since we are told by both Charlotte and Debbie that "House of Cards" is bad play. *The Real Thing*, having staked out its territory as the discussion of the aesthetics of authenticity, fails to deliver even a debate much less a resolution. In point of fact, the debate does not really exist here as it did in *Travesties* and *Night and Day*. This play demonstrates that "the real thing" in matters of love is not necessarily the right thing or the good thing – Stoppard having avoided either the ethical or the moral components of the debate entirely. And whether love and art are equatable terms in an argument, with some commonality of real-thing-ness inherent in both, seems dubious.

Stoppard's allusive twinning suggests ruinous contrasts to the play we are watching: Max's inarticulate heartbreak when he discovers his betrayal is both pitiful and genuine but lacks anything like the grandeur of Othello's heartbreak (and so all we get is what Debbie calls "Infidelity among the architect class. Again"; p. 61), nor does Stoppard's play provide the power of *'Tis Pity She's a Whore* as it not only overwhelms Billy and Annie but hushes the theatre audience as we feel its sudden passion and richness. As he did in *Rosencrantz and Guildenstern are Dead*, Stoppard reveals how difficult it is to be a contemporary playwright: what "real' dramatist would not sell his soul for genuine rather than merely parodic or quoting access to Renaissance English? Is this the way Procul Harem's "A Whiter Shade of Pale" uses Bach's "Air on a G String"? Stoppard via Henry acknowledges the problem of "the real thing" musically in the distance between Maria Callas singing and The Crystals singing "Da Doo Ron Ron": does this mean that whatever moves you is "the real thing?" As we hear in the second scene from *'Tis Pity She's a Whore*, "Music as well consists /In the ear as in the playing." It strikes me as odd that although "high" and "low" music is so crucial throughout the play, given Henry's preference for dated pop music and the plot device of Desert Island Discs, and additionally that musical taste is an on-going squabble between Henry and Annie, that it is not a generational issue, as it realistically would be, between Henry and his seventeen-year-old daughter Debbie, thereby sidestepping the issue of "the real thing" even in popular music. The intrepid leapfrog dialectic of the earlier plays has here been abandoned for contrivance as we watch Stoppard attempting to write a non-Stoppardian play.

Although the task in this chapter has been to point out similarities, the real interest in thinking about these three plays together may lie in the differences between them, and the way they build toward the greatness of *Arcadia*, where difficult ideas and fully human characters meet. Tom Stoppard may be the only living playwright in the English-speaking world from whom we can expect plays of such power and beauty.

NOTES

1 Tom Stoppard speaking at the University of Pennsylvania, Philadelphia, 7 February 1996.
2 Tom Stoppard in an interview with the author in Philadelphia, 5 January 2000. He would not reveal anything more about this new play, which he hoped to have ready "by Christmas 2000."
3 Tom Stoppard talking to the cast of *Arcadia* at the Wilma Theater in Philadelphia, 10 November 1996. The author was permitted to sit in.
4 Michael Billington, *Stoppard: the playwright* (London: Methuen, 1987), p. 130.
5 Tom Stoppard during an interview at the Bellevue Stratford Hotel, Philadelphia, 20 February 1998.
6 My article on *Hapgood* addresses this at length; see, "Blizintsy/Dvojniki, Twins/Doubles, Hapgood/Hapgood," *Modern Drama*, 34.2 (June 1991), pp. 312–321.
7 *Arcadia* (London and Boston: Faber and Faber, 1993), p. 38.
8 All references are to the revised edition of *Travesties* (New York: Grove Press, 1996).
9 Ross Wetzsteon, "Tom Stoppard Eats Steak Tartare with Chocolate Sauce," reprinted in Paul Delaney, ed. *Stoppard in Conversation* (Ann Arbor: University of Michigan Press, 1994), p. 83.
10 Thomas R. Whitaker, *Tom Stoppard* (New York: Grove Press, 1983), pp. 128–129.
11 Rodney Simard, "Seriousness Compromised by Frivolity: structure and meaning in Tom Stoppard's *Travesties*," in John Harty, III, ed., *Tom Stoppard: a Casebook* (New York: Garland, 1988), p. 187.
12 Jim Hunter, *Tom Stoppard's Plays* (New York: Grove Press), 1982, p. 240.
13 Hersh Zeifman, "Tomfoolery: Stoppard's theatrical puns," in Anthony Jenkins, ed., *Critical Essays on Tom Stoppard* (Boston: G. K. Hall, 1990), p. 190.
14 Jon Bradshaw, "Tom Stoppard, Nonstop: word games with a hit playwright," reprinted in Delaney, ed., *Stoppard in Conversation*, p. 95.
15 Whitaker, *Stoppard*, pp. 113–114.
16 All references are to *Night and Day* (New York: Grove Press, 1979).
17 Billington, *Stoppard*, p. 123.

18 Quoted in Whitaker, *Stoppard*, p. 147.

19 Quoted ibid., p. 147.

20 Melvyn Bragg, "The South Bank Show," reprinted in Delaney, ed., *Stoppard in Conversation*, p. 123.

21 All references to *The Real Thing* are to the revised Broadway edition (Boston: Faber and Faber, 1984).

22 Tim Brassell in *Tom Stoppard: an assessment* (New York: St Martin's Press, 1985) writes that "although Stoppard's extraordinary agility at handling ideas and explanations does not let him down in *The Real Thing*," (p. 258), he finds that the main characters never move us fully. Richard Corballis finds its language "slick and trendy rather than genuinely clever" and the plot plodding (*Stoppard: the mystery and the clockwork* [New York: Methuen, 1984], p. 147). Richard Allen Cave allows that "though fine, it is not Stoppard at his very best" because it lacks the dimension of surrealism and fantasy (found in *Jumpers* and *Travesties*); it is too conventional and Henry is "too positive a figure" (*New British Drama on the London Stage: 1970 to 1985*, [Gerrards Cross: Colin Smythe, 1987], p. 93) and Anthony Jenkins (*The Theatre of Tom Stoppard*, Cambridge: Cambridge University Press, 1987) sees it as "a major achievement" despite his view that the female characters are inconsistently drawn and implausible. He feels that "Henry presents a chimerical version of his creator's public self and behind that lies a vulnerability, a rawness which Stoppard had not felt able to expose – and mock – since 'Reunion,' the early short story" (p. 172).

23 Mel Gussow, *Conversations with Tom Stoppard* (London: Nick Hern, 1995), pp. 41–42.

24 Mel Gussow, "The Real Tom Stoppard," *New York Times Magazine*, 1 January 1984, p. 28.

25 Hersh Zeifman, "Comedy of Ambush: Tom Stoppard's *The Real Thing*," in Hersh Zeifman and Cynthia Zimmerman, eds., *Contemporary British Drama, 1970–90: Essays from Modern Drama* (Toronto: University of Toronto Press, 1993), p.220.

26 Ibid., p. 218.

8

JOHN BULL

Tom Stoppard and politics

In an early Tom Stoppard play, *After Magritte* (1970), Detective Inspector Foot seeks to explain the opening tableau, announcing a series of increasingly bizarre theories that are capped only by the real explanation. What is here used playfully, elsewhere in Stoppard's work takes on more serious dimensions. Tom Stoppard is as fascinated by systems of logic as was Jonathan Swift, and as suspicious of them. From Stoppard's very earliest work, audiences were drawn into worlds that declared themselves as rationally coherent, even as the events of the plays set out to demolish the evidence. This dualistic structuring is reflected in the way in which Stoppard balances and opposes thematic material in his plays: classicism and romanticism; imagination and science; free-will and determinism; and so on. Stoppard's suspicion of logical constructs is predicated on a belief in the supremacy of the individual and the particular over the determined and the enforced; his fascination with them comes from his firm sense that there must be order for the aspirations of the individual to flourish.

This duality is central to any political consideration of Stoppard's work. For his sternest critics, it is taken to be at best evasive; for his admirers it is simply a part of the questioning stance that Stoppard has made peculiarly his own, and is looked for in each new piece. A perfect example can be found in *Squaring the Circle* (1984), where the narrator talks of the efforts of Solidarity to reconcile the irreconcilable in Poland: "an attempt was made to put together two ideas which wouldn't fit, the idea of freedom as it is understood in the West, and the idea of socialism as it is understood in the Soviet empire." The attempt would fail because it was as impossible as turning "a circle into a square with the same area – not because no one has found out how to do it, but because there is no way in which it can be done."[1] Stoppard is here talking about a local situation, but it is easy to open up the terms of his metaphor to create a larger structural model of oppositions. For the "idea of freedom" we can read the aspirations of the individual *per se*, and for the "idea of socialism" the aspirations of the state – any state, though some far more than others – to restrict, curtail, and generally control the aspirations of the individual.[2] In all of Stoppard's work the individual operates in a continual state of flux beween being the "free man" of his ironically entitled first stage play,[3] and being part of the mechanism of a larger informing structure, whether it be the office, the palace, or the state.

In his earliest work, Stoppard tried hard to avoid an intervention into the realms of political debate. It was not that he was uninterested in politics as such, but rather that he put more trust in the process of questioning than in attempts to create a fixed ideological position. For instance, talking of *Jumpers* two years after its first production in 1972, Stoppard vehemently denied it was a play about politics or ideology, but that "it reflects my belief that all political acts have a moral basis to them and are meaningless without them."[4] In talking thus he was making an explicit comparison with left-wing theatre. In 1978, he was still clear about his attitude toward the polemical school: "I had a reaction against making heroes for plays who had positive points of view and no qualifications about them . . . But I was always morally, if not politically involved."[5] Stoppard's sense of himself as, above all, a *moral* writer is, then, the necessary precondition for any consideration of his interventions into the public arena. It is now possible to see, in a way that it was very difficult for writers considering Stoppard's career up to that point,[6] that his entire dramatic output has been one that placed the minutiae of moral philosophy at its center, and that his deployment of philosophical debate, whilst remaining playful in dramatic terms, is deadly serious in Stoppard's attempts to reconcile the apparently irreconcilable, to square the circle.

The year 1978 was actually a strange one for Stoppard to be continuing his efforts to distance himself from politics, because by then he had to a great extent abandoned his position of political neutrality. In November 1978, his *Night and Day* opened in London. Set in an African country, it was concerned largely with the activities of rival British journalists attempting to obtain a scoop on the rebel skirmishes that they hoped might turn into a full-scale war. Stoppard already had the double bill of *Dirty Linen* and *New-Found-Land* running at the Arts Theatre. Where the double bill dealt farcically with public corruption in Britain, including a sideswipe at the gutter press in *Dirty Linen*, *Night and Day* was a more serious piece, quite unlike anything Stoppard had previously offered. The chief conflict is between Wagner, a straight-down-the-line trade union man, and Milne, a freelance journalist who has previously broken a union picket line. Although there is no obvious "hero" figure, "there was no doubt that Stoppard's sympathies lay with Milne . . . and that they reflected informed [the play is dedicated to Paul Johnson[7]] and popular opinion in advance of the 1979 General Election."[8] It was the general election of 1979 that brought the

Conservative Party back into power, with Margaret Thatcher as prime minister. In this same year Stoppard confided to Paul Delaney: "I'm a conservative with a small c. I'm a conservative in politics, literature, education and theatre." [9] This was a significant time at which to have made such a remark, for from the outset of the new administration it was clear that the terms of political debate were to be completely altered. Stoppard, thus, both distances himself from the specifics of the Conservative Party even as he claims an allegiance to some wider moral and cultural definition of "conservatism"; his is a political ideology that is not, and could not be, wedded to any party. The rest of his career to date has involved a struggle to understand and come to terms with this allegiance.

These plays are unusual in that they deal directly with British political life in a way that Stoppard would never again attempt. However, that *Night and Day* should do so, though set in Africa, is characteristic of Stoppard's other work around this period. For, it was not British politics that first moved him away from a declaredly non-engaged position. In 1971 James Saunders claimed that Stoppard was "basically a displaced person. Therefore, he doesn't want to stick his neck out. He feels grateful to Britain because he sees himself as a guest here, and that makes it hard for him to criticise Britain." [10] If this was true then, and if it did, indeed, affect his writing about Britain, it is scarcely so today. In what follows I want first to consider Stoppard's entry into the political arena where he looked towards Eastern Europe, and then consider the implications of this change for his later writing when his thoughts were very much back with Britain.

Stoppard's first success, *Rosencrantz and Guildestern are Dead* (1967) is a good place to start, for it set the pattern of a movement backwards and forwards through history that is at the center of Stoppard's questionings. Stoppard's choice of plays to use as base texts welded together the established classic, *Hamlet*, to a modern avant-garde play, *Waiting for Godot*, in ways that continued the existentialist rereading of Shakespeare's play presented by Jan Kott in *Shakespeare our Contemporary* (first published in English in 1964[11]). Stoppard's appropriation of a drama of existentialist *angst* is not, however, confined to *Rosencrantz and Guildenstern*, where it could well be traced to the use of Beckett's play. The point is, rather, that the use of *Godot* appealed to Stoppard not only for its contemporaneity but for the very circularity of its form: a dialogue that never leads to answers but only to more questions. Furthermore, Stoppard's play refuses to present a reliable voice: uncertainty is all. This characterizes all Stoppard's early work.

Stoppard's roots as a playwright are perhaps best seen as a part of that Anglicization of the "absurdist" tradition that I outlined in *Stage Right*.[12] The pattern of repetition, suggesting that nothing in human history will or can be changed, which is central to absurdist theatre, opposes the central tenet of political theatre as defined by Brecht, that man is "alterable and able to alter."[13]

This distinction is crucial, for the start of Stoppard's theatrical career coincided almost exactly with that of a whole generation of new playwrights, playwrights who were not only anthithetical towards absurdist philosophy, but who would, in many cases, be profoundly influenced by Brechtian theory and practice in their theatre work in the 1970s.[14] This meant that Stoppard's early work not only declared itself in terms that disavowed any direct interest in the political but did so in a context in which the very existence of a contemporaneous oppositional theatrical movement made that declaration the more overt.[15] Stoppard was, indeed, only too anxious to stress the point; in 1968 he declared: "I burn with no causes. I cannot say I write with any social objective."[16] Stoppard's work was, however, never free from a political dimension, and his early attempts at denial are always open to the same kind of questioning that his plays demand. That critics should have overlooked this aspect of his work is because dialogue (in the sense of debating voices) was not used by him to either promote the views of a single voice or to present a dialectical model in which a synthesis is to be arrived at. For Stoppard the questions, and the questioning, had initially been more important than any move towards providing answers. What this does not take account of, however, is that a play has a life outside the ostensible intentions of its author. *Rosencrantz and Guidenstern* can be read politically simply in terms of its relationship to the political ideologies of its two base texts; the movement of the spotlight away from the activities of the royal figures to the bemused alienation of the two outsider figures, who have brought with them from their university studies all the post-1945 existentialist *angst* of Beckett's protagonists. Indeed, in a Hungarian revival of *Rosencrantz and Guildenstern* in 1996,[17] the potential significance of this was elaborated on. In Gabor Mate's production, the two friends were recognizable as Hungarian strangers let loose in the police state of a Russian court in a way that not only demonstrated the play's flexibility but also released much of the inherent general political content of the text.

As late as 1976, Stoppard was still seeking to distance himself from the political arena: "I tend to overreact against the large claims of committed theatre . . . I used to feel out on a limb, because when I started to write you were a shit if you weren't writing about Vietnam or housing. Now I have no compunction about that . . . *The Importance of Being Earnest* is important, but it says nothing about anything."[18]

His invocation of Oscar Wilde's play is not coincidental. It had provided the base text for *Travesties* (1974), the first Stoppard play to concern itself even peripherally with a directly political perspective. It is as if, in the light of his words about Wilde's play, its deployment in *Travesties* acts to defend him against charges that he was becoming "too serious": for, how can this be if Wilde's play "says nothing about anything?"

Although a series of arguments occur in *Travesties*, they either resist the move towards resolution or – more usually – do little more than reinforce the "absurdist" line about the impossibility of change. Stoppard develops the framework for the debate through a gigantic historical fiction, the fictionality of which is continually stressed throughout the play, particularly at the end, and through the misremembrances of the play's "narrator," Henry Carr. The fiction rests on bringing three men together in Zurich in 1917 – James Joyce, the dadaist Tristan Tzara, and a Lenin about to embark on a train to Russia on hearing the news of the outbreak of the revolution. That their simultaneous presence is Stoppard's own creation is in itself a caution against an over-literal reading of the narrative; but it is done in order to allow a debate about the relationship of art and politics to take place. What is problematic is that the three characters move constantly from caricature to quasi-naturalism whilst engaging in a debate that is frequently hijacked by the need for an intertextual reprise of elements of the plot of *The Importance of Being Earnest*, being rehearsed and then performed whilst the action of *Travesties* is taking place. However, *Travesties* is a pivotal play for any consideration of Stoppard's entry into the arena of political drama. Originally Stoppard conceived of the play as being concerned with a debate between Tzara and Lenin; only later did Joyce enter the frame.[19]

That Joyce brings with him the production of Wilde's play, with which historically he was concerned in a production in Zurich, undoubtedly makes the play more entertaining, and it adds a third strand of debate, which further (and deliberately) complicates the argument. In 1974, the second act opened with a long lecture by Cecily, Lenin's ex-officio secretary. In it, she offers a history of events leading up to the Russian Revolution and an account of the ideological split between the Bolshevik and the non-Bolshevik positions in relation to Marx's original formulation that the "conditions for a socialist revolution as he saw it did not exist in Russia at all."[20] The lecture is prefaced by one of the most extraordinary stage directions ever to have been offered by a playwright: "The performance of the whole of this lecture is not a requirement, but is an option" (p. 66). Whether or not Stoppard's direction stems from a political doubt about allowing such a direct piece of revolutionary discourse into his play – and we know that he was, anyway, worried about the figure of Lenin being too dominant in the second act[21] – or whether it was "aesthetic" doubt, a concern that the lecture is too long to hold audience interest, the result is a political decision in any case.

Travesties was frequently reprinted through the 1970s and 1980s, with both the lecture and the stage direction in place; but then, in 1993, the play was revived by the Royal Shakespeare Company, and the text was reissued, incorporating revisions made for the new production. Most of the changes are fairly minor, but the stage direction has disappeared completely, as has all of the lecture that it prefaced. However, Stoppard retains the important account of the argument given by Carr's butler, Bennett, in the first act:

> According to Marx, there is no way for a country to leap from autocracy to socialism: while the *ultimate* triumph of socialism is inevitable, being the necessary end of the process of dialectical materialism, it must be preceded by a bourgeois–capitalist stage of development . . . However, there is a more extreme position put forward by the Bolshevik party . . . that some unspecified but unique property of the Russian situation, unforeseen by Marx, has caused the bourgeois–capitalist era of Russian history to be compressed into the last few days, and that the time for the proletarian revolution is now ripe.
>
> (pp. 30–31 in 1975 edn; pp. 14–15 in 1993 edn)

What had happened in the gap between the editions of *Travesties* of 1975 through the mid-1980s and 1993 was that from 1988 the process of unravelment of the Russian Empire had started (symbolized by the pulling down of the Berlin Wall in November 1989), and was pretty well complete by the time of the revival. The specifically Marxist debate that had been submerged in the original production can, with the advantage of historical hindsight, now be foregrounded by Stoppard as a piece of political prediction; and the significance of Lenin's presence in the play thus suitably toned down. When Stoppard first tentatively introduced a directly political dimension into his work – however much he sought to conceal or subvert it – he did so with an eye not to Britain where he was living and working but to Eastern Europe, where his own roots lay, and to its political struggles that would increasingly concern and involve him. In this sense, the debate about the feasibility of a genuine proletarian revolution in Russia in 1917 becomes for Stoppard a diminished theoretical issue to be discussed as part of a wider intellectual game about "art and politics" – and one that needs to be addressed less ambiguously.

In 1977, he stated his position strongly again: "the most widespread misapprehension about playwrights . . . is that they set out to say something and then say it, in short that a play is the end product of an idea."[22] Although aesthetically this sense of his plays – as an act of creative imagination in which no specific end is in sight at the outset – continues to hold good, something was about to change. For this was the year of Charter 77, a document originally signed by 242 people, including the playwright Václav Havel, the year that signaled the public start of the civil rights movement in Czechoslovakia. The Charter 77 manifesto was published in *The Times* on 7 January, and by this time the activities of its creators in arguing for basic civil rights in Czechoslovakia were known about across the globe. The creators of the charter were insistent that theirs was not a party struggle of any kind: "Charter 77 is not an organization; it has no rules, permanent bodies or formal membership. It embraces everyone who agrees with its ideas and participates in its work. It does not form the basis for any oppositional political activity. Like many similar citizen initiatives in various countries, West and East, it seeks to promote the general public interest."[23] The disclaimer of any "party" intent would have appealed to Stoppard on top of its call for liberty.

Given that Stoppard had been born in Czechoslovakia, it was inevitable that he should have a particular interest in the Charter 77 movement, but it is important to realize that his political engagement with Communism did not start here and is, indeed, importantly prefigured in *Travesties*. However, it is from this point that the playwright first begins to make publicly political pronouncements. For Stoppard, State Communism is the ultimate embodiment of a system that uses its rules to inhibit individual behavior rather than to allow the expression of free will. His involvement with the Charter 77 movement is, then, one with a profoundly philosophical base, and not just an empathetic response to the plight of his one-time countrymen; although it is, of course, this also.

Beginning in 1974, Stoppard was slowly but gradually being drawn into taking a direct political stand. André Previn, then conductor with the London Symphony Orchestra, suggested that Stoppard write a play that incorporated a real orchestra. The play itself stubbornly refused to be formed. It lacked a central coherent reason for its dramatic dilemma, and its long gestation is indicative of a shift in Stoppard's relation to the political. In April 1976, Stoppard met Victor Fainburg, a Czech dissident who had been arrested, imprisoned in a hospital-prison for five years having been adjudged insane, and then exiled. His actual crime had been to protest against the Russian invasion of his country following the "Prague Spring" of 1968. In August of 1976 Stoppard addressed a London rally organized by the Committee Against Psychiatric Abuse, and tried unsuccessfully to deliver a petition to the Russian Embassy. His play at last began to take shape, *Every Good Boy Deserves Favour* duly being produced at the Festival Hall in July 1977, with Previn conducting the London Symphony Orchestra. Six months earlier the Czech playwright Vaclav Havel had been arrested for his participation in the Charter 77 movement. Stoppard wrote in direct response to this imprisonment the following month:

Connoisseurs of totalitarian double-think will have noted Charter 77, the Czechoslovakian document which calls attention to the absence in that country of various human rights beginning with the right of free expression, has been refused publication inside Czechoslovakia on the grounds that it is a wicked slander.[24]

The play that was eventually performed at the Festival Hall centered on the related fates of two prisoners in Czechoslovakia. Ivanov is mad, and believes that he has a full orchestra to accompany his triangle. His cell-mate, Alexander, is a dissident, imprisoned and declared insane after his involvement with the kind of political activities outlined above. Throughout the play, Ivanov labors to persuade his fellow cell-mate of the reality of his orchestra, a madness that extends to his insistence that Alexander must also be a musician. The irony of Ivanov's delusion is stressed by the orchestral accompaniment to Alexander's long account of the activities that have led to him being incarcerated. It echoes the punishment that the teacher tells his son, Sacha, is even now being imposed on his father – that he write out one million times, "I am a member of an orchestra and we must play together." The echo of mass state-directed culture as against the efforts of the lone artist is one that haunts Stoppard, and not just in his Eastern European plays. The state imposes a harmony that denies the efforts of such as Alexander to question, and the lunatic's view of reality in this world is seen as more desirable than that of the honest dissident.

As he was slowly shaping the play, Stoppard was becoming increasingly drawn into a direct consideration of the treatment of dissidents – and particularly dissident writers – in the Eastern Bloc. He had agreed to write a television play about Russia for Amnesty International's Prisoner of Conscience Year, and had traveled to Moscow in February 1977. There he met a number of dissidents, and returned to write about his visit in the *Sunday Times* on 27 February. In May, Havel was released from prison, and the month before *Every Good Boy* received its first performance, Stoppard returned to his native Czechoslovakia for the first time since leaving it with his family at the age of two. There he met Havel at last. In a sense, the two strands of the absurdist theatre, the domestic English and the politicized Eastern European, were united at the very point at which the move towards the disintegration of the Russian Empire began to gather real momentum.[25] Stoppard would provide an Introduction for the republished English version of *The Memorandum*, and in 1986 his version of Havel's *Largo Desolato* (dedicated by Havel to Stoppard) would be performed by the Bristol Old Vic.

Although *Every Good Boy* shares with Stoppard's earlier work a strong reliance on humor, its subject meant that the tone was inevitably bleaker

4 Photograph of Tom Stoppard and Václav Havel taken during Stoppard's Eastern European travels, *c.* 1977.

because of its connections with a directly contemporary abuse. The deployment of absurdist tactics in this context is one that would have seemed distinctly familiar to Václav Havel, one of the drafters of Charter 77. For, as Czechoslovakia had moved towards the troubles and the tanks of 1968, an absurdist tradition began to develop, and one that had a directly political intent, albeit one usually and necessarily disguised. John Grossman directed Václav Havel's first staged play, *The Garden Party*, at the Balustrade Theatre in 1963 – the same year that Tom Stoppard, for whom Havel was later to assume such importance, had his first play produced.[26] *The Garden Party* was a perfect example of "absurdism" with a specifically political slant. In 1965 Havel's *The Memorandum* was first performed, and the following year *The Times* was able to report on a "wind of change in the Czech theatre,"[27] leaving its readers in no doubt about the link between the use of the absurdist tradition to satirize and attack the bureaucratic machinery of state government and the larger urge for reform. So ingrained was the practice that both absurdist pieces and others received a subversive reading. A year after the 1968 uprising, Irving Wardle talked of the way in which the new Czech drama had been able to offer an oblique criticism of oppression: "Politics are inseparable from the rest of life – and from the sense of history:

and any piece that seems to refer to the Russians will probably relate equally to the Hapsburgs and the Nazis. It is a theatre of allegory, metaphor and double meaning."[28]

Already familiar with Havel's work, Stoppard sought consciously to bridge the gap between East and West with *Cahoot's Macbeth* (1979), a play that looks away from a western and towards an Eastern European sense of the "absurd." It is a play that uses the familiar structural device of a play-within-a-play, but not in the cosy context of the formulaic West End thriller. It plays with that subversion of the history play text discussed above, welding on to it an absurdist structure of real (that is to say, Eastern European) menace. The intertextuality thus extends beyond the themes of the play; its very use becomes a pointedly political statement both of solidarity (the connection of texts) and condemnation (the separation of contexts).

The Cahoot of the title refers to the Czech playwright Pavel Kohout, who shares Stoppard's place of birth, Gottwaldov (formerly Zlin). Kohout had been forced underground after the Russian tanks invaded in 1968, and Stoppard's play is, amongst other things, an enactment of the circumstances of illegal performances of his work, staged secretly in private apartments and played by actors such as Pavel Lanovsky, who was driving the car when the first known copies of the Charter 77 documents were seized by the police. A private performance of Shakespeare's *Macbeth* is taking place in a Czech flat. To make the connection with the Czech productions of Kohout even stronger, in his opening directions Stoppard suggests how the parts might be doubled up, adding: "In the Czech productions, Kohout distributed the roles as follows."[29] He shortened this version to make the connections between the text being played out in the room and the political drama being played out in the state outside the more pertinent. For instance, the performance, and Stoppard's play, opens as Shakespeare's does, with the three witches. But their incantations take on a far more direct significance when placed in the Czech context:

1ST WITCH. When shall we three meet again?
            In thunder, lightning, or in rain?
2ND WITCH. When the hurly-burly's done,
            When the battle's lost and won. (p. 47)

The "battle" becomes easily relocated both in terms of the nature of the struggle and, therefore, of its geographical placement. When Macbeth returns to say that he has murdered Duncan, Stoppard accompanies his "I heard the owl scream and the crickets cry" with the offstage sound of a police siren approaching the house. The connections continue to be made:

MACBETH. Wake Duncan with thy knocking! (Sharp rapping.)
    I would thou couldst!
(*They leave . . . and the* INSPECTOR *enters an empty room . . .*)
INSPECTOR. Oh – I'm sorry – is this the National Theatre? (pp. 52–53)

The secret policeman's awareness of the political significance of Brecht's work – "putting yourself at the mercy of any Tom, Dick or Bertolt who can't universalize our predicament without playing ducks and drakes with your furniture arrangements," and his assurance, "You've got your rights" (even as he is violating them, and thus denying their existence), to a hostess reduced to monosyllabic responses to his very "actorly" performance introduces a sinister quality to the comedy unusual in English absurdism.

Stoppard's secret policeman, aware of the subversive potential of the event, arranges for the proscenium arch to be bricked over: "What we don't like is a lot of people being cheeky and saying they are only Julius Caesar or Coriolanus or Macbeth. Otherwise we are going to start treating them the same as the ones who say they are Napoleon" (pp. 60–61).

Stoppard continued to focus his attention on Eastern Europe, and did so in ways that called directly into question his own earlier stance as a nonpolitical writer – a stance which was, as I will argue, always problematic. In so doing, the dramatic tension in his subsequent plays becomes centered on the role of the playwright as mouthpiece for the ideas that the plays embrace, or at the least seek to discuss. It is a vital change of direction in the work of a man who had always sought to swerve away from supplying a reliable perspective, and for whom the flow of wit, the clashing of ideas and styles had been all.

The television play that he eventually produced for Amnesty International was *Professional Foul*. The plot of the play was suggested to Stoppard by his visit to Russia in 1977 (although, significantly, he places the action in the country of his birth, rather than in Russia). Stoppard had traveled to collect signatures for a petition protesting against the mistreatment of prisoners. The authorities dealt with his actions quite simply, by having Soviet customs officers steal the documents.[30]

Stoppard's play (which he dedicated to Havel) is concerned with the visit of three English academics to Czechoslovakia for an academic conference. Given Stoppard's insistence on seeing a philosophical base to political argument, it is significant that the three are philosophers. We are first shown them on the plane to Prague: Chetwyn has become known for writing letters to *The Times* protesting the treatment of "persecuted professors with unpronounceable names," according to the second, McKendrick, a moral pragmatist from Stoke University, who is attracted to the idea that the third, Anderson, might become directly involved in dissident politics on his arrival.

It is on Anderson, and what happens to him, that the play centers. Invited to read a paper on "Ethical Fictions as Ethical Foundations," his planned truancy is not, as McKendrick thinks, political, but is intended to coincide with a World Cup football match qualifier between Czechoslovakia and England; he will use fiction to watch a game. Hollar, an ex-student who had returned optimistically to his homeland in 1968 and is now employed as a lavatory cleaner, asks Anderson to take a copy of his thesis back for publication in England. The terms of Anderson's refusal to comply are perfectly in keeping with the safe world of Oxbridge ethics from which he has been briefly transported: "Perhaps the correct thing for me to have done is not to have accepted their invitation to speak here. But I did accept it. It is a contract, as it were, freely entered into. And having accepted their hospitality I cannot in all conscience start smuggling . . . It's just not ethical" (*Professional, Foul*, p. 9).

However, the security of the theoretical position is about to be removed. Stopping at Hollar's flat on his way to the match to hand back the manuscript, he becomes involved in the police search of the rooms after the man's arrest. Released, he returns to the conference and gives an impromptu paper on the rights of the individual and the rights of the state. The football match that he missed has been won by Czechoslovakia as a result of a successful penalty after a "professional foul." But Anderson eventually commits the most professional of all fouls. Knowing that he will be searched at the airport, he secretly plants the thesis in McKendrick's suitcase, and moral expediency literally carries the day.

The English football team had lost as a result of foul play, foul play that the drunken McKendrick argues allies them with the ungentlemanly yobs on the terraces, but the English gentleman will achieve a small victory by his "professional foul." As always, the game is fixed, as the consummate stylist, admittedly more alert to the realities of the outside world, weaves his way past an unthinking, uneducated defense. The ball is a thesis on the importance of the individual, and the goal will be credited to the English liberal tradition.

Confronted with a world in which the domestic absurdism of his early plays unexpectedly gives way to the more frightening absurdism of the bureaucracy of totalitarianism, his characters have no retreat, no comforting word games or philosophical conundrums left. Many critics had found a way of reading *Travesties* by attempting to identify a dominant voice.[31] But even if such an exercise could be successful, there would be no certainty that this dominant voice in the discourse could be identified with Stoppard. Throughout his career, right up until his most recent stage play, *The Invention of Love* (1999), he has made frequent use of other past writer figures who, again, present arguments that may or may not coincide with those of Stoppard. No single viewpoint can be taken as the author's.

However, in *Squaring the Circle: Poland 1989–91*, a 1984 television film, he attempted (unsuccessfully) to present the narrative, using a narrator clearly identified as the author who would stress the dangers of taking on trust any material presented in the form of a drama-documentary; and thus carrying forward his long-time unease with polemical and pseudo-documentary play-writing, as was to be seen most memorably in the attack on Private Brodie's attempt at agitprop theatre in *The Real Thing* (1982).

Thus, although the play follows events from the formation of the union through its official disbanding in December 1981, Stoppard is less interested in the chronicling of history as such, than with questioning the way in which that chronicling is presented. He foregrounds the narrator's role, the reliability of his accounts deliberately problematized. So the play opens, for instance, with two different enactments of Brezhnev's meeting with Gierek in July 1980, enactments interrupted by the narrator's insistence that the audience is simply watching a fiction – "That isn't them, of course – and this isn't the Black Sea. Everything is true except the words and the pictures." – and concludes with his aside to the camera, "Who knows?"[32]

The wish to ally himself with a narrator uncertain of the exact components of the story he is telling indicates Stoppard's own uncertainty about his newly adopted role as political spokesman; but it also accurately reflects his sense of being a part of two cultures simultaneously. This was a theme he was to explore most memorably in his 1991 radio play, *In the Native State*,[33] where – in what is one of his most impressive works to date, and one that moves him further than ever before from his absurdist roots – the action moves between India (where Stoppard had also lived briefly as a boy) in 1930 and the English home counties in the present, forging links that are both psychological and political.

Stoppard made the connections for the last time to date in *Hapgood* (1988), written well into the era of seismic change in Eastern Europe. The central character is Elizabeth Hapgood, an English secret agent compromised by her relationship with Kerner, a Russian double-agent. Hapgood ends the play watching encouragingly as her son plays rugby at his public school. We have already seen her similarly engaged in scene 3, but now she is accompanied by her Russian lover, Kerner, who as the play ends seems incapable of moving away from this quintessentially English scene – a scene in which the Anglo-Russian child is being initiated into the rituals of the English establishment. She had already spelt out its significance after the first rugby game: "Anyway, there's the male society thing . . . I like all that manners maketh man stuff, and competition and talking properly and being magnanimous in victory and defeat – middle-class values, I'm in favour and I'm not going to chuck them because they happen to be shared by a fair number of people you wouldn't want to be seen dead with, they always were."[34] The invocation of rugby football, a fight by two sides with clearly defined rules, has echoes of Stoppard's use of cricket in *The Real Thing* (1982), where Henry argues for the importance of craft over ideology: "What we're trying to do is to write a cricket bat, so that when we throw up an idea and give it a little knock, it might . . . *travel*."[35] Her son, like Stoppard himself, has had his side chosen for him – a move away from Russia for Hapgood's son, and from Czechoslovakia for the playwright, and towards an enthusiastic embracement of middle-class English values.

Stoppard's interventions into Eastern European politics were unproblematic for him in political terms. The opposition was easy to define. But it is important to emphasize that the struggle was seen by him as precisely an example of the freedom of the individual/constraint of the state model that I started with. In his two most recent original plays, *Arcadia* (1993) and *The Invention of Love* (1997), he has returned to England and, having confronted politics directly in his European plays, sought to resolve the political dualisms of his earlier work. The former is set in a Derbyshire stately home in the early nineteenth century and the present day, as the various characters seek to reconcile their notions of the pursuit of "truth" with the changes in a surrounding but never seen landscaped garden that mirrors the changes in British society; and the latter in an Oxford University college in which the action moves backwards from and forwards to 1936.

For the first time in his theatrical career, Stoppard had found with *Arcadia* a containing structure that would allow him to properly examine the problematics of the "conservatism" that had preoccupied him for so long. For what is immediately apparent is that this "Arcadia" has little in common with the "little England" invoked by the now ousted Margaret Thatcher through the long years of her "reign." It invokes a world of class privilege, certainly, but it does so in a context that stresses the unbreakable connection between past and present. As the action moves from the early nineteenth to the late twentieth century, the audience is allowed to see not only the way in which history is shaped, but the disparity between attempts at theoretical models of that shaping and the interventions of individuals who render any construction of a line of predication absurd. As one of the contemporary characters says: "It's all because of sex . . . That's what I think. The Universe is deterministic all right, just like Newton said, I mean it's trying to be, but the only thing going wrong is people fancying people who aren't supposed to be in that part of the plan."[36]

Stoppard's use of "chaos theory" allows him to argue for the supremacy of the individual in a way that would have gladdened the hearts of Rosencrantz and Guildenstern, had their studies led them in that historically unlikely direction. Stoppard starts from Newton's classical views of motion which, as one reviewer (Roger Highfield, a scientist himself) put it, "are insensitive to time and seem to leave no room for unpredictability or free will." This essentially mechanistically and fatalistically constructed universe "has been shattered by a contemporary field called non-linear mathematics . . . It is a rich area of study that rescues free will and chance, giving full rein to the uncertainties of love and sexual attraction that unfold in the play."[37]

Where Stoppard had "played" with philosophy in earlier plays, here its deployment is central to his establishment of what is, in effect, a political credo: that the individual is more, or at least capable of being more, than just a construction of the political state; that all ideologies will crumble in the face of individual will; but that the result is not an ungovernable chaos, rather a set of unpredictable patterns. That the play also makes creative use of Newton's Second Law to suggest the inevitability of a move from what Highfield calls "the Big Bang of creation towards heat death, when all that is left is a thin cool gruel at constant temperature" means that, in the long term, the news is pessimistic. What this play does so excitingly, however, is to present a case for the kind of conservatism with a little *c* that Stoppard had declared for in 1979.

That passion ("It's all because of sex") might provide an opposition to the attempts to create rigidly deterministic structure is something that Stoppard had been conjuring with ever since *The Real Thing*, the very title of which refers to love. Significantly, in that play it is eventually revealed that the supposedly political protest staged by Private Brodie was actually embarked upon with the intention of impressing Annie, who is to take up his cause. In Stoppard's most recent play, interestingly entitled *The Invention of Love*, he uses the context of the Oxford College to compare the lives, aspirations, and achievements of two writers, A. E. Housman, who is the central protagonist of the piece, and Oscar Wilde, who is frequently mentioned but only belatedly puts in an appearance. Housman insists continually that his activities as a scholar are those of a "scientist" (by which he means someone who applies an inflexible logic to the recovery of reliable versions of classic texts). This rigidity is mirrored in his private life, where he refuses to admit to his lifelong love for his once fellow male student, Moses Jackson. All his emotional life goes into his one collection of poetry, *A Shropshire Lad*, for which ironically he is now far more remembered than for his scholarship.

Wilde's intrusion into the narrative calls into question the very logic on which Housman has constructed his existence, one of repression and self-denial. As the play ends – both men now safely dead – Charon rows Wilde across the Styx, and his final words stand as a reproach to the other poet's entire life: "Wickedness is a myth invented by good people to account for the curious attractiveness of others. One should always be a little improbable. Nothing that actually occurs is of the smallest importance."[38]

What this play does is once more to put the spotlight firmly on the lives of individuals and, furthermore, once again on individual writers. It is not difficult to see that from the first introduction of Oscar Wilde and his contemporaries in *Travesties* to Wilde's final bow in *The Invention of Love*, Stoppard has in a sense been trying out the potential of narrator figures; but always in a series of dialogues that offer opposition and uncertainty. For one of the chief questions posed by this most recent play is put quite neatly on the back of the published version of the text, which talks of the play as giving a "sympathetic account of Housman and Oscar Wilde" and asking "with hindsight – whose passion was really the fatal one?"

The political significance of these most recent devlopments in Stoppard's work is that he has found not only a way of arguing for the supremacy of the individual – not in itself a very startling political credo perhaps – but something of an answer to the questions posed in his pre-European work. For Stoppard has moved towards a new definition of freedom, a definition which is faithful to his 1979 declaration, "I'm a conservative with a small *c*. I'm a conservative in politics, literature, education and theatre." This conservatism is rooted in a sense of tradition that predates modern *laissez-faire* capitalism – hence the replaying of older history – and that places the emphasis on the exceptional individual; in Stoppard's world not all men can be free, nor all men equal. Whilst sharing something of the ideology of Margaret Thatcher's vision of how things would be, it is completely opposed to the efforts of such as the ex-prime minister to impose order on the chaos that is life to Stoppard or to deny the creativity of the individual in the supposed cause of the greater good.

What all this means can, perhaps, be best summed up by referring back to *Professional Foul*. Stoppard tells us, in his Introduction, that the Introduction was being written whilst Havel was being tried for "attempting to damage the name of the State abroad." He writes that "in mentioning his name only, I am putting undue emphasis on his part in the Czechoslovakian human rights movement," and concludes, "But I have in mind not just the Chartist but the author . . . It is to a fellow writer that I dedicate *Professional Foul* in admiration."[39] That Havel, the playwright of opposition, should become leader of his state is, of course, not without a certain irony. It is an irony that would not be lost on Stoppard.

NOTES

1 *Squaring the Circle; Every Good Boy Deserves Favour; Professional Foul* (London and Boston: Faber and Faber, 1984), p. 29.
2 Interestingly, there is a 1928 Soviet play by Valentine Katayev, translated into

English as *Squaring the Circle*, which is concerned with just such efforts in the period of the New Economic Policy, in Eugene Lyons, ed., *Six Soviet Plays* (New York: Greenwood Press, 1968).

3 *Enter a Free Man*, first staged as *A Walk on the Water*, Hamburg, 1964; as *Enter a Free Man*, St. Martin's Theatre, London, 1968.

4 Interview in *Theatre Quarterly*, 14 (May–July 1974), p. 12.

5 Milton Shulman, "The Politicizing of Tom Stoppard," *New York Times*, 23 April 1978.

6 Consider, for instance, Philip Roberts, "Tom Stoppard; serious artist or siren," *Theatre Quarterly*, 20 (1978), pp. 84–92.

7 In an earlier emanation the journalist Johnson had edited the left-wing *New Statesman*, but was by this time firmly established well to the right of the Conservative Party.

8 Richard Foulkes, "Tom Stoppard," in John Bull, ed., *British and Irish Dramatists Since World War II*. (Colombia (S.C.: Bruccoli Clark Layman, 2000), p. 285.

9 Paul Delaney, ed., *Stoppard in Conversation*. (Ann Arbor: University of Michigan Press, 1994), p. 133.

10 See Kenneth Tynan, "Withdrawing with Style from the Chaos," *Gambit*, 10.37, (1980), p. 27; reprinted from *New Yorker Magazine*, 1977.

11 Jan Kott, *Shakespeare our Contemporary* (London: Methuen, 1964).

12 John Bull, *Stage Right: crisis and recovery in British contemporary mainstream theatre* (Basingstoke: Macmillan, 1994).

13 "The Modern Theatre is the Epic Theatre," in John Willett, ed., *Brecht on Theatre* (London: Eyre Methuen, 1978), p. 37.

14 See Bull, *Stage Right*, chapters 3 and 4.

15 See John Bull, *New British Political Dramatists* (Basingstoke: Macmillan, 1984).

16 "Something to Declare," *Sunday Times*, 25 February 1968.

17 It was performed by the Kayona Jozsef Szinhaz Theatre Company in their Studio Theatre, Kamra in 1994, and revived there in 1996/97, where a performance was seen by my colleague Brian Woolland, to whom I am grateful for allowing this intriguing connection to be made.

18 "'Serious Frivolity': Steve Grant interviews Tom Stoppard," *Time Out*, 18–24 June 1976, p. 7.

19 See C. Werner, "Stoppard's Critical Travesty, or Who Vindicates Whom, and Why . . .," *Arizona Quarterly*, 35 (1978), pp. 228–236.

20 *Travesties* (London and Boston: Faber and Faber, 1975), pp. 66–71.

21 See Stoppard as quoted in Richard Corballis, *Stoppard: the Mystery and the clockwork* (New York: Methuen, 1984), p. 77.

22 "But for the Middle Classes," *Times Literary Supplement*, 3 June 1977.

23 *The Times*, 7 January 1977.

24 *New York Times*, 11 February 1977.

25 See Bull, *Stage Right*, pp. 63–66.

26 *A Walk on the Water*, which was screened by Rediffusion, later being reworked for the stage as *Enter a Free Man* (1968).

27 *The Times*, 20 January 1966.

28 *Guardian*, 29 November 1969.

29 *Dogg's Hamlet, Cahoot's Macbeth* (London and Boston: Faber and Faber, 1980), p. 45.

30 See Stoppard's account in "The Face at the Window," *Sunday Times*, 27 February 1977.

31 See Werner, "Critical Travesty," also Neil Sammells, *Tom Stoppard: the artist as critic* (Basingstoke: Macmillan, 1988), pp. 73–74; and David Rodd, "Carr's Views on Art and Politics in Tom Stoppard's *Travesties*," *Modern Drama*, 29 (1983), pp. 536–542.

32 Tom Stoppard, *Squaring the Circle; Every Good Boy Deserves Favour; Professional Foul* (London and Boston: Faber and Faber, 1984), pp. 27–28.

33 *In the Native State* (London and Boston: Faber and Faber, 1991). Stoppard adapted the play for the stage, as *Indian Ink*. (London and Boston: Faber and Faber, 1995).

34 *Hapgood*, revised edn (London and Boston: Faber and Faber, 1988).

35 *The Real Thing*, revised edn (London: Faber and Faber, 1983), p. 52.

36 *Arcadia* (London and Boston: Faber and Faber, 1993), p. 73.

37 Roger Highfield, *Daily Telegraph*, 15 April 1993.

38 *Invention of Love* (London and Boston: Faber and Faber, 1997), p. 102.

39 *Every Good Boy Deserves Favour*; and *Professional Foul* (London and Boston: Faber and Faber, 1978, p. 9.

9

JILL L. LEVENSON

Stoppard's Shakespeare: textual re-visions

> [We] always get back to Shakespeare, but I think
> with good reason, because he's sort of there like
> a decanter, with that silver label around its neck
> saying "World Champ."
>
> Stoppard, "The Event and the Text"[1]

The record of Stoppard's engagement with Shakespeare shares the feature Stoppard values most in his own plays, "a series of conflicting statements made by conflicting characters."[2] In his nondramatic writing, interviews, and lectures, Stoppard himself may enact the conflicting characters who make conflicting statements. The simile of Shakespeare as decanter is reductive, an equivalent of the ashtrays and other inanimate objects to which Stoppard repeatedly compares inert play texts. But Shakespeare is also "World Champ," an athlete who has defeated all competitors and attracted spectators like Stoppard, the cricket fan. In Stoppard's plays, this ambivalence takes the usual form of conflicting statements by conflicting characters. During an argument in *The Real Thing*, for example, a similar analogy states the same type of contradiction. The playwright Henry will identify and defend his craft in terms of sport, an elaborate description of a cricket bat. His wife Annie, an actress, anticipates him with an image of Shakespeare outrunning everyone else in a foot race for an immaterial prize, "Eng. Lit."[3] In lecture and play, Shakespeare is both a winner and something less.

The icon, ambiguous and inescapable, appears everywhere in expressions of Stoppard's thought: "Shakespeare theatre-going, Shakespeare-watching and so on, is . . . a rich enough field to explicate any point that I might make and more beyond. I hardly know where to stop."[4] True to his word, Stoppard draws on Shakespeare – not only the plays but the sonnets – to illustrate points ranging from the very concrete to the very abstract. In particular, he refers repeatedly to *The Comedy of Errors*, *King Lear*, and *The Tempest* when distinguishing between text and event, script and performance. On the one hand, imaginative productions of Shakespeare show how theatrical events depart from the playwright's text in memorable ways. On the other, "[a] great production of a *Black Comedy* is better than a mediocre production of a *Comedy of Errors*."[5] Yet Shakespeare without a theatrical dimension can still be extraordinary. In two exchanges with the journalist Mel Gussow, the sonnets help Stoppard to clarify his skepticism about evolution and the existence of God.[6]

It is no surprise that Shakespeare appears everywhere in Stoppard's plays. Undoubtedly some of the references are almost gratuitous, like the scattered phrases from *A Midsummer Night's Dream* and *Hamlet* in *Arcadia* and *The Invention of Love*.[7] But Stoppard has always made glancing allusions to Shakespearean lines, adding resonance to the speeches around them.

> Day and night, night and day,
> Shall I compare me to a summer's day,
> 'Cos I can't get me out of my mind
> *Albert's Bridge*[8]

Other references to Shakespeare the icon enhance comic moments in plays from *The Real Inspector Hound* to *The Invention of Love*, as when Jerome K. Jerome locates the wellspring of "English life and letters": "Wholesome humour and a rattling good yarn. Look at Shakespeare" (p. 85). But the occasional allusion deepens, or darkens, Stoppard's text. In *Jumpers*, for example, Dotty voices her panic in lines from *Macbeth* after the death of another Duncan, and Archie rings variations on the words of Richard III at the close of Stoppard's play.[9] *The Real Thing* makes powerful use of the handkerchief from *Othello*, an authentic sign of betrayal in its modern context (pp. 36–37).

The most extensive use of such quotations occurs in *Travesties*, whose well-known first-act episode has been interpreted by Katherine E. Kelly as "a Dada demonstration": "the entire scene reenacts in the terms of a Wildean romance the Dada intention of destroying traditional art and replacing it with poetry 'written in the hand of chance.'"[10] In the reenactment, Tristan Tzara literally deconstructs Shakespeare's eighteenth sonnet, "Shall I compare thee to a summer's day?," by writing it down, cutting it up, and placing single words in a hat. He sets the hat before Gwendolen Carr: "I offer you a Shakespeare sonnet, but it is no longer his" (p. 53).

With the exchange that follows, the episode condenses the Shakespeare canon into eight plays (representing the major genres) and two sonnets transmitted through little more than a dozen speeches delivered over a hat. What happens to Sonnet 18 may, as Nicole Boireau suggests, reflect the chaos of World War One; but the cleverness of its execution makes the case for the modern aesthetic even as it provides a medium for Gwendolen and Tzara to articulate their mutual attraction.[11] Stoppard has created a Shakespeare who is both transcendent and transient, a fixture and an appropriation.

As this brief survey indicates, Stoppard's Shakespeare fits into a larger picture distinguished by the eclecticism which has long been recognized as a prominent feature of Stoppard's art. In Stoppard's network of allusions, Shakespeare takes his place not only among great artists of the past but also among Stoppard's contemporaries: Wilde, Beckett, and Pinter; Joyce, Eco, and Byatt; Wordsworth, Tennyson, T. S. Eliot, and lyrics from popular music. The network extends to nonliterary genres, including painters like Magritte and Duchamp, philosophers like G. E. Moore and Wittgenstein. Drawn from Stoppard's vast reading and his interest in cultural trends, it incorporates figures from the worlds of exploration, science and mathematics, and politics.

Reconfigurations of Shakespeare in text and event are nothing new: they began to appear during the Restoration.[12] According to Ruby Cohn, twentieth-century directors had modernized Shakespeare on stage by the 1960s, and postwar playwrights negotiated Shakespeare's presence in a number of ways.[13] Both kinds of rewriting have continued in adaptations that cross the boundaries of genre (for example, into pastiche and film) but clearly announce their origins in Shakespeare. Both coincide with what Kelly calls "a surge in interartistic quotation, mimicry, and appropriation of various kinds in Western arts of the past several decades."[14]

As more than one recent theorist has noticed, such intertextuality can both subvert and celebrate the original.[15] Stoppard's does both in a "plurality of contexts," generating "a dramatic universe of perpetual transformations."[16] In this sense, Stoppard's Shakespeare belongs to the second half of the twentieth century, a product of its artistic styles and political views. What makes this Shakespeare different from the rest is the persistence with which the dramatist reproduces him, the originality of each new conception, and the continuity of influence over more than three decades.

The keys to Stoppard's uniqueness are the plays based on Shakespearean tragedies, *Rosencrantz and Guildenstern Are Dead* (*R&GAD*) and *Dogg's Hamlet, Cahoot's Macbeth*. Each ended a process of composition, a series of plays which reworked *Hamlet*; the first was produced in the 1960s, the second in the 1970s. When the earlier process began, it immediately incorporated a nonliterary text that would remain an identifiable part of Stoppard's work: the playwright's own life, specifically his experience as an artist. Stoppard would tell a group of professional Shakespeareans in 1982, "in my innocence I just wrote along, a bit of Shakespeare, off they went, a bit of me, a bit more of that, off with me, on with some Shakespeare."[17]

The collaboration with Shakespeare did not begin until young adulthood. At school Stoppard had been "totally bored and alienated by everyone from Shakespeare to Dickens besides."[18] His first experience of a live performance in the mid-1950s radically changed those impressions. When he was a newspaper reporter in Bristol he watched Peter O'Toole play Hamlet for the Bristol Old Vic; and that, he later said, "began the whole thing."[19] As theatre critic for *Scene* between September 1962 and April 1963, Stoppard covered Shakespeare productions. Kelly has examined this phase of his writing and concludes that "The Shakespeare reviews show him awed by the text even when critical of a particular director's production concept."[20]

According to the established narrative about the genesis of *R&GAD*, Stoppard seems to have become less reverential toward the end of 1963. In an attempt to cheer him after the rejection of a sixty-minute television script, Stoppard's agent, Kenneth Ewing, revealed a long-cherished notion about *Hamlet*: "in his opinion the King of England at the time of [Rosencrantz and Guildenstern's] arrival might well have been King Lear. And, if so, did they find him raving mad at Dover? Stoppard's spirits rose."[21] "The possibility appealed to me," Stoppard would explain in an interview, "and I began work on a burlesque Shakespeare farce."[22]

Stoppard wrote *Rosencrantz and Guildenstern Meet King Lear* (*R&GMKL*) in West Berlin, where he spent five months from spring 1964 on a Ford Foundation grant. Among four dramatists in the subsidized group of artists was James Saunders, author of *Next Time I'll Sing to You* (1963), a play Stoppard admired and later incorporated in *R&GAD*. By autumn 1964 Stoppard had produced what he judged a failure.[23] Nevertheless, he would include passages from the first half of this one-acter in *R&GAD*, borrowings which have led John Fleming to compare the unpublished typescript (at the Harry Ransom Humanities Research Center) with one version of the three-act play (New York: Samuel French, 1967).[24] It turns out that the first attempt is not "a burlesque Shakespeare farce"; King Lear has a small role near the end; and *R&GMKL* centers on the boat voyage to England which would become the third act of *R&GAD*.

Stoppard accurately summarized *R&GMKL* in a letter dated August 1964 to Anthony C. H. Smith, the arts editor and writer who became a close friend:

> The gist is that Ros, Guil, and Ham are joined on the boat by the Player from the play-in-Hamlet, . . . Hamlet and the Player change identities on boat; the Player is captured by Pirates and goes off to fulfill Hamlet's role in the rest of Shakespeare's play. Hamlet goes on to England, returning to Elsinore . . . just in time for the final tableau of carnage.[25]

Stoppard had drafted in this one-acter what would be his greatest departure from Shakespeare's *Hamlet* in *R&GAD*, filling in the gap between Hamlet's leaving for England and Horatio's receipt of his letter.[26] During the summer of 1964, a 25-minute excerpt from *R&GMKL* was performed in West Berlin. Afterward Charles Marowitz recollected that "It struck me, and most everyone else, as a lot of academic twaddle."[27] When Stoppard returned to England, an excerpt was staged by the Questors at Ealing, the company that produced Saunders's plays.[28]

R&GMKL outlined Stoppard's Shakespeare in its transformation of the *Hamlet* plot, its eclectic mix of Renaissance drama and contemporary thought, and the wittiness of the whole enterprise. Yet Stoppard would deny the obvious continuities, claiming that he scrapped the early effort and began a different play in October 1964.[29] He would admit later that he has great difficulty in working out plots, and using *Hamlet* relieved the pressure of composition.[30] By April 1965, Stoppard had written two acts of *R&GAD*. A commission from the Royal Shakespeare Company inspired him to complete a third act, but the play was not performed until the Oxford Theatre Group picked it up and presented it, revised, at the Edinburgh Festival Fringe in 1966.[31]

As soon as *R&GAD* appeared in performance, reviewers and academic commentators became preoccupied with the "twaddle" dismissed by Marowitz. They recognized the play's derivation not only from Shakespeare's *Hamlet* but also from Beckett's *Waiting for Godot*. They noticed other influences as well: theatrical and literary traces from Pirandello, T. S. Eliot, Wilde, Kafka, and Pinter; philosophical bearings from Wittgenstein's late *Investigations*. Until the early 1980s, most of these critics described the composition of Stoppard's play as if all the parts existed in equilibrium: plot and characters from Shakespeare set in a Beckettian ambiance, or vice versa; discrete borrowings of concept, phrasing, or tone from the other dramatic or literary sources; and Wittgenstein's philosophy used as a frame. But *R&GAD* is dynamic, like a field of force, all of its components constantly changing in relation to one another. More recent critics, drawing from Clive James's lexicon, draw analogies from physics to describe Stoppard's art, and Shakespeare takes his place among the shifting paradigms.

Stoppard began with *Hamlet* for a second time, and on this occasion he was asked why. When questioned by Giles Gordon, he responded that he had no other choice for his kind of drama: he considers this Shakespearean tragedy probably "the most famous play in any language, it is part of a sort of common mythology"; and Rosencrantz and Guildenstern "are more than just bit players in another play . . . I see them much more clearly as a couple of bewildered innocents rather than a couple of henchmen."[32] In writing

5 A scene from the Broadway production of the N. Y. Drama Critics' Prize Play, *Rosencrantz and Guildenstern Are Dead*. Left to right: Brian Murray (Rosencrantz), John Wood (Guildenstern), Noel Craig (Hamlet).

R&GAD, Stoppard seemed to view *Hamlet* not only as a means for solving practical problems of composition but also as a familiar text whose interpretation he could share with his audience.

When Stoppard acknowledges his debt to Beckett, he emphasizes what he calls "a Beckett joke," meaning a technique Beckett uses in his novels as well as his plays: "It appears in various forms but it consists of confident statement followed by immediate refutation by the same voice."[33] *R&GAD* therefore shares with *Waiting for Godot* not only "the image of two lost souls waiting for something to happen," but Stoppard's idea of Beckett's humorous, dialectical mode of expression. Although he makes this idea clear, Stoppard is vague or noncommittal about the other components of *R&GAD*.[34] Yet there is a third important presence. No one has pressed Stoppard about Wittgenstein's influence on *R&GAD*, but striking reflections of ideas and language from the *Philosophical Investigations* suggest that this text was the third major paradigm for Stoppard's.

In *R&GAD* Stoppard seems to have borrowed his strategies from at least three important works which vary in chronological or generic terms. As these works – content, form, and style – are superimposed upon one another in perpetually shifting combinations, likenesses appear for a moment between generally unlike texts and then disappear with the next configuration.[35] Perhaps *R&GAD* performs like the theatrical version of a metaphysical conceit: it draws connections which can be seen and heard between unlikely partners, and it does not dwell on any single combination or explain its significance. Stoppard himself would use an extreme version of this metaphor in characterizing all of his plays to 1993: "what I'm doing is forcing something that isn't quite natural. What Johnson says about metaphysical conceits, you know – yoking together by violence."[36]

Stoppard's Elsinore and his *Hamlet* are unfamiliar, unpredictable, and often comic arrangements of Shakespeare's text. In this second rewriting of *Hamlet*, Stoppard appropriated some 250 lines from the original, introducing them more than halfway through his first act.[37] But Shakespeare's play, dismantled and revised, had begun to appear in Stoppard's at the very beginning with two anonymous Elizabethans on an unlocalized stage; and it became more apparent with the entrance of traveling players (p. 15) and a pantomime version of Hamlet's melodramatic gestures in Ophelia's closet (pp. 24–25), an episode not enacted but described in Shakespeare's tragedy at the end of Act 2, scene 1. In effect, *R&GAD* starts by remodeling *Hamlet* 2.2, the longest scene in that long play, an episode which goes through many modulations in tone and which introduces Rosencrantz, Guildenstern, and the players.

From this point on, Stoppard's play edits *Hamlet* chronologically, reproducing Shakespeare's narrative in unexpected and frequently humorous ways. Early in the second act, for example, Rosencrantz and Guildenstern analyze their first meeting with Hamlet instead of performing it (p. 40). Shortly after, they discuss Hamlet's melancholy/madness with the Player, turning a central issue of theatre and literary criticism to patter (pp. 48–49); and they treat Polonius's misconception of Hamlet's love for Ophelia, a motivating factor from 2.1 to 3.1, as a play on words (p. 49). Rosencrantz anticipates Hamlet's most famous soliloquy, "To be or not to be," with his fantasy of death as sleep in a box: "Eternity is a terrible thought. I mean, where's it going to end?" (p. 51); almost immediately Shakespeare's 3.1 begins (p. 52) and Hamlet performs the soliloquy in pantomime (p. 53).

As he rearranges and defamiliarizes Shakespeare's sequence, Stoppard also directs attention to correspondences between *Hamlet* and his other sources. Besides direct quotation – Rosencrantz and Guildenstern speak phrases from *Waiting for Godot*[38] – well-known theatrical or literary conventions link the plays: time dislocated from strictly ordered chronology; a minimally localized scene; address to the audience; play within a play; and shifting from a less poetic to a more poetic idiom in order to indicate some other kind of change. Further, Stoppard's manipulation of language produces many points where the texts meet. Resonances of *Hamlet* and *Waiting for Godot* sound clearly in the multitudes of puns, both serious and frivolous, which are integral to the meaning of *R&GAD*. The three plays meet as well in other kinds of wordplay which are also intrinsic to thematic content, such as the exposure of clichés.

Paradigms connect with one another not only through language but through philosophy, especially logic. In the three plays, philosophical tools like syllogism frequently break down. The modern texts share with *Hamlet* and Wittgenstein's work preoccupations with specific obstacles to the proper functioning of reason: lapses of memory and the variables of perception. When the philosopher Jonathan Bennett interprets the role of memory in *R&GAD*, he also throws light on *Hamlet* and *Waiting for Godot*: "The point is made that memory is needed for access to the past . . . Their inability to initiate action stems partly from the lack of memory."[39] Even more than memory, "The concept of 'seeing' makes a tangled impression," as Wittgenstein contends.[40] Stoppard makes this point tellingly when he enacts a problem set by Wittgenstein – "'Is this foot *my* foot?' . . . 'Is this sensation *my* sensation?'" (p. 123[c]) – in a dialogue between Rosencrantz and Guildenstern at the beginning of the third act (p. 70).

In part, Stoppard conflates theatre history and modern philosophy according to dialectical principles. It is through this process that he writes himself into the text. As he told Gordon in 1968, Rosencrantz and Guildenstern "both add up to me in many ways in the sense that they're carrying out a dialogue which I carry out with myself."[41] "What I'm always trying to say is 'Firstly, A. Secondly, minus A.'"[42] The latter statement echoes Stoppard's definition of Beckett's theatrical dialectic. Still another model for Stoppard's method can be detected in Wittgenstein's view of philosophy: "Philosophy simply puts everything before us, and neither explains nor deduces anything" (p. 50e). *R&GAD*, typical of Stoppard's work, "is essentially dialectical, but without a final synthesis ever being reached."[43]

If Shakespeare's *Hamlet* is the most famous paradigm for this kind of dialectic, mid-twentieth-century culture provided Stoppard with a distinctive medium for its expression. The medium is nonheroic and self-consciously derivative. Its idiom not only echoes written texts central to modern culture in the West but also refers to complex new ideas about science, psychology, and the texts themselves. By expressing Shakespeare's dialectic in the contemporary medium, Stoppard appropriates it for modern culture. John Freeman argues that Stoppard's play, in its shifting perspectives, is both of its time and ahead of it: "Indeed, *Rosencrantz* anticipates the postmodern/deconstructive questioning and dismantling of the individual authorial self."[44] Stoppard's adaptation claims *Hamlet* for the whole second half of the twentieth century, even as it reduces high tragedy to offbeat comedy; and Stoppard claims Shakespeare as a fellow artist, even as he dismantles the individual authorial self.

Shortly after the initial success of *R&GAD*, Stoppard commented on the vitality of plays: "They're organic things, they're not mineral. They change their composition in relation to the time they exist, or are seen to exist, and in relation to oneself."[45] Stoppard's relation to *R&GAD* may have changed – he has stated more than once that plays go off like fruit, and parts of this one have gone off for him – but the text has continued to flourish in different venues since its rapid transfer from the Fringe of the Edinburgh Festival to the National Theatre at the Old Vic in 1967. Currently it belongs to the international repertory of English-language drama, even alternating with *Hamlet*; it has been staged with variations in many foreign languages; and it is a prescribed text in British schools and North American universities. Stoppard's next encounters with Shakespeare would not thrive in the same way, perhaps because their politics confine them more narrowly to the time they exist.

"The comma that divides *Dogg's Hamlet, Cahoot's Macbeth* also serves to unite two plays which have common elements: the first is hardly a play at all without the second, which cannot be performed without the first."[46] Written when Stoppard had become an established playwright, this adaptation of *Hamlet* returns to the sources he had used before, but now it forms part of a play composed as a diptych. Stoppard himself identifies his sources and analogues in his preface to the published version; relatively few commentators have analyzed their formulation.

Like *R&GAD*, *Dogg's Hamlet, Cahoot's Macbeth* evolved over a number of years, from 1971 to 1979, but its components remained separate until Stoppard combined them in the full-length play. He devised the first part of *Dogg's Hamlet* as an opening ceremony for the Almost Free Theatre in 1971. A language game deriving from Wittgenstein's *Philosophical Investigations*, this entertainment took approximately twenty-five minutes to perform. "The [original] title [*Dogg's Our Pet*] is an anagram for Dogg's Troupe, a group of actors operating under the umbrella of Inter-Action whose guiding spirit is Ed Berman, sometimes known as Professor Dogg."[47] In 1972 Stoppard wrote the second part of *Dogg's Hamlet* – his fifteen-minute version of *Hamlet* for seven actors – for the Fun Art Bus, a double-decker bus serving as another performance space for Inter-Action. According to Berman, "We both coincidentally misplaced the script for four years," but in 1976 Dogg's Troupe played it "on the grey parapets of the National Theatre."[48]

Dogg's Hamlet, Cahoot's Macbeth conflates these two playlets – elaborating the first, barely changing the second – as a prelude to *Cahoot's Macbeth*. Stoppard has explained that the latter play, which includes an abbreviated version of *Macbeth*, was inspired by specific events: the situation of artists in Czechoslovakia since Charter 77; and, most immediately, a letter from Pavel Kohout in 1978 which describes Living-Room Theatre, a group of five actors "with one suitcase" who perform *Macbeth* in private homes.[49]

By 1976, Stoppard said he "felt . . . sick of flashy mind-projections speaking in long, articulate, witty sentences about the great abstractions."[50] His changed attitude may have resulted from the connection with Berman and Inter-Action, both representing theatre with an agenda, or an ideology.[51] It probably accounts for the composition of *Dogg's Hamlet, Cahoot's Macbeth*, which differs from that of his earlier plays, including *R&GAD*. In the finished text of 1979, paradigms are not superimposed but juxtaposed. Stoppard arranges long quotations from some of his favorite writers side by side with long quotations from his own experience, allowing the passages to comment on one another. All of the familiar borrowed devices appear – from play within a play to puns and syllogisms – but here dispersed through the action, often as parts of quotations and therefore in their original contexts. Compared with *R&GAD*, *Dogg's Hamlet, Cahoot's Macbeth* is neither intensely derivative nor analytical. Shakespeare and his affiliations with the twentieth century have become less complex, more accessible.

Stoppard begins *Dogg's Hamlet* where Wittgenstein begins his *Philosophical Investigations*: with the presentation of a primitive language. For the original *Dogg's Our Pet* he created a language from Wittgenstein's illustration

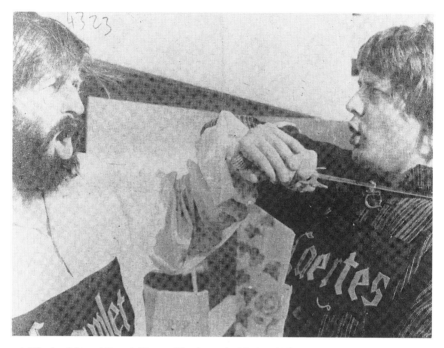

6 *The (15 Minute) Dogg's Troupe Hamlet* at the National Theatre (1976), with John Perry as Hamlet and Patrick Barlam as Laertes.

and five words: "plank," "slab," "block," "brick," and "cube." In *Dogg's Hamlet*, he produces a more elaborate primitive language with a much larger vocabulary. The published text of *Dogg's Hamlet* gives translations of this language called "Dogg" in square brackets; it does not advertise the misunderstandings among the characters that lead to insults and physical abuse, misunderstandings also significant in *Dogg's Our Pet*.

As the action unfolds among a group of schoolboys who speak Dogg, two other kinds of languages are heard briefly: a very concentrated form of contemporary English compounded by a truck driver, and bits and pieces of Shakespeare's *Hamlet*, which the boys rehearse without enthusiasm. After a series of events and a ceremony articulated in Dogg – the setting is actually an English prep school – "*The lighting changes and there is a trumpet fanfare*," and the same characters perform the fifteen-minute *Hamlet* (p. 31). This version is a *tour de force*: a seventeen-line prologue, an enactment of *Hamlet* which includes almost all of the characters (even Osric) and events, and an encore which reprises the whole in thirty-eight lines. Every word comes from the original text, although phrases, lines, and passages usually turn out to be composites from different acts and scenes.

Dogg's Hamlet ends with a bit of stage business, and *Cahoot's Macbeth* begins in a different setting: "*the living room of a flat. Thunder and lightning. Three* WITCHES *in minimal light*" (p. 47). The adult actors perform this Shakespearean tragedy in an abbreviated version without farcical effect. Elizabethan English serves as the basic idiom of Stoppard's play, interrupted by passages of modern English and finally by passages of Dogg. In *Cahoot's Macbeth*, the embodiment of repressive political forces, an Inspector, usually expresses himself in the kind of hyperventilated English heard briefly in *Dogg's Hamlet*; he also frequently echoes Stoppard's own observations of life in Husak's Czechoslovakia as they appeared in periodicals such as the *New York Review of Books*.[52] As Stoppard's play closes, the actors manage to perform the end of *Macbeth*, despite the Inspector, by speaking the final passages in Dogg as they build a platform with now familiar slabs, blocks, planks, and cubes.

Stoppard's ambivalence toward Shakespeare may be more pronounced in *Dogg's Hamlet, Cahoot's Macbeth* than anywhere else. In *Dogg's Hamlet*, as in *The (15 Minute) Dogg's Troupe Hamlet*, Shakespeare himself bows and delivers the prologue (p. 31). The farcical version of *Hamlet* is part of a formal occasion, the awarding of school prizes, and its setting makes an obvious statement: Shakespeare has become a cliché in British culture, virtually meaningless (that is, a foreign language) in the very institutions where he is most revered. But Stoppard qualifies this statement. The cleverness of his *Hamlet* calls attention to itself not only as self-parody but as acknowledgment of his freedom to rewrite a classic. *Dogg's Hamlet* also anticipates the link with Kohout, whose *Poor Murderer* (1972) plays on *Hamlet*; and it never loses completely its original sense of occasion, preserving in its title and in the language games from *Dogg's Our Pet* a tribute to Berman's concept of interactive theatre.[53]

In *Cahoot's Macbeth*, Shakespeare's later tragedy assumes immediacy in a repressive political regime: it functions as an agency of subversion and defiance; and its author, thus appropriated, takes on the dimensions of a hero. This is as close as Stoppard has come to creating in a play the Shakespeare he extolled for Shakespeareans.[54] Yet bits of clay adhere to the Shakespeare of *Cahoot's Macbeth*. For one thing, as Ralph Toucatt points out, the Inspector – controlling Stoppard's play and Shakespeare's, punning, mocking the audience – represents both playwrights. For another, Shakespeare's *Macbeth* performs its subversion only when it is articulated in Dogg, the language which previously undermined *Hamlet* and created opportunities for violence in the menacing rhythms of Pinter's *Caretaker* (1960).[55] At the close, victory is not decisive, threatened by the police who occupy the acting space.

Stoppard was engaged for a while by *Dogg's Hamlet, Cahoot's Macbeth*, adapting its political references to keep them up to date in production,[56] but he would not do another wholesale reconstitution of Shakespearean texts until the 1990s. At the beginning and end of the decade, he returned to the project through film, with the adapted *R&GAD* and the collaborative *Shakespeare in Love*. Clearly this medium has given Stoppard the freedom not only to rewrite Shakespeare but also to rewrite himself.

The earlier film allowed Stoppard to revise those parts of his successful play which had gone off for him. More than once he has said that cinema permitted him to "change the frame," the limited visuals and perspectives of theatre.[57] The film depends less on dialogue than on motion: Stoppard thinks he cut half the lines, affording the actors time to pursue events, to "show up in a place."[58] Redoing his play as a script for film, Stoppard altered the balance of the original composition. Beckett recedes, for example, and cultural references become more apparent and funnier, especially in the series of sight gags where Rosencrantz unwittingly toys with scientific discoveries.

In *Shakespeare in Love*, the screenplay written by Marc Norman and Stoppard, there are obvious signs of Stoppard's hand: eclecticism; conflating a previous era with a modern one; cultural observations about both; verbal wit. The film refers both to Shakespeare's life as it has been reconstructed by biographers, and to fictional renditions such as *No Bed for Bacon*, the novel by Caryl Brahms and S. J. Simon, or *Will Shakespeare – An Invention*, the play by Clemence Dane (pseudonym for Winifred Ashton).[59] Although it focuses on *Romeo and Juliet*, it cites other plays and verse in Shakespeare's canon, ranging from *Titus Andronicus* to the sonnets to *Antony and Cleopatra*. It ends with *Twelfth Night*, and along the way there are many allusions to *Hamlet*.

All of this coexists with the world of modern entertainment, from the West End to Hollywood. *Shakespeare in Love* plainly presents this world as a continuum in which Shakespeare's early life in London corresponds with Stoppard's, in particular the Stoppard who first attempted to enter the theatre scene; it offers a parody of the artist as a young man. "One room, scratching a living":[60] Stoppard describes his arrival in London with an image that parallels the film's introduction of Will. The changing titles of Stoppard's plays, the distractions, the borrowing of ideas are reflected in the film. Stoppard felt like a "bag of nerves";[61] Will sees an apothecary, an early modern psychiatrist.

Both young playwrights, under pressure, evade their obligations. One of Stoppard's letters to Smith in October 1963 epitomizes a key element of the film: "Kenneth [Ewing, his agent] keeps on me about the play . . . which (I lie) I am progressing with."[62] Most strikingly, both dramatists attend chaotic rehearsals of their first major successes – Will of *Romeo and Juliet*, Stoppard of *R&GAD* – guiding the performances through obstacles arranged and paced like a Feydeau farce.[63]

In the end, of course, both plays were breakthroughs for their authors: in the film, Henslowe realizes "*It's a hit*"; Ron Bryden, theatre critic for the *Observer*, recognized *R&GAD* as a "brilliant debut by a young play-wright."[64] Collaborating on the screenplay apparently encouraged Stoppard to contemplate his beginnings after three decades in the theatre. With the callow and frenetic Will of *Shakespeare in Love*, he seems to refashion Shakespeare the "World Champ" as a double for his earlier self, a figure not without charm. He varies the formula "a bit of Shakespeare, . . . a bit of me," producing a new ambivalence which balances caricature and sentiment, wit and affection, me and sympathy.

NOTES

1 The Whidden Lectures, McMaster University, Hamilton, Ontario, 24 October 1988, transcribed and edited Doreen DelVecchio, reprinted in *Stoppard in Conversation*, ed. Paul Delaney (Ann Arbor: University of Michigan Press, 1994), p. 210.

2 Quoted in Roger Hudson, Catherine Itzin, and Simon Trussler, "Ambushes for the Audience: towards a high comedy of ideas," *Theatre Quarterly*, 4 (1974), reprinted in Delaney, ed., *Stoppard in Conversation*, p. 58.

3 *The Real Thing* (London and Boston: Faber and Faber, 1983), pp. 52, 49.

4 Stoppard, "The Event and the Text," pp. 204–205.

5 Quoted in Shusha Guppy, "Tom Stoppard: the art of theater VII," *Paris Review*, 109 (1988), reprinted in Delaney, ed., *Stoppard in Conversation*, p. 180.

6 See Gussow, "Stoppard Refutes Himself, Endlessly," *New York Times*, 26 April 1972, and "*Jumpers* Author is Verbal Gymnast," *New York Times*, 23 April 1974, reprinted in Delaney, ed., *Stoppard in Conversation*, pp. 31, 75.

7 See *Arcadia* (London and Boston: Faber and Faber, 1993), pp. 40, 79, and *The Invention of Love* (London and Boston: Faber and Faber, 1997), p. 49. Citations of Shakespeare come from *The Riverside Shakespeare*, ed. G. Blakemore Evans with J. J. M. Tobin, 2nd edn (Boston and New York: Houghton Mifflin, 1997).

8 In *Albert's Bridge; and, If You're Glad I'll Be Frank: two plays for radio* (London and Boston: Faber and Faber, 1969), p. 29, quoting Sonnet 18.

9 *Jumpers* (London and Boston: Faber and Faber, 1986), pp. 15 and 76.

10 Katherine E. Kelly, *Tom Stoppard and the Craft of Comedy: medium and genre at play* (Ann Arbor: University of Michigan Press, 1991), pp. 108, 109, quoting the play, p. 53. See *Travesties* (London and Boston: Faber and Faber, 1975).

11 Nicole Boireau, "Tom Stoppard's Metadrama: the haunting repetition," in *Drama on Drama: dimensions of theatricality on the contemporary British stage*, ed. Nicole Boireau (Houndmills and London: Macmillan, 1997), p. 143.

12 See Gary Taylor, *Reinventing Shakespeare: a cultural history, from the Restoration to the present* (New York: Weidenfeld and Nicolson, 1989).

13 Ruby Cohn, *Retreats from Realism in Recent English Drama* (Cambridge: Cambridge University Press, 1991), pp. 49, 53.

14 Katherine E. Kelly, "Staging Repetition: parody in postmodern British and American theater," in *Repetition in Discourse: interdisciplinary perspectives*, ed. Barbara Johnstone (Norwood, N.J.: Ablex, 1994), vol. 1, p. 55.

15 This type of theory, generous in allowing a wide range of interactions between texts, derives from Linda Hutcheon, *A Theory of Parody* (New York: Methuen, 1985).

16 These phrases come from Clive James, who recognized the dynamism of Stoppard's eclectic art in 1975 ("Count Zero splits the infinite," *Encounter*, 45 [1975], reprinted in a shorter version in *Critical Essays on Tom Stoppard*, ed. Anthony Jenkins [Boston: G. K. Hall, 1990], pp. 29, 30).

17 Tom Stoppard, "Is It True What They Say About Shakespeare?," International Shakespeare Association Occasional Paper no. 2 (Oxford: International Shakespeare Association, 1982), p. 11.

18 Stoppard quoted in "Ambushes for the Audience," p. 53.

19 Stoppard, "Is It True What They Say About Shakespeare?," p. 10.

20 Kelly, *Stoppard and the Craft of Comedy*, p. 18.

21 Kenneth Tynan, "Profiles: withdrawing with style from the chaos," *New Yorker*, 19 December 1977, reprinted in *Show People: profiles in entertainment* (New York: Simon and Schuster, 1979), pp. 69–70.

22 Tom Stoppard, "The Writer and the Theatre: the definite maybe," *Author*, 78 (1967), p. 19.

23 See ibid., and "Ambushes for the Audience," p. 57.

24 John Fleming, "Tom Stoppard: his life and career before 'Rosencrantz and Guildenstern,'" *Library Chronicle of the University of Texas at Austin*, 26.3 (1996), pp. 139–146.

25 Quoted ibid., pp. 139–140.

26 See Thomas Whitaker, *Tom Stoppard* (New York: Grove Press, 1983), pp. 62–63.

27 Charles Marowitz, *Confessions of a Counterfeit Critic: a London theatre notebook, 1958–1971* (London: Eyre Methuen, 1973), p. 123.

28 Neil Sammells suggests that the text may have changed under the influence of Saunders and actors familiar with his work (*Tom Stoppard: the artist as critic* [Houndmills and London: Macmillan, 1988], p. 39).

29 See Stoppard, "Definite Maybe," p. 19, and "Ambushes for the Audience," p. 57.

30 Stoppard, quoted in "Ambushes for the Audience," p. 60.

31 Stoppard, "Definite Maybe," pp. 19–20.

32 Quoted in Giles Gordon, "Tom Stoppard," *Transatlantic Review*, 29 (1968), reprinted in Delaney, ed., *Stoppard in Conversation*, p. 18.

33 Ronald Hayman, "First interview with Tom Stoppard 12 June 1974," in Ronald Hayman, *Tom Stoppard*, 4th edn, Contemporary Playwrights (London: Heinemann, 1979), p. 7.

34 Stoppard quoted in Gordon, "Tom Stoppard," p. 21; see also Hayman, "First Interview with Stoppard," p. 8.

35 See James's description of Stoppard's work in "Count Zero Splits the Infinite," pp. 27–34.

36 Quoted in Katherine E. Kelly and William W. Demastes, "The Playwright and

the Professors: an interview with Tom Stoppard," *South Central Review*, 11.4 (1994), p. 5.

37 *Rosencrantz and Guildenstern Are Dead* (London: Faber and Faber, 1967), p. 25.

38 See Ruby Cohn, *Modern Shakespeare Offshoots* (Princeton: Princeton University Press, 1976), p. 216, and "Tom Stoppard: light drama and dirges in marriage," in *Contemporary English Drama*, ed. C. W. E. Bigsby, Stratford-upon-Avon Studies 19 (London: Edward Arnold, 1981), p. 113.

39 Jonathan Bennett, "Philosophy and Mr. Stoppard," *Philosophy*, 50 (1975), reprinted in Jenkins, ed., *Critical Essays on Stoppard*, pp. 85–87.

40 Ludwig Wittgenstein, *Philosophical Investigations*, trans G. E. M. Anscombe, 3rd edn (Oxford: Oxford University Press, 1974), p. 200^e.

41 Stoppard quoted in Gordon, "Tom Stoppard," p. 19.

42 Stoppard quoted in Hayman, "First Interview with Stoppard," p. 10.

43 Hersh Zeifman, "Tomfoolery: Stoppard's theatrical puns," *Yearbook of English Studies*, 9 (1979), reprinted in Jenkins, ed., *Critical Essays on Stoppard*, p. 186.

44 John Freeman, "Holding up the Mirror to Mind's Nature: reading *Rosencrantz* 'beyond absurdity,'" *MLR*, 91 (1996), p. 32.

45 Stoppard quoted in Gordon, "Tom Stoppard," p. 22.

46 Stoppard, preface to *Dogg's Hamlet, Cahoot's Macbeth* (London and Boston: Faber and Faber, 1980), p. 7. All references to *Dogg's Hamlet, Cahoot's Macbeth* in this chapter come from this edition.

47 Stoppard, note to *Dogg's Our Pet*, in *Ten of the Best British Short Plays*, ed. Ed Berman, Ambiance/Almost Free Playscripts 3 (London: Inter-Action Imprint, 1979), p. 80.

48 Ed Berman, "How Long is an Ephemeron?," in Berman, ed., *Ten of the Best British Short Plays*, p. x.

49 Preface to *Dogg's Hamlet, Cahoot's Macbeth*, p. 8.

50 Stoppard quoted in Hayman, "Second Interview with Tom Stoppard 20 August 1976," p. 139.

51 See Berman's summary of the theatre's mission in "How Long is an Ephemeron?," pp. xiv, ix.

52 Compare the Inspector's speech on p. 54 with Tom Stoppard, "Prague: the story of the Chartists," *New York Review of Books*, 4 August 1977, pp. 11–15.

53 See Anthony Jenkins, *The Theatre of Tom Stoppard*, 2nd edn (Cambridge: Cambridge University Press, 1989), pp. 101–104.

54 The lecture "Is It True What They Say About Shakespeare?" contains an encomium on p. 11.

55 Ralph Toucatt, "Cross-cultural Stoppard," *Threepenny Review* (spring 1981), p. 20. On the echoes of Pinter, see Jenkins, *Theatre of Stoppard*, p. 156.

56 See Delaney's headnotes, *Stoppard in Conversation*, pp. 129, 199.

57 Stoppard quoted in Sid Smith, "Script Jockey: the flickering images of theater," *Theatre Magazine*, 1 (1991), and in Paul Allen, *Third Ear*, BBC Radio Three, 16 April 1991, both reprinted in Delaney, ed., *Stoppard in Conversation*, pp. 236 and 245.

58 Stoppard quoted in Robert Seidenberg, "*Rosencrantz & Guildenstern are Dead*: Tom Stoppard adapts Tom Stoppard," *American Film*, 16 (1991), p. 49.

59 In the British media after the film's release Michael Dobson and Stanley Wells

were the first to point out links with the novel (London: Michael Joseph, 1941); Stoppard has admitted to flipping through it in twenty minutes. I noticed the connections with the play, produced in 1921 and recently reprinted (Fidelis Morgan, ed., *The Years Between: plays by women on the London stage 1900–1950* [London: Virago, 1994], pp. 67–162).

60 Stoppard quoted in "Ambushes for the Audience," p. 55.

61 Stoppard in a letter to Smith, January 1964, quoted in Fleming, "Stoppard: life and career before 'Rosencrantz and Guildenstern,'" p. 127.

62 Stoppard quoted ibid., p. 118.

63 See Janet Watts, "Tom Stoppard," *Guardian*, 21 March 1973, reprinted in Delaney, ed., *Stoppard in Conversation*, p. 47.

64 Shakespeare in Love: *a screenplay* (New York: Hyperion, 1998), p. 146; Bryden quoted in Fleming, "Stoppard: his life and career before 'Rosencrantz and Guildenstern,'" p. 157.

10

PAUL EDWARDS

Science in *Hapgood* and *Arcadia*

> even the desperate abstractionist
> drives his car of ice into the great question of fire.
>
> Edward Dorn

Stoppard's two major science-based plays, *Hapgood* (1988) and *Arcadia* (1993) have met quite different receptions from audiences and critics. *Hapgood*, which uses some of the baffling aspects of quantum physics as a parallel to the bluff and double-bluff found in the plots of Cold War spy thrillers, simply confused and irritated much of its audience, while *Arcadia*, which uses the hardly less confusing mathematical theories of "Chaos" to structure its account of the passage of time in the "timeless" surroundings of an English country house and parkland, is regarded by many as Stoppard's greatest play. Stoppard is not a playwright who wants to engage only with an élite audience appreciative of an avant-garde aesthetic, so any account of these two plays, even one that makes high claims for *Hapgood*, must go some way to explain its relative failure. On the other hand, in 1992 Stoppard himself declared that he was interested in it "insofar as it *succeeded*."[1] For him, its technical successes were to be the foundation for the critical success of *Arcadia*.

   Clearly, part of the appeal of incorporating scientific theory into theatre is the sheer technical challenge. Quantum mechanics describes the interaction of particles at a subatomic level, where the "common sense" rules of classical mechanics no longer apply. The challenge for the playwright is to find analogies in the larger-scale, human world for the behavior of particles in the subatomic world where our human intuitions completely mislead us. Humans do not, on the face of it, behave like electrons. The playwright here can be seen as vying with popular science manuals or television documentaries like the BBC's *Horizon* series, which in the 1970s and 1980s aimed at imparting real understanding of complex scientific ideas. But Stoppard combines this ambition with one that, as it were, leads in the opposite direction: science should, through the sideways slant of its analogies, illuminate the human world, and perhaps show it in a more intense and emotional light than could be achieved through more direct treatment. Stoppard is a deeply Romantic writer in that the emotional heart of his plays has to lie in what cannot be articulated directly. It is smuggled in behind the glittering surface where words and ideas are juggled by a master showman. And it could be argued that the more his plays are occupied with matters that tax the intellect or flatter it with paradoxes and witty antitheses, the more unexpectedly and poignantly their emotional charge is felt. The risk is obvious: if the balance is wrongly weighted, or the production wrongly calculated, emotion and human meaning are not just unspoken but lost altogether.

The plot of *Hapgood* is complicated in the extreme, and the presentation of events that are explained only belatedly (if at all) can leave the audience struggling too hard to keep up. What follows is a bare summary. The British Secret Service is trying to find out who has been leaking technical details of the Strategic Defense Initiative (better known as President Reagan's Star Wars program) to the Russians. At the center of this attempt is Elizabeth Hapgood, steely, super-intelligent, and efficient in running her department, yet also, we find, appealingly scatty and emotionally dependent; sexually attractive and a crack shot to boot. She runs a "joe" (double agent), the defector Kerner, a physicist working on Star Wars, who regularly passes innocuous "secrets" of his work back to the KGB by swapping briefcases at a cubicle in a swimming pool. The play opens with just such a swap, but this time monitored both by Hapgood's agents and a team from the CIA; the CIA has discovered that real secrets as well as harmless ones have been turning up in Moscow as a result of Kerner's activities. This is only revealed later to the audience. Hapgood's agent, Ridley (who normally packs the briefcase with supposedly secret information) will on this occasion intercept the case and pass it to Hapgood (waiting in a nearby shower cubicle), so that it can be checked for any extra, genuinely secret information that might illicitly have been put in. If anyone opens this case (to remove any compromising extra material), a hidden isotope will leave a radioactive marker on them that can be detected by a miniature Geiger counter carried by the CIA agent Wates. The KGB agent will be given a duplicate also containing the innocuous "secrets"; this, it is assumed, he will swap as usual for another case.

Several things go wrong, the most baffling of which is that the intercepted briefcase does indeed prove to have been opened, and its rolls of film removed by someone (presumably along with a compromising extra roll of film, indistinguishable from the others, that would have confirmed the treachery), yet apparently nobody has opened the case, for no one registers on Wates's Geiger counter. A bug, also placed in the case, has disappeared too. The consequence of this is that, although it is now confirmed that extra information is passing by this channel, it is not clear who is responsible, Kerner, Ridley, or even (as Wates later decides) Hapgood herself, in league with Ridley. A further complication should be mentioned. Instead of sending the usual KGB agent, the Russians send two agents, twins, who make the sequence of exchange, substitution, and removal even more difficult to follow. These are apparently the celebrated "KGB twins" recruited by a Russian security officer with a background in particle physics.

Twinning and doubling are at the heart of the analogy this play makes with quantum physics, by making the "uncertainty principle" concrete on a human scale. Stoppard uses Richard Feynman's exposition of the dual nature of light – behaving like a stream of particles or like a succession of waves depending on which behavior one is trying to check for – as the basic example of this uncertainty.[2] Kerner himself explains the experiment and its connection with twins in one of several short but plodding lectures on physics he delivers to other characters:

> The particle world is the dream world of the intelligence officer. An electron can be here or there at the same moment . . . Its movements cannot be anticipated because it has no reasons. It defeats surveillance because when you know what it's doing you can't be certain where it is, and when you know where it is you can't be certain what it's doing.[3]

If one secret agent is really a pair of twins, then he or she can be doing something unknown while under close surveillance. Thus the surveillance of the western agents in the "experimental" exchange of briefcases can apparently be defeated by the "KGB twins." Only apparently, however, for it turns out that the real KGB twins are Hapgood's agent Ridley and his unknown brother; it is they who remove the films from Kerner's briefcase, and it is the unseen twin who is marked by the isotope in it. Ridley himself, though he removes the films and disposes of the bug, is unmarked. The two Russians collecting at the meet are simply a blind, sent as a distraction by the KGB because they knew from Ridley that the exchange would be watched. Once Hapgood and her associates have worked this out for themselves, the plot of the play centers on their attempt to entrap the Ridleys in yet another exchange.

There is not room here to explore the remaining intricacies of the plot. (It turns out, for example, that Kerner, as well as Ridley, has been passing genuine secrets.) What must be said, however, is that working these intricacies out does not – as ideally it should – take us deeper into the heart of the mysteries of quantum physics, even by analogy. On the contrary, we find ourselves concerned with much more traditional and mundane puzzles: how could Ridley have enough time to enlist his brother and two extra Russian

7　A scene from the Aldwych Theatre 1988 production of *Hapgood* – Nigel Hawthorne (Blair) and Roger Rees (Joseph Kerner).

twins in the operation after packing the briefcase but before the exchange took place? And when Ridley is trapped into participating in a second drop – believing he is helping Hapgood privately by delivering a disk to the Russians in exchange for her supposedly kidnapped eleven-year-old son – why does he need to perform another double sham exchange with the help of his twin, when all that seems required is to get the disk to the "kidnappers?" The whole "kidnap" scenario is Hapgood's bluff, so one is also compelled to ask why she and her colleagues are certain – in a play illustrating the Uncertainty Principle – that Ridley will indeed summon his twin and pass a dummy disk, keeping what he thinks is a genuine disk for himself. I labor these nit-picking points not so much because they are not answered as because any answers we come up with will not bring us any closer to the mysteries of quantum physics, even by analogy. Nor will they be of any human interest, for this aspect of the play is simply Cold War baroque; indeed, the history Stoppard was working with was slipping into obsolescence even as he wrote.[4]

There is other human interest in *Hapgood*, however, and it is evidently connected with some of the paradoxes of quantum physics. Until the behavior of an electron is "made public" as it were, by an experiment that gives knowledge about it, its state is indeterminate, both epistemologically and, the logic (inconceivably) suggests, ontologically: it can be thought of as having a "choice" of manifestations. Indeed the "many worlds" interpretation of quantum physics attributes an equal reality to the choice not taken, locating it in a world parallel to the one revealed by experiment. Stoppard transposes this to human psychology and places his characters in situations where choices are or have been made and identities fixed by them. But other choices or identities could equally well have been elected. In a neat reversal of the main device of the play, Hapgood convinces Ridley that she has a twin. Ridley then works with the "twin" to arrange the drop that will release Hapgood's son from the "kidnappers." This second Hapgood – a product of choices not taken – is slatternly, disorganized, and louche where the official Hapgood is neat, uptight, and controlled. Official Hapgood dislikes Ridley (or at least the Ridley that has been revealed to her); unofficial "twin" Hapgood takes to him (or at least the Ridley she is in a hotel room with) – even tries to persuade him not to deliver the disk – then surrenders sexually to him, telling him she is his "dreamgirl . . . Hapgood without the brains or the taste" (p. 71). Stoppard has explained his intentions: "the person who gets up in the morning and puts on the clothes is the working majority of a dual personality, part of which is always there in a submerged state."[5] The explicit pathos of the play comes when Hapgood later shoots Ridley, who has not only just made love to her but has revealed to her the futility of the spying business for which she has sacrificed yet another alternative identity as a mother devoting most of her life to her young son and the father (Kerner, it transpires) he has lost to the same business. The challenge for the actors is to make the audience feel that there is actually pathos rather than tasteless sentimentality behind these complicated transactions.

One of the weaknesses of *Hapgood* is the remoteness of its action from everyday life. *Arcadia*, on the other hand, turns such remoteness to its own advantage, being set quite deliberately in a world of social privilege that very few of its audience can be expected to have experienced. The "real world" does intrude on the apparently timeless "Arcadia" of the English country house, and the whole play can be seen as an exemplar of the inscription traced on the tomb by the shepherds in Poussin's reflection on the traditional pastoral idyll: "Et in Arcadia Ego." "Even in Arcadia, there am I," as it is translated by one of the characters; it is death that is present, even in this aristocratic idyll.[6] In fact, Sidley Park, the stately home where the action is set, proves to be far from immune to changes over time, and it is the irreversibility of such changes that provides both the human meaning and the scientific framework of the play.

That framework is Chaos Theory, a form of mathematic that plots (typically on a computer screen) the apparently random results of an unimaginably long series of repeated calculations; without computers the task would be impossible. The starting point of each round of calculation is the result of the previous one. The results are random and unpredictable, but given enough of them, an ordered pattern emerges. Just as in *Hapgood* Stoppard included a quantum physicist as one of the main characters to expound science for the other characters (and for the audience), so in *Arcadia* one of the characters, Valentine Coverly, is a mathematician working with Chaos Theory. His research project is to discover the equation that governs the apparently haphazard fluctuations in the populations of grouse on the moors where the Coverly family have always shot. He describes the emergence of such a pattern among the accumulating random points on the computer screen: "In an ocean of ashes, islands of order. Patterns making themselves out of nothing."[7] It is a description to which we will return, for it encapsulates the lure of Chaos Theory in this play: the capacity for nature, and us as part of nature, to recuperate our losses – ultimately, to circumvent time.

The brilliantly conceived structure of *Arcadia* enables the audience to witness the effects of time in Sidley Park, since the play is set in two different periods, but in the same garden room of the stately home. The audience actually witnesses, as far as possible, the events of April 1809, and can piece together what is only reported. In other scenes, set in the present day, the cocky careerist university lecturer, Bernard Nightingale, is seen constructing a sensational account of those events based on the fragments of evidence that have survived the 180-year interval. The audience can see where Bernard goes wrong and watch him propelled by vanity to publish his mistaken conclusions. This is broad comedy, but embellished with the wit and subtlety we would expect of Stoppard. Bernard's theory is that Lord Byron stayed at Sidley on an April weekend in 1809, slept with the wife of a minor poet, Ezra Chater, then fought a duel with Chater and killed him. The beauty of the theory is that it seems to explain why Byron left England for two years in July 1810. It also has an additional attraction for Bernard because it adds material to the Byron canon: two hostile reviews of books by Ezra Chater and some additional couplets for *English Bards and Scotch Reviewers*. It will make Bernard's reputation as a media don.

But Bernard's theory is almost completely wrong. Byron was at Sidley that weekend, and did make love to Mrs. Chater, but no duel took place; the surviving documents concerning the duel (actually two duels) were addressed not to Byron but to Septimus Hodge, the stylish wit working as the tutor to the thirteen-year-old Thomasina Coverly. Septimus also has slept with Mrs. Chater (the same weekend!), and is the author of the damning reviews. Lady Croom, on her way to Byron's bedroom during the night, encountered Mrs. Chater emerging from it, and the Chaters and Byron were all expelled from Sidley before any duel could be fought. All this is sufficiently clear to the audience.

In the modern period Valentine Coverly is also doing research, as I have mentioned, into grouse populations, while another researcher, Hannah Jarvis, is investigating the history of the gardens of the park, and is particularly interested in the transformation brought about by Richard Noakes, who around 1810 obliterated the "classical" eighteenth-century pastoral landscaping and replaced it with the gloomy and Romantic features of a Gothic novel: crags, waterfalls, thickets, artificial ruins and a "hermitage." The hermitage was equipped with a hermit, and he is the focus of her interest: an appropriately insane recluse who filled the hermitage with thousands of papers scrawled with incomprehensible "cabalistic" formulae, all of which were burnt at his death. For Hannah this mad hermit represents the end of a cultural decline that began with the elimination of the geometrical and symmetrical layout of the gardens (expressing classical, rational order) and continued with successively irregular redesigns. "The whole Romantic sham, Bernard! It's what happened to the Enlightenment, isn't it? A century of intellectual rigour turned in on itself. A mind in chaos suspected of genius . . . The decline from thinking to feeling, you see" (p. 27). But though her cultural history might be sound enough, Hannah proves to be as wrong about the hermit as Bernard is about Byron, and she builds up a stranger but more accurate account of him by the end of the play.

The play turns around the intuitive – romantic versus rational – classical dichotomy sketched by Hannah, even in its treatment of science and the recoverable or irrecoverable past. It turns out that one of the chief sources of Stoppard's information about Chaos Theory, James Gleick's *Chaos*, is, in one of its aspects, an anticlassical paean to Romanticism – something that Stoppard could hardly have missed.[8] The presiding genius of Gleick's book is Mitchell Feigenbaum, a modern pioneer of Chaos, who Gleick says had "managed not to purge himself of some seemingly unscientific ideas from eighteenth-century Romanticism." Gleick presents a picture of this Romantic genius on a solitary walk, Feigenbaum observing the movements of his fellow-beings, and momentarily alienated, finding them incomprehensible: "*The ceaseless motion and incomprehensible bustle of life.* Feigenbaum recalled the words of Gustav Mahler . . . [He] was listening to Mahler and reading Goethe, immersing himself in their high Romantic attitudes."[9] Elsewhere Gleick puts forward the view that the regular geometrical forms in modern buildings (and, by implication, in classically ordered gardens) are inherently ugly, while shapes like that of a storm-blasted tree on a hillside are attractive.[10] Gleick would be the "classical" Hannah Jarvis's temperamental opposite, it seems.

There is a serious scientific point behind this perennial culture war; just as the classical garden is symmetrical and geometric, so the universe of Isaac Newton is governed by symmetries that are demonstrated through geometry. It is an ordered, determinate universe, and in principle its future changes are predictable and past states discoverable by calculation based on the knowledge of forces and masses involved in events. Discussing physics with her tutor in 1809, Thomasina Coverly precociously perceives this implication: "If you could stop every atom in position and direction, and if your mind could comprehend all the actions thus suspended, then if you were really, *really* good at algebra you could write the formula for all the future; and although nobody can be so clever as to do it, the formula must exist as if one could" (p. 5).[11] Leaving aside the question of knowledge, this universe is a self-maintaining system not going in any particular direction: "Newton's equations go forwards and backwards, they do not care which way," as Thomasina recognizes (p. 87). Valentine Coverly explains that if this were the whole truth about the universe, however, we could run a piece of film backwards and not know whether we were seeing it in the right direction. But in the real universe, though some phenomena could pass this test of reversal (Valentine instances a pendulum, or a ball falling through the air; p. 93), others cannot – Valentine instances a ball smashing a pane of glass, but the reduction of anything to ashes by fire would be an equally good example. These processes do not reverse themselves.

Thomasina's tutor Septimus maintains a classical, Newtonian faith that they do reverse themselves, or that the principle of the conservation of energy means that the prior conditions will return again. When Thomasina bemoans the loss of so many of the works of the ancients in the burning of the great library of Alexandria ("All the lost plays of the Athenians! Two hundred at least by Aeschylus, Sophocles, Euripides"), he confidently explains to her that her regret is misplaced:

> We shed as we pick up, like travellers who must carry everything in their arms, and what we let fall will be picked up by those behind. The procession is very long and life is very short. We die on the march. But there is nothing outside the march so nothing can be lost to it. The missing plays of Sophocles will turn up piece by piece, or be written again in another language . . . Mathematical discoveries glimpsed and lost to view will have their time again.   (p. 38)

There are two ironies here. I shall discuss only the first, most obvious one, which is at Septimus's expense (though he seems unwittingly to have engineered it for himself, to tease his pupil). He has set Thomasina a passage in Latin to translate into English. Unknown to her, it is a Latin version of Enobarbus' speech from *Antony and Cleopatra* (2.2, ii, 191ff.), describing Cleopatra, "The barge she sat in, like a burnish'd throne," etc. Here is a great work "written again in another language." Thomasina's stumbling version proves that translation is a one-way process, and that what is once lost remains lost. Classical, "optimistic" cosmology fails to take account of this.

Arcadia is full of instances that confirm the irreversibility of time. Stoppard is careful to specify that certain props (books, folders) that appear in both time frames of the play should exist in both "new" and "worn" versions. The garden is changed, game is slaughtered. Letters by Byron and Septimus are burnt and reduced to ash. Candles and oil lamps burn. Most poignantly of all, we learn from a retrospective comment of Hannah's in the final scene, Thomasina herself will be burnt to death on the eve of her seventeenth birthday in an accident presumably involving a candle: "et in Arcadia ego" indeed. This final scene is a brilliant example of Stoppard's stagecraft, in which the two periods of time merge as the audience see superimposed on each other, as it were, the actions of 1993 and 1812 (just before Thomasina's seventeenth birthday and her death, thus three years later than the earlier scenes). Thomasina will not die, however, until she has made various anachronistic discoveries and observations. In the 1809 scenes she has puzzled over the fact that jam stirred into her rice pudding cannot be "unstirred" out of it by reversing the movement of her spoon. This is not a particularly radical observation itself, of course, but Thomasina, unlike Septimus at this stage, realizes some of its importance; perhaps God is not a "Newtonian," she suggests. Valentine explains the science of this to Hannah when she is beginning to suspect, from examining Thomasina's surviving exercise book, that she may have been a genius who anticipated later scientific and mathematical discoveries. Valentine's example is of a cup of tea that gradually cools to room temperature: Thomasina's jam disperses into the rice pudding like the heat of the tea into the surrounding atmosphere. Thomasina has made an intuitive discovery of the second law of thermodynamics, which was not formulated until 1865 by the German physicist Rudolf Clausius, the inventor of the term "entropy" to refer to the quantification of the dispersal of heat into its surroundings. Although the first law of thermodynamics announces the "Newtonian" fact that the energy of the universe is constant (nothing, therefore, is lost, just as Septimus had asserted), energy is not always available, for it dissipates into a uniform diffusion and cannot be recovered.

It was at least in part the invention and development of heat engines, particularly steam engines, that led scientists to the second law of thermodynamics. Joseph Fourier's *Analytic Theory of Heat* (1822) and Sadi Carnot's *Reflections on the Motive Power of Fire* (1828) were the necessary precursors to its formulation. In the final scene of *Arcadia*, Noakes, the landscape gardener who has played havoc with Sidley's ideal landscape, brings his "Improved Newcomen steam pump" to the park. Thomasina, casually reading "a prize essay for the Scientific Academy in Paris," immediately perceives that "Newton's equations go forwards and backwards, they do not care which way. But the heat equation cares very much; it goes only one way. That is the reason Mr. Noakes's engine cannot give the power to drive Mr. Noakes's engine" (p. 87). It is also the reason, she implies, why the whole universe must be gradually evening out in temperature and declining to a state of maximum entropy. Just as Noakes's engine, when its fuel is burnt out, will cease, so the "Improved Newtonian Universe" (p. 93), when all its heat has burnt up, will also cease, except as a randomly distributed mass of irrecoverable energy: chaos.

Thomasina is a far more appealing and charming character than her preoccupation with thermodynamics and the irreversibility of time would suggest. She makes her discoveries serendipitously and announces them with a winning, throwaway manner that makes her the perfect foil for her tutor. One discovery that Stoppard holds back from attributing to her is the consonance of entropy in thermodynamics with "noise" in Information Theory.[12] An increase in entropy corresponds to a loss of information. Stoppard nevertheless builds this dimension into the structure of the plot itself, as the modern characters struggle to recover lost information. It is illustrated also by the occasional playing of a piano that recurs in the play: entropic "noise" disrupts the melody and makes it difficult to pick out. Alternatively, at one point, when the offstage pianists, Thomasina's mother and the Count Zelinsky, have worked themselves up a passionate head of steam, the stage direction instructs that the music doubles its notes and passion – "the action of bodies in heat," as Thomasina with perhaps unintentional wit declares. Valentine, in an earlier (modern-day) scene, has already explained the significance of the piano by instancing it in an analogy for the difficulty of his research into grouse population. The many variables (food supply, predation, weather) confuse the information: "Like a piano in the next room, it's playing your song, but unfortunately it's out of whack, some of the strings are missing, and the pianist is tone deaf and drunk – I mean, the *noise!*" (p. 46). There is a paradox involved in this: disorder, chaos, entropy are at least partly subjective phenomena, as Ludwig Boltzmann noticed when remarking that entropy is related to "missing information."[13] Stoppard tacitly illustrates this point by instructing that the work-table in the room should not be readjusted after each scene to conform with the chronology of the story (p. 15). A coffee mug set down in a "modern" scene at the beginning of the play should remain on the table in a nineteenth-century scene that occurs later in the play (and vice versa for props placed there in the nineteenth century). At the end of the play, the table has accumulated a variety of objects that, if one saw them without having seen the play, would seem completely random and disordered. Entropy is high. But if one has seen the play, one has full information about the objects and the hidden "order" of their arrangement, brought about by the performance itself. Entropy is low; this can be proved by reflecting that tomorrow night's performance of the play will finish with the table in a virtually identical "disorder" – which therefore cannot really be disorder at all.

Chaos mathematics is about the recovery of information from apparently chaotic and random systems where entropy is high. Valentine is using it to find the pattern underlying the changing grouse population. It is "asymmetric" (unlike the equations of classical physics), yet it finds regularities that prove to be the regularities of nature itself. Strikingly, this mathematics can generate patterns of amazing complexity ("fractals" and the famous Mandelbrot set), but it also has the power to generate seemingly natural or organic shapes that defeat Newtonian geometry. The promise, then, (however questionable it is in reality) is that information and, by extension, nature itself, can overcome the tendency to an increase in entropy.

We now see the full significance of Valentine's description of the emergence of a pattern on a computer from the equations he has found in Thomasina's mathematics notebook. The pattern presumably plots apple leaf shapes, for it was in order to do this that Thomasina developed – in the most daring and "impossible" anachronism of the whole play – her mathematics that would make "all the forms of nature . . . give up their numerical secrets and draw themselves through number alone" (p. 43). As Byron, through Romantic imagination rather than rational deduction, anachronistically intuited in his poem, "Darkness," the universe may suffer heat death and the earth be reduced to ashes, but "in an ocean of ashes, islands of order. Patterns making themselves out of nothing."

Stoppard scrupulously has Valentine limit the optimism or meliorism apparently inherent in this overcoming of entropy (the world is "still doomed. But if this is how it started, perhaps it's how the next one will come"; p. 78), but it explains, finally, Hannah's mystery of the mad hermit scribbling thousands of sheets of calculations. It was Septimus Hodge, who begins the play as a "classical" optimist, blithe, witty, and apparently completely imperturbable. Thomasina has shown him the gloomy future implied by the second law of thermodynamics that she has discovered. A contemporary account of the hermit is discovered stating that "Frenchified mathematick . . . brought him to the melancholy certitude of a world without light or life . . . as a wooden stove that must consume itself until ash and stove are one, and heat is gone from the earth" (p. 65). His "madness" consists in spending twenty-two years reiterating Thomasina's equations after her death, desperate to overturn this pessimistic conviction through restoring pattern and the promise of life in the ocean of ashes. This is "mad" because it can only be done through a computer; the classical Septimus has become his opposite, a full-blooded Romantic (just as, far less affectingly, Hapgood became her temperamental opposite).[14] The truth, the emotional core of this madness, left typically unstated by Stoppard, but all the more poignant for that reason, is that by the eve of Thomasina's seventeenth birthday, Septimus and she are in love, though they are not even aware of it themselves.[15] The pain of her irrecoverable loss in the fire must be at the root of the hermit's desperate attempts to restore hope "through good English algebra" (p. 65).

At the end of the story, after all the researches, and despite entropy, just about everything has been recovered, and, by an irony I have reserved from my discussion of Septimus's earlier speech, "Mathematical discoveries glimpsed [by Thomasina] and lost to view . . . have their time again." The final scene of the play shows us an image of perfect harmony, time overcome through the copresence of past and present as the modern couple Hannah and the new, silent genius of the Coverly family, Gus, dance alongside Thomasina and Septimus to the tune of a waltz. But the audience knows that "tomorrow" or "tonight," Thomasina will take a candle, mount the stairs to her bedroom and be burnt to death. She cannot be brought back – certainly not by algebra. The overcoming of time at the conclusion of *Arcadia* is a triumph of art, not of science, and like all such triumphs it is momentary, fragile, and all the more poignant for being quite useless.

NOTES

1 Stoppard, quoted in Angeline Goreau, "Is *The Real Inspector Hound* a Shaggy Dog Story?" (1992), reprinted in Paul Delaney, ed., *Stoppard in Conversation* (Ann Arbor: University of Michigan Press, 1994), p. 259.

2 Kerner's exposition to Blair in Act 1 scene 2 of the experiment by which the paradox of the duality of light, and of the role of the experiment in determining its own outcome, is paraphrased from two of Feynman's own accounts, the more technical one of which is in his *Lectures on Physics* (vol 1; Reading, Mass.: Addison-Wesley, 1963, Ch. 37; reprinted in Richard Feynman, *Six Easy Pieces: The fundamentals of physics explained*, Harmondsworth: Penguin, 1998, pp. 115–138). The less technical account is in Feynman, *The Character of Physical Law* (1965; reprinted Harmondsworth: Penguin, 1992, pp. 127–148). The epigraph to *Hapgood* combines passages from both books; *Six Easy Pieces*, p. 117, and *Character*, p. 130.

3 Tom Stoppard, *Hapgood* (1988), revised edn (London and Boston: Faber and Faber, 1994), p. 40.

4 The politics of *Hapgood* are fairly perfunctory, especially when compared with *Professional Foul*. The Cold War thriller is simply a convenient genre for Stoppard, though he makes revisions in the 1994 text to make the defector Kerner more aware of a forthcoming crisis in the Communist bloc than he had been in the 1988 version (compare *Hapgood* [London and Boston: Faber and Faber, 1988], p. 73, with the 1994 text, p. 63: in the former Kerner implies that the East, unlike a western democracy, cannot "reverse itself," while in 1994 it is a British agent who can see no prospect of change in the East, and Kerner who asserts that "the system can change"). The 1994 revision retains the pre-1989 setting of the play. The other, more significant revisions considerably reduce the scientific details of Kerner's expositions of physics. Perhaps Stoppard has realized that the physics was more important as an inspiration than as an actual ingredient in the play.

5 Stoppard, quoted in Michael Billington, "Stoppard's Secret Agent" (1988), reprinted in Delaney, ed., *Stoppard in Conversation*, p. 194.

6 Nicholas Poussin's painting, *The Arcadian Shepherds* (about 1638), is in the Musée du Louvre, Paris The translation of the inscription on the tomb the shepherds are examining in the painting is given by the character Septimus Hodge (*Arcadia*). Corrected edn (London: Faber and Faber, 1993), p. 13. A more complacent translation, "Here I am in Arcadia!," has already been provided by Lady Croom (p. 12).

7 *Arcadia*, p. 76. The main source for the image is Byron's "Darkness," but Stoppard may also be recalling Beckett's *Endgame*: "I once knew a madman who thought the end of the world had come . . . I'd take him by the hand and drag

him to the window. Look! There! All that rising corn! . . . He'd snatch away his hand and go back into his corner. Appalled. All he had seen was ashes." Samuel Beckett, *Endgame*. (1958), reprinted (London: Faber and Faber, 1969), p. 32.

8 James Gleick, *Chaos: making a new science* (1988), reprinted (London: Abacus, 1995).

9 Ibid., p. 163.

10 Ibid., pp. 116–118, citing Gert Eilenberger and John Fowles. The point of view put forward is so directly contrary to Hannah's that a researcher not made wary by the errors of Hannah and Bernard would confidently declare the passage to be the trigger for Stoppard's composition of *Arcadia*.

11 Historically, Thomasina's ideas, and the cosmos she describes, are those of Pierre-Simon Laplace (1749–1827) rather than Newton.

12 The discovery that equations used for measuring entropy in physical systems apply also to information was made by Charles Shannon in the 1940s. For a useful explanation of the concepts involved, and a consideration of the significance of this "coincidence," see Jeremy Campbell, *Grammatical Man: information, entropy, language and life*. (Harmondsworth: Penguin, 1984).

13 Quoted ibid., p. 16.

14 Stoppard commented to Mel Gussow: "At the same time, I was thinking about Romanticism and Classicism as opposites in style, taste, temperament, art. I remember talking to a friend of mine, looking at his bookshelves, saying there's a play, isn't there, about the way that retrospectively one looks at poetry, painting, gardening, and speaks of classical periods and the romantic revolution and so on. Particularly when one starts dividing people up into classical temperaments and romantic temperaments – and I supppose it's not that far from *Hapgood* in a way. The romantic temperament has a classical person wildly signalling, and vice versa." Mel Gussow, *Conversations with Stoppard* (London: Nick Hern, 1995), p. 90.

15 The play is full of random, meaningless (entropic?) sexual couplings and proposals of more; it is sexual restraint – particularly Septimus's with the now-grown Thomasina – that really signifies.

I I

HERSH ZEIFMAN

The comedy of Eros: Stoppard in love

In his 1967 review of the New York production of *Rosencrantz and Guildenstern Are Dead*, Robert Brustein dismissed its author as a mere "university wit" who achieved his success by offering audiences "a form of Beckett without tears."[1] That specific criticism has continued to dog the plays of Tom Stoppard throughout his now lengthy and distinguished career. The major argument with Stoppard's theatre has always been that it is far too cerebral, too emotionally barren: all head and no heart. "That particular duality has become a bit of a cliché about me," Stoppard concedes.[2] And it is a cliché that gets repeated in almost every profile of the dramatist ever written: thus his plays are perceived, one journalist states, as "avoid[ing] emotion";[3] another describes them as often appearing "cold, frigid, impossibly remote";[4] a third comments that, to many spectators, "a dynamo and not a heart lay beneath his work's surface, . . . and it pumped a kind of icy adrenaline, not blood."[5] "If I filed my cuttings," Stoppard has wryly noted, "I would no doubt have a pretty thick too-clever-by-half envelope."[6]

This critical tide was stemmed to some degree by the appearance of *The Real Thing* in 1982, which surprised audiences in much the same way that the publication of A. E. Housman's collection of romantic verse *A Shropshire Lad* reputedly surprised Housman's own family; in Stoppard's recent play about Housman, *The Invention of Love*, one of Housman's sisters is said to have exclaimed, "Alfred has a heart!"[7] Suddenly, it seemed, Stoppard too had a "heart" – except, of course, that it was hardly sudden. Stoppard's early plays were indeed clever (perhaps even, in some instances, too clever by three-quarters), but there was always an emotional pulse beating steadily beneath all that surface erudition and irony. What "suddenly" changed with *The Real Thing* was that this self-confessed "very private sort of person"[8] was no longer afraid to wear his heart openly on his sleeve in a play dealing specifically with the emotionally charged topic of love. "Love is a very interesting subject to write about," Stoppard noted in a 1983 interview. "I've been aware of the process that's lasted 25 years, of shedding inhibitions

185

about self-revelation. I wouldn't have dreamed of writing about it 10 years ago." At the same time, however, he seemingly closed the door on any future explorations of the subject: "As far as I'm concerned, this is all I'll do. For better or worse, that's it – the love play!"[9]

But that assertion proved to be false, for in his stage plays of the 1990s – especially *Arcadia* (1993) and *The Invention of Love* (1997) – Stoppard has continued to write movingly about love, thus confirming, as one interviewer has noted, the critics' contention that he has become "emotionally less guarded." Stoppard agreed: "Yes, [they] can't all be wrong. And it's not difficult to work out. I'm a very shy, private person and I camouflaged myself by display rather than by reticence. I became a repressed exhibitionist. I found emotional self-exposure embarrassing – and now I don't, or less so. The older I get, the less I care about self-concealment."[10] Although the love theme constitutes only one thread among many in the rich tapestry of these two dense and difficult plays, it is an absolutely central one, ultimately informing every aspect of the plays' overall designs. While affairs of the heart lie at the very heart of these plays, however, Stoppard still remains dauntingly cerebral and daringly theatrical: in each play, Eros is compelled to pick a dilly of a circus in which to perform its emotionally complex high-wire act. Both Stoppard and the god of love are working here, as always, without a net.

Arcadia is alternately set in two radically different time frames – 1809–1812 and the present – but within a single theatrical space: a room in the garden front of Sidley Park, a large country estate in Derbyshire. The play's original impetus, Stoppard has said, was his desire to write about the contrast between the classical temperament ("those who have particular respect for logic, geometry and pattern") and the romantic temperament ("those with a much more spontaneous, unstructured communion with nature")[11] – in other words, about the conflict specifically between head and heart, between thinking and feeling. The primary representative of a classical temperament in the play is the present-day writer/biographer Hannah Jarvis, researching a book on the hermit of Sidley Park, her peg for "the nervous breakdown of the Romantic Imagination."[12] This reportedly mad nineteenth-century hermit, Hannah claims, is the "perfect symbol" of "The whole Romantic sham": "It's what happened to the Enlightenment, isn't it? A century of intellectual rigour turned in on itself. A mind in chaos suspected of genius." Hannah reads the same symbolism into the history of the landscape in which the hermit was placed. "There's an engraving of [the garden of] Sidley Park in 1730 that makes you want to weep," Hannah notes. "Paradise in the age of reason." But "the whole sublime geometry" (p. 27) was ultimately ploughed under, to be replaced by romantic notions of the garden as "untamed nature . . . the Gothic novel expressed in landscape. Everything but vampires" (p. 25). Both hermit and garden, Hannah thus concludes, perfectly symbolize the "decline from thinking to feeling" (p. 27).

Earlier, in the 1809 portion of *Arcadia*, the teenaged prodigy Thomasina had inquired of her tutor: "Septimus, do you think God is a Newtonian?" (p. 5). Doubting Thomasina will later answer her own question; but whether God is a Newtonian or not, Hannah certainly is. As her vocabulary attests, she believes in "intellect," in "reason," in "geometry," in "thinking"; her world, like Newton's, is deterministic – ordered and logical. "Newton's equations go forwards and backwards," Thomasina at one point explains, "they do not care which way" (p. 87). So, not so incidentally, does Hannah's palindromic name, thus marking her as the very embodiment of Newtonian classicism.

As a consequence, hard-hearted Hannah has shut herself off from anything even remotely connected with a romantic sensibility – including, not surprisingly, romance itself: the erotic is, for her, too erratic. Stoppard dramatizes Hannah's anti-romantic temperament in many ways – from her clothing ("She wears nothing frivolous"; p. 15) to her refusal to dance ("I don't dance," she twice exclaims; pp. 33, 64) to her aversion to being kissed ("Don't kiss me!"; p. 49). When her antagonist and fellow researcher Bernard Nightingale, the representative of romantic sensibility in the play, invites her to escape with him to London for some recreational sex, Hannah automatically demurs:

> BERNARD. You should try it. It's very underrated.
> HANNAH. Nothing against it.
> BERNARD. Yes, you have. (p. 63)

"You've been deeply wounded in the past, haven't you, Hannah?" (p. 57), accuses Chloë, one of the present-day inhabitants of Sidley Park – and perhaps Chloë is right. For in the multiple romantic roundelays that punctuate the action of *Arcadia*, Hannah positions herself deliberately as an outsider. When asked to dress up in Regency clothes for the fancy-dress party Chloë's parents are throwing and join the others in a group photograph, Hannah responds, "I'll come and watch" (p. 90).

Although Bernard's romanticism is portrayed by Stoppard as deeply (and hilariously) flawed, so too is Hannah's "classical reserve" (p. 75). The problem with Hannah's attempt to inhabit her own private version of "Arcadia," a paradise of rationality and predictability, is that God ultimately is *not* a Newtonian: there is a "serpent" in the garden, and that serpent, as always, is the irrational and seductive power of Eros. At the end of scene 2, the first scene set in the present, Chloë's teenaged brother Gus, who is in love with Hannah, offers her an apple; at the beginning of scene 3, set in the past, the same apple is eaten by Septimus. That iconic apple reminds us simultaneously of Newton's apple (the law of gravity) and the apple with which Eve tempted Adam (the law of desire) – a law of equal gravity that will prove to be the far stronger force. For what finally defeats Newton (and the Newtonian/classical sensibility of Hannah) is, as Thomasina will discover, "The action of bodies in heat" (p. 84). Thomasina is referring here to the physical structure of the universe; what she has stumbled on, long before its time, is thermodynamics, the study of heat that first burned away some of the certainties of Newtonian determinism. But she is also alluding to the action of *human* bodies in heat, the forbidden fruit of Eros.[13]

Stoppard slyly emphasizes this connection between bodies in heat in physics and bodies in heat in the throes of erotic passion in a stage direction in the play's final scene. In the offstage music room, Lady Croom, Thomasina's mother, is playing a romantic piano duet with Count Zelinsky, the latest in her long string of lovers (for Lady Croom, it's not just the heat – it's the tumidity); in the offstage garden, landscape architect "Culpability" Noakes is proudly employing the Improved Newcomen steam pump, a heat engine with which he is reshaping the garden: "*The piano music becomes rapidly more passionate, and then breaks off suddenly in mid-phrase. There is an expressive silence next door which makes* SEPTIMUS *raise his eyes . . . The silence allows us to hear the distant regular thump of the steam engine . . .*" (p. 81). The sounds of heat collide with the sounds of heat, and the heat of Eros is at least as fatal to Newtonian order as the heat of thermodynamics – as Chloë later suggests in a conversation with her mathematician brother Valentine:

> CHLOË. The universe is deterministic all right, just like Newton said, I mean it's trying to be, but the only thing going wrong is people fancying people who aren't supposed to be in that part of the plan.
> VALENTINE. Ah. The attraction that Newton left out. All the way back to the apple in the garden. (pp. 73–74)

"The attraction that Newton left out" leads inevitably to chaos – and thus to Chaos Theory. For Thomasina similarly manages to discover the science of chaos long before its time: in scene 3 she picks up Hannah's/Septimus's apple (that apple again!) and vows to plot its leaf and deduce its equation, thus anticipating the mathematics of fractals, "the New Geometry of Irregular Forms" (p. 43).[14] "Where chaos begins, classical science stops," writes James Gleick in *Chaos: making a new science*; specifically, Gleick notes, "chaos cuts away at the tenets of Newton's physics" by eliminating the "fantasy of deterministic probability."[15] In the present-day scenes of *Arcadia*, Valentine attempts to explain chaos theory to Hannah:

The unpredictable and the predetermined unfold together to make everything the way it is . . . The ordinary-sized stuff which is our lives, the things people write poetry about – clouds – daffodils – waterfalls – and what happens in a cup of coffee when the cream goes in – these things are full of mystery . . . The future is disorder . . . It's the best possible time to be alive, when almost everything you thought you knew is wrong.   (pp. 47–48)

Poor Hannah – thermodynamics to the left of her, chaos to the right of her, and Eros (which, Hesiod informs us in *Theogony*, is literally Chaos's child) sneaking in behind, all making a mockery of her classical sensibility.

And it gets worse: in a chaotically uncertain world, the only certainty is death – even in Arcadia, as Septimus at one point reminds Thomasina. "'Even in Arcadia, there am I!'" (p. 13), Septimus quotes, translating and interpreting the tomb inscription "Et in Arcadia Ego" in Poussin's celebrated seventeenth-century painting of the same name. But Thomasina does not need reminding, because she knows something still worse: according to the second law of thermodynamics, which she has intuited, it is the entire universe that is dying, inevitably heading towards an entropic dead end. "Heat goes to cold," Valentine explains to Hannah. "It's a one-way street . . . It'll take a while but we're all going to end up at room temperature" (p. 78). Thomasina had grasped this more than a century before: the heat equation, she deduced, "goes only one way" (p. 87). As Stoppard's Rosencrantz acknowledged: "for all the compasses in the world, there's only one direction, and time is its only measure."[16]

"So, we are all doomed!," Septimus is forced to conclude, to which Thomasina replies: "(*Cheerfully*) Yes" (p. 93). That stage direction speaks volumes; despite what she knows, Thomasina refuses to give in to despair. At this moment, however, she is thinking of heat in more than one sense: not just the heat of thermodynamics but the heat of Eros. For she is falling in love with Septimus, and begs him to teach her to waltz – that most romantic of dances. In the remarkable final scene of *Arcadia*, past and present seamlessly, and heartbreakingly, merge: Thomasina's and Valentine's explanations of entropy speak to each other simultaneously across the ages:

SEPTIMUS. So the Improved Newtonian Universe must cease and grow cold.
  Dear me.
VALENTINE. The heat goes into the mix.
    (*He gestures to indicate the air in the room, in the universe.*)
THOMASINA. Yes, we must hurry if we are going to dance.
VALENTINE. And everything is mixing the same way, all the time, irreversibly
  . . .
SEPTIMUS. Oh, we have time, I think.
VALENTINE. . . . till there's no time left. That's what time means.

SEPTIMUS. When we have found all the mysteries and lost all the meaning, we will be all alone, on an empty shore.

THOMASINA. Then we will dance. Is this a waltz? (pp. 93–94)

Septimus, alas, is wrong: they do *not* have time – not only cosmically but within their own lifetime. For, as we know from the vantage point of the scenes set in the present, this is the very night that Thomasina will die – ironically enough, in a fire: "Be careful with the flame," Septimus warns as he lights the candlestick that will ultimately lead to her death (p. 96). Eros tragically melts into Thanatos; heat consumes in all possible ways. And yet, what other response is there in a world without predictable pattern or meaning except, as Thomasina suggests, to "dance?"

Earlier in the play, in her discussion with Bernard about her proposed book on the follies of romanticism (a book she intends to title, sardonically, *The Genius of the Place*, in reference to the Sidley Park hermit), Hannah declared: "I don't like sentimentality." "Are you sure?" Bernard replied. "You seem quite sentimental over geometry" (p. 28). What Hannah truly dislikes, however, is not so much sentimentality as sentiment itself – feeling with her heart rather than thinking with her head. Thomasina, on the other hand, who possesses unquestionably the most profound brain in a play bursting with brainy characters, likewise knows full well that Eros "addles the brain" (p. 14), yet it does not stop her from wanting to waltz or to make love to Septimus. This is precisely what Hannah must learn from the past, from the *true* "genius of the place": in the midst of a chaotic, disordered world, even in the face of death – *especially* in the face of death – we must still leave ourselves open to romance, to the vagaries of erotic desire.

And Hannah *does* learn; luckily for her, there are chinks in her classical armor. "None of us is tidy," Stoppard has commented; "none of us is classifiable. Even the facility to perceive and define two ideas such as the classical and romantic in opposition to each other indicates that one shares a little bit of each."[17] As Kerner states in *Hapgood*, "We're all doubles"; Hannah's "working majority" may be classical, but there's a romantic "sleeper" buried deep within her.[18] To cite just one example, we have only to examine the opening lines of *Arcadia*:

THOMASINA. Septimus, what is carnal embrace?

SEPTIMUS. Carnal embrace is the practice of throwing one's arms around a side of beef.

THOMASINA. Is that all?

SEPTIMUS. No . . . a shoulder of mutton, a haunch of venison well hugged, an embrace of grouse . . . *caro, carnis*; feminine; flesh. (p. 1)

The puns are, as usual, outrageous, but, as always with Stoppard, they lead us into the very heart of the play. "Carnality" is precisely what Hannah has set herself in opposition to; yet her bestselling-biography of Byron's lover Caroline Lamb ("the closet intellectual shafted by a male society"; p. 60), was titled, Stoppard slyly notes, *Caro* (p. 20). *Caro*, of course, is simply short for Caroline; but the pun on *caro* as "flesh" subtly implies that Hannah may not be entirely immune to the potential pleasures of "carnal embrace" (though not, presumably, of a rack of lamb).

By the end of the play, the sweet security of Newtonian physics (and metaphysics) has been literally shot down in flames, leaving Hannah to sift forlornly among the ashes. Even her book is in ruins: the mad Sidley Park hermit, she now knows, is not some abstract symbol of "the decline from thinking to feeling" but the very real Septimus, forever mourning the loss of his love – though Hannah, at this stage, has no tangible proof. Nor does she have to journey into the past to find concrete examples of the mess Eros leaves in its wake: Chloë is a present-day victim, her romantic feelings for Bernard having been cruelly rejected by him. When Hannah attempts to console her, Chloë "*rounds on her*: And you mind your own business! What do you know about anything?" "Nothing," Hannah replies bleakly, and then repeats it two lines later: "Nothing" (p. 95). Her entire belief system has been completely shattered, defeated by the sheer arbitrariness of erotic desire: "the attraction that Newton left out."

Stoppard, however, does not leave her there, for suddenly Gus appears in the doorway. Or is it Gus? In the scenes set in the past, we briefly meet Thomasina's young brother, Augustus, played by the same actor who plays his descendant, the present-day Gus. The character who now appears is dressed in Regency clothes, but that does not necessarily narrow the field: so are all the modern characters in this scene, guests at the fancy-dress party. And throughout this final scene, as previously noted, characters from the past freely intermingle with those from the present: while Chloë yells at Hannah, Thomasina and Septimus waltz in circles around them. So: is it Gus or Augustus? The present or the past? In a sense it is both; the confusion created here by Stoppard is deliberate. The character in fact turns out to be Gus, but in a way he is an "emissary" from the past – specifically from Thomasina, imparting her wisdom to Hannah. For the silent Gus, like Thomasina a "genius" (p. 33), has a present for Hannah: just as he previously offered her an apple, now he offers her the proof for what she already knew through "gut instinct . . . the part of [her] which doesn't reason" (p. 50) – a drawing of Septimus that establishes him as the hermit.

But Gus has an additional "present" for her; through gestures he asks her to dance. "Oh, dear, I don't really . . ." (p. 97), Hannah starts to reply, and then stops herself. It was only the old, "classical" Hannah who refused to dance; *this* Hannah finally knows better:

> (*After a moment's hesitation, she gets up and they hold each other, keeping a decorous distance between them, and start to dance, rather awkwardly.* SEPTIMUS *and* THOMASINA *continue to dance, fluently, to the piano.*)
>
> (p. 97)

The play closes, then, with a dance, or rather two dances – one past, the other present, simultaneously sharing the same space. A dance, of course, is the traditional ending for comedy, the symbol of order finally restored; but this twinned dance in Stoppard's dark comedy of Eros is infinitely more complex. Both couples – and especially Hannah, who has journeyed the furthest – have passed through order and come out the other side, to an acknowledgment of the oxymoronic "orderly disorder" at the chaotic heart of existence. And yet they still choose, bravely, to embrace romance, to dance – a dance not of innocence but of knowledge sorely gained, an act of grace in the face of unspeakable loss. It is perhaps the most moving moment in all of Stoppard's theatre.

A. E. Housman, on the other hand, the protagonist of Stoppard's most recent play, *The Invention of Love*, chooses *not* to dance – only to dream of dancing.[19] Once again Stoppard is dramatizing the conflict between a romantic and classical sensibility, but this time within a single character. When asked in an interview in 1998 what originally inspired him to write a play about Housman, Stoppard replied: "It's the Romantic/classicist contrast, isn't it, it's *Arcadia* again. I just realized there was something basically dramatic in the man who was two men."[20] In *The Invention of Love*, Stoppard portrays Housman as *literally* two men, played by two different actors: the old man of seventy-seven at the end of his life (AEH) and the young man between the ages of eighteen and twenty-six (Housman). This bifocal vision structurally encapsulates the play's central thematic metaphor, a metaphor that will be dramatized in a number of significant ways in the play: the concept of the divided self.

In "Dream Song 205," poet John Berryman wrote of Housman: "he was a fork / saved by his double genius."[21] Whether he was "saved" or not is one of the main issues raised by the play, but there is no question that Housman was indeed a "fork." On the most obvious level, Housman was bifurcated in terms of profession: he was both a scholar and a poet, as the opening lines of the play immediately establish. The ferryman Charon is waiting patiently to transport two dead souls across the river Styx to the underworld:

8 A scene from the National Theatre 1997 production of *The Invention of Love* – Paul Rhys (A. E. Housman) and John Wood (AEH).

CHARON. A poet and a scholar is what I was told.
AEH. I think that must be me.
CHARON. Both of them?
AEH. I'm afraid so.
CHARON. It sounded like two different people.
AEH. I know. (p. 2)

As a classical scholar and a romantic poet, Housman was very much "two different people." The scholar was all "head"; a professor of Latin, Housman produced rigorous textual criticism which he regarded as a "science" (p. 38), the tools of which were "logic" (p. 79) and rationality: "scholarship is a small redress against the vast unreason of what is taken from us" (p. 71). The poet, by contrast, was all "heart"; the "peculiar function of poetry," Housman stated in a public lecture at Cambridge, was "to transfuse emotion – not to transmit thought."[22]

The combination of scholarship and poetry in a single person could easily be regarded as an ideal balance rather than a conflict; what made it "divisive" in Housman's case was that the head far outweighed the heart. Housman published only two slim volumes of verse during his lifetime, devoting the vast majority of his time to intellectual pursuits. Significantly, we never see him engaged in any way with his own poetry in *The Invention of Love*, and only a few snippets from a handful of his poems are actually cited in the text. But the relative meagerness of Housman's poetic output is not really the issue here; it is that the emotions that inspired his poetry were *confined* to his poetry rather than acted out in his life. If Housman's head (the classicist) outweighed his heart (the romantic), it is because the head was given full rein while the heart was intentionally repressed. As Auden noted in his poem "A. E. Housman": "Deliberately he chose the dry-as-dust, / Kept tears like dirty postcards in a drawer."[23]

This is the true sense in which Housman was a "fork," a divided self: while his romantic sensibility was allowed to come out in poetry, the man himself was unable to "come out" in life. If "The laws of God, the laws of man," he writes in one of his poems, were determined to "make me dance as they desire,"[24] then Housman would refuse to dance. Eros played a cruel trick on Housman: it made the object of his desire a heterosexual man – Moses Jackson, whom he first met as an undergraduate at Oxford and continued to love, chastely and from afar, for the rest of his life. When Housman sent his beloved "Mo" a copy of *Last Poems* in 1922, he inscribed it from "a fellow who thinks more of you than anything in the world," and added, significantly, "you are largely responsible for my writing poetry."[25] In *The Invention of Love*, Stoppard assesses the enormous cost of that emotional sublimation.

Thus the real barrier to Housman's emotional fulfillment was not so much Moses Jackson's heterosexuality as it was his own homosexuality, which was considered taboo by the society at large – and, more importantly, by Housman himself. When he was a youth, the great minds who taught him at Oxford simultaneously revered the classics and condemned (or, worse, erased) all classical instances of "beastliness" – minds so deeply repressed that they were unaware of their own hypocrisy, as Stoppard commented in an interview: "My chorus of old Oxford wrinklies . . . consists of Pater who wanted to have sex but never dated, Jowett who didn't want to, and Ruskin who couldn't – 200 combined years of celibacy and impotence."[26] (Wickedly, Stoppard first introduces these men in *The Invention of Love* playing a game of croquet with an imaginary ball!) And when Housman was an adult, equally powerful men – a trio of politicians and journalists played, in the original National Theatre production, by the same actors – were instrumental in criminalizing homosexual acts. Is it any wonder, then, that Housman internalized society's judgment, converting his own guilt and shame into abject denial, unma(s)king Eros through transmut(il)ation into something less threatening – brotherhood, say, or comradeship. "Was there ever a love like the love of comrades," rhapsodizes the youthful Housman in the play, "ready to lay down their lives for each other?" (p. 39). But the older AEH is not so easily fooled: "Love will not be deflected from its mischief by being called comradeship or anything else" (p. 43).

"My life was marked by long silences" (p. 3), AEH acknowledges at the beginning of the play – something the youthful Housman would not so readily admit. Stoppard's strategy of splitting the character in two thus brilliantly illuminates the theme of repressed sexuality, for AEH, unlike his younger self, has much less to lose, and therefore less reason to remain silent. *The Invention of Love*, like *Travesties*, is at heart a memory play; despite AEH's (and the play's) opening line ("I'm dead, then"; p. 1) or his later revision ("Not dead, only dreaming!"; p. 5), he is "Neither dead nor dreaming, . . . but in between" (p. 101). Physically, as indicated by the play's running gag about incontinence, AEH is on his deathbed at the Evelyn Nursing Home; mentally, he is rehashing his life in those final few moments left to him before death obliterates all. As in *Arcadia*, death permeates every scene of *The Invention of Love*, thereby imparting to the play a heightened urgency. In life, as in law, deathbed confessions carry special weight; imminent death suddenly renders pointless life's central evasions. And so the dying AEH finds himself confessing to his younger self: "If I had my time again, I would pay more regard to those poems of Horace which tell you you will not have your time again. Life is brief and death kicks at the door impartially . . . Now is the time, when you are young, to deck your hair with myrtle, drink the best of the wine, pluck the fruit" (p. 39) – even, or perhaps especially, if that erotic fruit is forbidden.

"I'm not as young as I was," AEH addresses his younger self in their first conversation in the play. "Whereas you of course are" (p. 30). These confrontations between old age and youth across the chasm of time are invariably poignant; but the dying old man's most emotionally wrenching memories center primarily not on his lost youth but on the elusive Mo, thus further emphasizing his repression of Eros. Stoppard dramatizes this repression in two especially haunting images of Mo repeated throughout the play. One of these images, which occurs twice in the first act, is of Mo running towards us in the distance but never getting any closer – an image which perfectly encapsulates AEH's longing and regret. Here as elsewhere, Mo is being specifically compared to the athlete Ligurinus, whose beloved memory was mourned by Horace in his ode "To Venus": "At night I hold you fast in my dreams, I run after you across the Field of Mars, I follow you into the tumbling waters, and you show no pity" (p. 49). AEH cites these lines at the close of Act 1, again accompanied by the image of Mo running yet never advancing; like Horace, he too is praying to the goddess of love for mercy.

The other, more powerful image, occurring three times in the text, replays AEH's most stirring memory of his student days at Oxford, an idyllic moment frozen in time: "*Three men in a boat row into view, small dog*

yapping" (p. 4). Although the context of this memory is obviously comic –
a parodic evocation of the 1889 novel *Three Men in a Boat (To Say Nothing
of the Dog!)* by Jerome K. Jerome, who will later appear briefly in that same
boat as a character in the play[27] – there is nothing at all humorous in AEH's
deeply emotional reaction. And that reaction clearly stems not from seeing
his younger self in the boat, whom he in fact fails to recognize, but from
seeing his beloved Mo: "Oh, Mo! Mo! I would have died for you but I never
had the luck!" (pp. 5, 46, 100). (In the play's first production, actor John
Wood modulated that "Oh" into the long-drawn-out sigh of "Ah"; what the
audience heard, then, was "Ah, Mo!" – *amo*, Latin for "I love.") AEH's
lines, a buried allusion to the concluding couplet of Housman's eight-line
"Poem xx" in *Additional Poems* – "For I was luckless aye / And shall not
die for you"[28] – are, typically for Stoppard, filled with puns and heavily
ironic. AEH's willingness to "die" for Mo both denies, on the surface, his
erotic desire, through the evasion of "comradeship," and simultaneously
reveals it: one of the secondary meanings of "die" is achieving sexual
orgasm. In yet another sense, however, Housman can be said to have indeed
"died" for Mo, by suppressing his erotic feelings and thus becoming emotionally dead. (The activist slogan "Silence = Death" has a resonance that
extends far beyond simply the AIDS pandemic.) As he later acknowledges in
the play, citing his own "Poem vii" in *Additional Poems*: "He would not stay
for me; and who can wonder? / He would not stay for me to stand and gaze.
/ I shook his hand and tore my heart in sunder / And went with half my life
about my ways" (p. 78).

As a man only "half alive," Housman's denial of Eros is dramatized by
Stoppard through yet another form of character division in the play: the
implicit contrast between Housman and his fellow Oxford undergraduate
and writer Oscar Wilde. Referring to the source of much of Wilde's humor,
the young Housman comments: "It'll be a pity if inversion is all he is
known for" (p. 15). Wilde is indeed best remembered for his "inversion":
linguistically, in his famous epigrams; sexually, in his identification with
"the love that dare not speak its name" ("inversion" was the nineteenth-
century psychiatric term for homosexuality); and, in *The Invention of
Love*, theatrically, in his function as the thematic opposite of Housman –
to use an appropriately classical and poetic metaphor, the antistrophe to
Housman's strophe. Wilde's ghost constantly haunts the margins of
Stoppard's text, his epigrams and exploits repeatedly invoked. Ironically,
Housman is at one point actually taken for Wilde by a comically confused
Jowett: "If you can rid yourself of your levity and your cynicism, and find
another way to dissimulate your Irish provincialism than by making
affected remarks about your blue china and going about in plum-coloured

velvet breeches, which you don't, and cut your hair – you're not him at all, are you?" (p. 22).

The precise extent to which Housman is not Wilde becomes abundantly clear at the very end of the play, when Wilde transforms from the diegetic to the mimetic and finally makes an appearance. Ostensibly a broken man, the postprison Wilde is in all respects the "inversion" of Housman: impecunious, emotionally volatile, disgraced, and reviled. When AEH tries to console him – "I'm very sorry. Your life is a terrible thing" – Wilde replies:

> Better a fallen rocket than never a burst of light . . . Your "honour" is all shame and timidity and compliance . . . I had genius, brilliancy, daring. I took charge of my own myth. I dipped my staff into the comb of wild honey. I tasted forbidden sweetness and drank the stolen waters . . . Where were you when all this was happening? (pp. 96–97)

Where indeed? Wilde's riposte is especially wounding because it reproaches Housman with his own words; Wilde's image of drinking "the stolen waters" is a buried allusion to "Poem xxii" in Housman's *More Poems*: "Ho, everyone that thirsteth / And hath the price to give, / Come to the stolen waters, / Drink and your soul shall live."[29] Housman, however, could only write those words, not live them (and even then only in a poem published posthumously); dying of thirst but terrified to drink, he in effect murdered his soul. As Wilde concludes: "The betrayal of one's friends is a bagatelle in the stakes of love, but the betrayal of oneself is a lifelong regret" (pp. 94–95). In "the invention of love," then, which of them made the better choice?

The answer to that question partly depends on how one interprets the significance of Stoppard's title: *The Invention of Love*, not surprisingly, is a multilayered pun. On the surface, it appears to refer to those Roman poets who, in the first century before Christ, invented the love poem – the substance of much of Housman's classical scholarship and of his own verse. At the end of the play, however, Wilde offers an alternative meaning: "before Plato could describe love, the loved one had to be invented. We would never love anybody if we could see past our invention" (p. 95). And there is, finally, yet another meaning: in addition to inventing the object of our love, the play suggests, we also invent *ourselves* through the act of loving; we "become" on some level whom we love (and, especially, *how* we love). Although the answer to the play's central question is left deliberately open, Stoppard has made his own feelings on the issue very clear. "When Housman died," he commented in a 1998 interview, "he got the memorial service at Trinity and a leading editorial in the *Times*, yet he was the one who failed in life – emotionally, if not intellectually. Though Wilde crashed in flames, and ended as a disgraced, pathetic, maladjusted, poverty-stricken wreck, he had the successful life."[30]

A. E. Housman's death-drenched, darkly melancholic, deeply romanticized poetry has always been ripe for parody. The most wicked takeoff is probably Hugh Kingsmill's poem beginning "What, still alive at twenty-two, / A clean, upstanding chap like you?"[31] Even Stoppard himself cannot resist having a go; in *The Invention of Love*, one character comments of *A Shropshire Lad*: "I never read such a book for telling you you're better off dead . . . No one gets off; if you're not shot, hanged or stabbed, you kill yourself. Life's a curse, love's a blight, God's a blaggard, cherry blossom is quite nice" (p. 86). But the most telling parody, because the most incisive, is Ezra Pound's "Mr. Housman's Message": "O woe, woe, / People are born and die, / We also shall be dead pretty soon / Therefore let us act as if we were dead already."[32] Yes, the world is frequently bleak and painful, and no one gets out of it alive; but why court death before it comes calling? By denying Eros, Housman condemned himself to an emotional imprisonment far more ruinous than Wilde's physical incarceration; by acting "as if [he] were dead already," he never allowed himself truly to live.

In *Arcadia*, erotic love is compared to heat – suddenly ablaze, dangerously seductive, as likely to destroy you as to save you. In *The Invention of Love*, on the other hand, erotic love is compared to ice. When the young Housman complains "I don't know what love is," AEH replies: "Oh, but you do . . . Love, said Sophocles, is like the ice held in the hand by children. A piece of ice held fast in the fist" (p. 43). Ice, as it freezes, sticks to the skin; like love, it hurts when you hold it and it hurts when you pull away. Ice or heat, the end result is almost invariably pain as well as pleasure; yet however painful Eros can be, it is far more painful to consciously will oneself to exist without it. Intellectual passion, Stoppard would be the first to admit, is certainly to be celebrated, but not when purchased at the expense of emotional fulfillment. For what else is there, finally, that reminds us so powerfully that we are alive? In Stoppard's recent film *Shakespeare in Love*, the heroine Viola insists that she must have love in her life: "not the artful postures of love, but love that overthrows life. Unbiddable, ungovernable, like a riot in the heart, and nothing to be done, come ruin or rapture. Love like there has never been in a play."[33] Stoppard's plays of the 1990s, while paradoxically still remaining as intellectually clever, complex, and challenging as ever, dramatize precisely that kind of love; the most cerebral of contemporary playwrights has become, ironically, the foremost romantic dramatist of our time.

NOTES

1 Robert Brustein, "Waiting for Hamlet: *Rosencrantz and Guildenstern Are Dead*," *New Republic*, 4 November 1967, p. 26.

2 Mel Gussow, *Conversations with Stoppard* (London: Nick Hern, 1995), p. 83.

3 Joan Juliet Buck, "Tom Stoppard: Kind Heart and Prickly Mind," *Vogue* (March 1984), p. 454.

4 Randy Gener, "Unstoppered Stoppard," *Village Voice*, 4 April 1995, p. 80.

5 Benedict Nightingale, "A Human Blender Creates an Arcadia," *New York Times*, 19 March 1995, H46.

6 Bryan Appleyard, "So What's it All About, Mr. Stoppard?," *Sunday Times Magazine*, 21 September 1997, p. 2.

7 Tom Stoppard, *The Invention of Love*, revised edn (London and Boston: Faber and Faber, 1998), p. 90.

8 Giles Gordon, "Tom Stoppard," reprinted in Paul Delaney, ed., *Stoppard in Conversation* (Ann Arbor: University of Michigan Press, 1994), p. 17.

9 Gussow, *Conversations with Stoppard*, p. 12.

10 Benedict Nightingale, "Long Haul Back for a Laidback Lad," *The Times*, 26 September 1997, p. 38.

11 David Nathan, "In a Country Garden (if it is a Garden)," reprinted in Delaney, ed., *Stoppard in Conversation*, p. 262.

12 Tom Stoppard, *Arcadia*, revised edn (London and Boston: Faber and Faber, 1993), p. 25. Note, by the way, Stoppard's pointed subversion of a sexist assumption here: it is not the female but the male – Hannah's antagonist Bernard Nightingale – who is portrayed as the romantic.

13 "Heat" as a metaphor of erotic desire is similarly used by Stoppard in both the radio play *In the Native State* (London and Boston: Faber and Faber, 1991) and its revision for the stage, *Indian Ink* (London and Boston: Faber and Faber, 1995), the play's that bookend *Arcadia*. "My poem is about heat" (*ITNS*, p. 2; *II*, p. 11), declares the play's protagonist, poet Flora Crewe, when describing her current project. But its "rasa" (its "juice" or essence), Flora acknowledges, is "[s]ex" (*ITNS*, p. 23; *II*, p. 29).

14 A number of critics have commented on the multilayered significance of the apple in *Arcadia*. See especially Anne Barton, "Twice Around the Grounds," *New York Review of Books*, 8 June 1995, p. 32; and David Guaspari, "Stoppard's *Arcadia*," *Antioch Review*, 54.2 (1996), p. 223.

15 James Gleick, *Chaos: making a new science* (Harmondsworth: Penguin, 1998), pp. 3, 6.

16 Tom Stoppard, *Rosencrantz and Guildenstern Are Dead* (London and Boston: Faber and Faber, 1967), p. 51.

17 Nathan, "In a Country Garden," p. 263.

18 Tom Stoppard, *Hapgood* (London and Boston: Faber and Faber, 1988), p. 72.

19 Housman makes his first (albeit diegetic) appearance in Stoppard's work in *In the Native State*, where one of the characters recalls being taught by him at Cambridge: "When it comes to love, he said, you're either an Ovid man or a Virgil man. *Omnia vincit amor* – that's Virgil – 'Love wins every time, and we give way to love' – *et nos cedamus amori*. Housman was an Ovid man – *et mihi cedet amor* – 'Love gives way to me'" (p. 55). The same speech, with only minor revisions, also appears in *Indian Ink* (p. 46).

20 Alastair Macaulay, "The Man Who Was Two Men," *Financial Times*, 31 October/1 November 1998, p. 31.

21 John Berryman, "Dream Song 205," *The Dream Songs* (New York: Farrar, Straus and Giroux, 1969), p. 224.

22 A E. Housman, "The Name and Nature of Poetry," *Collected Poems and Selected Prose*, ed. Christopher Ricks (Harmondsworth: Penguin, 1989), p. 352.

23 W H. Auden, "A. E. Housman," *Collected Shorter Poems 1927–1957* (London and Boston: Faber, 1966), p. 126.

24 Housman, "Poem xii," *Last Poems*, in Ricks, ed., *Collected Poems and Selected Prose*, p. 109.

25 Richard Percival Graves, *A E. Housman: the scholar-poet* (New York: Scribner's, 1979), p. 230.

26 Peter Conrad, "Thomas the Think Engine," *Observer*, 1 November 1998, p. 5.

27 This is not the first time this particular boat has floated through Stoppard's work: in 1975 Stoppard adapted Jerome's novel, which he has acknowledged as "one of my favourite books," for BBC television. David Gollob and David Roper, "Trad Tom pops in," *Gambit*, 10.37 (1981), p. 13.

28 Housman, "Poem xx," *Additional Poems*, in Ricks, ed., *Collected Poems and Selected Prose*, p. 219.

29 Housman, "Poem xxii," *More Poems*, in Ricks, ed., *Collected Poems and Selected Prose*, p. 168.

30 Conrad, "Thomas the Think Engine," p. 5.

31 Hugh Kingsmill, "Two Poems (After A. E. Housman)," *The Best of Hugh Kingsmill*, ed. Michael Holroyd (New York: Herder, 1971), p. 394.

32 Ezra Pound, "Mr Housman's Message," *Collected Shorter Poems* (London and Boston: Faber, 1968), p. 57.

33 Marc Norman and Tom Stoppard, *Shakespeare in Love* (London and Boston: Faber and Faber, 1999), p. 21 Although Stoppard is not the sole author of this work, anyone familiar with his writing will be able to identify the vast majority of the screenplay's dialogue as unmistakably "Stoppardian."

3
CULTURE AND CONTEXT

12

ENOCH BRATER

Tom Stoppard's Brit/lit/crit

Stoppard's use of the literary past – naming names, mixing and matching time and place and trope, and manhandling familiar quotations – runs the theatrical gamut from farce to parody to show(off)manship to somber intellectual inquiry. As successful productions of his plays have shown, especially when persuasively performed and articulated on the London stage, such territories are rarely, if ever, exclusive. Yet untangling the rich mixture of discourses, a heady allusive style that embraces quick wit, the surprising turn of phrase, and a bit more than a nodding acquaintance with relativity, quantum physics, and the provability (or lack thereof) of Fermat's last theorem, has proved to be both a delight to his audiences and a challenge to dramatic criticism. In this chapter I would like to trace the development of Stoppard's engaging "Brit/lit/crit" as well as consider its implications for the kind of audience that continues to be attracted to his plays.

Rosencrantz and Guildenstern Are Dead, Stoppard's early and spectacular work, already shows the telltale signs of what would quickly become an idiosyncratic and highly eclectic dramatic voice. Let the world take note: Shakespeare's *Hamlet* would never be quite the same again. When the Fringe was still the fringe, two minor characters took center stage and turned the English-speaking theatre's most famous revenge tragedy upside down and inside out. Actors were suddenly hankering to play Rosencrantz and gentle Guildenstern (or is it the the other way around?), roles formerly assigned as consolation prizes for not making it big-time. Philosophically, of course, this retooling of *Hamlet*'s endgame offers its audience no such dumbing-down: death is no longer the "consummation devoutly to be wished," but rather the price you pay for being in the wrong place at the wrong time, then realizing it too late, just when the curtain's about to fall. *To be* is in this unenviable stage situation simply – and fatally – *not to be*, reckoning closed and story ended. "Wham, bam, thank you Sam." That's what happens to a clever undergraduate who has read too much Beckett.

Stoppard relies on an audience who has done precisely that; the hurlyburly will not work unless you are with Stoppard all the way and most of the time, including this first of his very particular excursions into *The Importance of Being Earnest*. Yet for all its literary finery, *Rosencrantz and Guildenstern Are Dead* is essentially parodic; that it is so of both Shakespeare's tragedy *and* the human condition is what brings weight and texture to such an elaborate revisionist display. What you can count on here is that the politics *in* this play and the politics *of* this play are not necessarily trumpeted as the same real thing.

One of the most attractive elements of *Rosencrantz and Guildenstern Are Dead* occurs in the dynamics of performance, when the production efficiently subverts the traditional relationship between background and foreground as it has been generally understood within the western theatre's conventions for the staging of "high" drama. The geography of Stoppard's play will capitalize on this motif in terms of downstage, upstage, and offstage action; and yet it is important to note that such theatrical reversals are prominently featured in this script's textual authority. *Hamlet* is to be staged, as it were, in the distance, one more icon undone, a pale shadow of its former self. What is the point of all these fancy-dress actions that a man might play? Why such strutting and fretting to get in character in the right place in the right scene? Rosencrantz and Guildenstern, this text's not so "indifferent children of the earth" who stand and wait and collaborate, are, by contrast, the observers unwittingly observed. That they have little sense of what is really going on in terms of the politics of the play or the pragmatics of its staging serves to make their dramatic moment all the more hilarious – and compelling. Shakespeare's *Hamlet* is now the play-within-the-play, though this dumb-show will prove to be these passive onlookers' ultimate undoing.

What an odd play Stoppard has written, especially in terms of scenography and *mise-en-scène*. And it is here that Beckett's influence is most chillingly apparent. Apart from the pirate ship, which is straight out of Gilbert and Sullivan – more real, of course, because only cunningly imagined in Shakespeare – the landscape for this play is mostly a lighting job, stark and atmospheric, a minimalist's *Waiting for Godot* minus rock and tree. No more court scenes, graveyards, or ghostly apparitions. Stoppard is relying on his audience to fill in the blanks.

Too clever by half, those absences tell us a lot, and they will do so on several complementary levels. What happens on the level of stagecraft also happens on the level of this play's reinvented dialogue. By no means constrained by the "prison-house" of *Hamlet*'s iambic pentameter ("full," as Iago says, "of bombast circumstance"), Stoppard will refashion lines from *The Importance of Being Earnest* and *Waiting for Godot* as well. He does so in order to meet his characters' pressing need for "words, words" as they attempt to hold the stage with ever-diminishing authority. When Rosencrantz and Guildenstern quote, but more often misquote, from Wilde and Beckett, do they realize that they are doing so? Probably not (in performance that would be fatal), but the audience does. Profiling the inherited language of the English-speaking stage with uncanny assurance, Stoppard makes *his* onlookers, no longer passive, hear his richly allusive new line at the same time that they overhear its simulacrum, a k a the original. Here tantalizing sources – Beckett's Winnie will memorialize them as "what are those wonderful lines?" in *Happy Days* – are energized as precious resources, and in both senses of the word. Purists beware. Dramatic *bon mots* are now set in unexpected, even ironic motion. This can work in one of two ways. With Wilde, Stoppard likes to burrow into the line to reposition it, to out, then out-wit the epigram, so to speak. But with Beckett, Stoppard's excavations are at once more formal and precise. In the shape of Ros and Guil's dialogue encounters, we are meant to overhear what every drama critic knows, the always missing, return-the-ball-once-in-a-way verbal misadventures of Didi and Gogo as they wait, this time *in earnest*, for a Godot who never comes.

What does the exploitation of such an intellectual – and talky – technique tell us about the audience Stoppard is writing for? First and foremost, that it is literate in precisely the same way that shares and appreciates and above all recognizes his telling points of reference. Stoppard's vocabulary in *Rosencrantz and Guildenstern Are Dead* is nothing if not conventionally dramatic; it is hard to imagine an audience for this play that has not previously overdosed itself, at the very least, on *Hamlet*, *Waiting for Godot*, and *The Importance of Being Earnest*. This is drama for the A-level and AP-English crowd. And though it may not be politically correct to say so, this is also the same audience that knows this traditional canon backwards and forwards (and in this case preferably backwards). For Stoppard is counting on an audience more than a little predisposed to playing with what it has already seen on mainstream stages before. Placing a high gloss on sixties' irreverence, the play Stoppard initiates can be found in the play of ideas, especially as represented in those plays that have come before.

Although it is possible, even tempting, to read *Rosencrantz and Guildenstern Are Dead* for a consistent existentialist narrative – "unaccommodated man" once more cut short by an indifferent, meaningless universe which he fails to comprehend – the play's sheer delight in extravagant minimalism belies such a tough philosophical through-line. *Rosencrantz and Guildenstern Are Dead* is very much a young man's play, part of whose attractiveness is the exuberant playwright's wink and the receptive audience's nod. We've all read the same texts and we're all "in" on this together, even and especially when the joke is on us.

In *Travesties* Stoppard works his way through a similar paradigm, though in this case the assumptions he makes about this play's audience are perhaps even more circumscribed. In this true history that never happened, at least in the way this show tells it, Stoppard imagines a Switzerland of 1917/18 where the busy lives of Joyce, Lenin, and Tristan Tzara intersect at the very moment when the British Consulate is staging an amateur theatrical version of *The Importance of Being Earnest*. That James Joyce briefly served in Zurich as business manager for the English Players is the only verifiable data Stoppard needs to set this kaleidoscope going; the rest is – how shall we say? – pure dramatic license. The fulcrum for so much "play," however, is the minor functionary Henry Carr; and it is through his memory ("not with entire accuracy") that *Travesties*' scenes unfold and refold. Carr is the embodiment of middle-class, establishment England, well-meaning, well-dressed, and well-spoken, self-satisfied but blissfully unaware and incompetent. While the Great War rages all around him, Carr remains "especially interested in the cut of his trousers." Manners before morals.

Just as the Eng/lit/Anglo tradition colonizes the great Irish writers Joyce, Beckett, and Wilde, only to teach them and recreate them in its own image, *Travesties* appropriates the continental figures of Lenin and Tzara for the light they specifically do not shed on Carr's memory and its fractured parts, those fluid scenes staged before us with ever-increasing idiosyncracy. The Russian Lenin, the Irish Joyce, and the French/Romanian Tzara we meet in retrospect are the projections of British, good-old-boy Henry Carr; but as his wife, the Old Cecily, patently warns him at close of play, where she serves as an eleventh-hour *aide-mémoire*, he seems to have got most of it all wrong. She knows a *red*-herring when she sees one. This Cecily (not, it must be emphasized, to be confused with Wilde's ingenue of the same name) may be a "pedant" and a termagant wife, but at least it isn't she who has made a bollix of artistic life and a travesty of twentieth-century political history.

If in *Travesties* Stoppard emerges as farceur extraordinaire, he nonetheless relies on his audience to stabilize the many dislocations that bring so much theatricality to this work. Paring his fingernails and striving for perfection, Joyce is the artist's artist, just as Lenin is the revolutionary's revolutionary. Tzara represents the anti-everything, the Dada sensibility in all its provocative extremis. "Da, da," echoes Lenin, though his incomprehension of Dada's intent may very well be matched by Stoppard's Anglo-American audience, for whom Tzara remains, at best, a shadowy twenties figure of the Paris avant-garde. Stoppard's audience must know, too, the historical significance of Lenin's daring train ride back to Russia; what to make of antiartists like Marcel Janco and Hans Arp; and remember enough about the tea-service scene between Gwendolyn and Cecily in *The Importance of Being*

Earnest to get the point and punch of its parody to the tune of "Mr. Gallagher and Mr. Shean." And that is just for starters. As might be expected, Stoppard will save his most trenchant parting-shot until the end of the play. If, in Wilde's original, the comedy concludes with the English theatre's most famous curtain line, when the hero, admonished, reports what he has learned from the long journey that is Wilde's play, the importance, finally, of being earnest, Stoppard builds to a similar climax when Carr abruptly states that he has learned no fewer than three things. Only in Stoppard's case Carr cannot remember what that third thing is. *Curtain*. The characters in *Travesties* are in the play for their intellectual, not their emotional weight. The playwright uses his literary sources accordingly. Like Shaw, Stoppard aims for a presentational, not a representational style, one in which the conflict is arranged in the thrust and parry of ideas.

Everything changes in *The Real Thing*. When this play makes use of the literary past, it does so to support or enhance its characters' complex emotional states. Shakespeare, John Webster, and John Keats are on hand, but they are now here to take the measure of the human heart. Such a major shift in tone has an effect on almost every element of Stoppard's drama, but most particularly in terms of characterization, psychological motivation, and the evocative use of literary allusion.

That the central figure in *The Real Thing* is a writer – and a playwright to boot – goes a long way in explaining the wide frame of reference Stoppard allows himself in this work. But when the curtain goes up on *The Real Thing*, Stoppard is far more concerned with illusion than allusion. It is not until well into the second scene that we realize that the first has not been "real" at all, just the final act in a performance of a West End play by the same fictive dramatist – one, moreover, in which his "real" wife takes the role of quondam lover. The play-within-the-play has been full of deception; reality follows from there, as frail as any make-believe house of cards.

The Real Thing features another Henry, this one the playwright who loves words even more than Motown. In the course of this play he will learn that they conceal as much as they reveal, though before he does so he will be forced to recognize their full and painful potential for irony, self-deception, and intrigue. Stoppard risks a great deal with this piece, for it is an emotional cavalcade, not an intellectual one, that is on display here. Theatre is more than metaphor: when two characters rehearse the lines assigned to them for a forthcoming Glasgow production of *'Tis Pity She's a Whore*, Ford's dialogue only thinly disguises their own mounting passion. Henry remembers a verse from "On First Looking into Chapman's Homer," though Keats yields only cold comfort here. To his sexually active daughter he quotes from

9 A scene from the Strand Theatre 1982 production of *The Real Thing* – Felicity Kendal (Annie) and Roger Rees (Henry).

Hamlet, but these lines fall on indifferent, even skeptical ears. Later the same Shakespeare turns gruesome: it will be Henry, like Rosencrantz and Guildenstern, who will be "hoist" on his own "petard." That duplicity worked on wife number one will come back to haunt him in the shape of wife number two.

As originally played in London by Roger Rees in 1982, Henry's vulnerability was all the more poignant because of the actor's persuasive understatement. Rees's intellectual approach to the role powerfully read the cues for the play's strong emotional pull; under Peter Wood's direction his Henry was always on the edge where subtext meets text. David Leveaux's 1999 London revival at the Donmar Warehouse was more intimate; Stephen Dillane's spry athleticism more convincingly revealed the sexual kineticism that lies at the heart of this play and damns Stoppard's characters to their fiery *ronde*. "To marry one actress is unfortunate, to marry two is simply asking for it." This time the echo from *The Importance of Being Earnest*, a telling paraphrase of Lady Bracknell's famous line, rings true in a way Stoppard would never have risked before. The emotional stakes are high.

The safety and security of a literary past, once so unwittingly useful to Stoppard's characters in keeping up their guard, has suddenly turned fickle; it now frames stage presence in an unexpected way, cauterizing it, ironically, with its own volatility.

Arcadia, a rich and ambitious play that ranges widely over complex emotional and intellectual territory, can only be partially understood in terms of the way Stoppard has dressed his stage before. In this play the literary past deliberately invades and colors the present, and vice versa, as the garden historian Hannah Jarvis and the self-styled "Media Don," designer-critic Bernard Nightingale, duke-it-out. What happened at a large country house in Derbyshire during a visit Lord Byron abruptly cut short in April 1809? Jarvis longs for some romantic tie-in; Nightingale wants a headline: "Even in Arcadia – Sex, Literature and Death in Sidley Park / Byron Fought Fatal Duel, Says Don."

In *Arcadia* time rarely stands still, even when Stoppard's characters go to enormous lengths to structure and stabilize it, depending on the limitations of their own sensibilities and their need to seize the day. Byron never appears. The play opens instead on what looks like an early nineteenth-century costume drama, the deceptively simple setting of a makeshift study on the garden front of a great house in England's green and pleasant land. Thomasina Coverly, precocious and pubescent, is struggling over a mathematics primer while her dashing young tutor, Septimus Hodge, ponders in dismay the brand new quarto edition of someone else's lame verse, a vanity production called "The Conch of Eros." His own work is kept in place by Plautus, a tortoise resurrected, literally, from Stoppard's *Jumpers* and this time "sleepy enough to serve as a paperweight." The characters may be dressed like turn-of-the-century Romantics, but their talk of private lives and "carnal knowledge" makes it sound as though we have mistakenly walked into a no-nonsense drawing-room comedy by Noël Coward.

Thus begins the first of this play's many dislocations. Stoppard counts on an audience savvy enough to know that onstage things are never *then* and *now* but always and enigmatically *there*, ". . . till there's no time left." Time past and time present can "happen" not only between the scenes but also and primarily within them. Late in the play, "past" and "present" will be staged simultaneously and within the same scene, *á la* Alan Ayckbourn, as Stoppard's characters literally dance to the music of time. Real time, like stage time, will not stand still: "That's what time means," Valentine tells a mystified Hannah Jarvis in the final moments of *Arcadia* – especially in the hands of a dramatist willing to play a game of chance with temporality. In *Arcadia* Stoppard's time signatures are bound to vary, for what takes place in the foreground of this play's scenic action is everywhere supported by the heavy historical drama taking place in the background, right outside the stately windows of Sidley Park.

Stoppard sets his *Arcadia* at the very disruptive moment when the classsical sensibility is about to be overwhelmed by the romantic. The *zeitgeist* is unhinged. Septimus Hodge is a Byronic *confrère* who looks and plays the part (most especially so in Rufus Sewell's bravura performance of the role in Trevor Nunn's 1993 production for the Royal National Theatre). And as he does so, Capability Brown's idealized landscape, full of *faux* temples, architectonic fountains, and artificial lakes is slated for destruction, all 500 acres of it. How vainly men themselves amaze; Andrew Marvell would be scandalized ("How could such sweet and wholsome Hours / Be reckon'd but with herbs and flow'rs!"). Plans are afoot for a revamped garden, this one "picturesque," fashionable, and Gothic, complete with resident hermit. All the while the restless Thomasina (Nunn's luminous Emma Fielding), who ages in this play all the way from thirteen to "sixteen years and eleven months . . . and three weeks," is working on a major breakthrough of her own, this one all but strictly mathematical. Only in her case it will take something like another 180 years for someone to appreciate the cutting-edge work she has done: new equations that explain "the actions of bodies in heat."

Is there death in this Arcadia? If so, the early nineteenth-century inhabitants of Sidley Park, hell-bent on "satisfaction," sexual as well as honorific, seem blissfully unaware of it. As they go about the play's business of writing poems, learning their maths, criticizing the literary critics, planning assignations in offstage gazebos, or unexplainably running off to the Levant, Time surreptitiously assigns them forever to their harsh and unpredictable fates. Byron will die in Greece only fifteen years later, three months after he had passed his thirty-sixth birthday. More poignantly, the young Thomasina will die long before she reaches her prime, unmarried, unloved, and unheralded.

The characters we meet in Sidley Park's present, despite their personal computers, will not fare much better, though they, too, hardly know it. Limited by their time, their place, and their petty ambition, their fate is to know only a small part of that enormity that is the truth. What really happened at Sidley Park in 1809 will elude them, even as these researchers (originally played in London by Bill Nighy and Felicity Kendall) struggle to make sense of the props and properties this play renders so melodramatically as kernels of enticing evidence. "Septimus with Plautus," sighs Hannah as she opens the folio containing Thomasina's drawing. "I was looking for that." Gus, Augustus Coverly's modern-day namesake, offers this prize as an ultimate love token, though Hannah has her eye on another sort of prey. Nightingale, whose name hoists both Keats and the London drama critic for

The Times on their own very different petards, deconstructs the past without ever considering the virtue or the wonder or the sheer impossibility of reconstructing it. A David Lodge academic if there ever was one, this brash trendenista spends most of his time in *Arcadia* in two sorts of play: one with the lively and available Chloë Coverly, the other with himself, as he imagines – or as he might say, fetishizes – a stunning press release. Unbeknownst to them, however, the characters of "today" are all the while replaying an updated version of what really took place in Derbyshire on that fateful April day in 1809. The mathematical genius of the present, the young Valentine, perhaps comes closest to this truth, at least theoretically; yet even he goes after Thomasina's lost algorithm backwards.

In *Arcadia* Stoppard is working with a full palette, only part of which his characters come to understand. Stoppard's audience, on the other hand, is sited in a far more privileged position, one that allows them to capitalize, if they can, on both the histrionics and the historicity of the moment. In this challenging play, the emotional complexity may be more difficult to unravel than any of the intellectual puzzles, and yet the play's structure presupposes a dramatic world in which one is always the gateway to the other. The drama of time and place laid out before us with so much formal control is once more invigorated by a liberating use of a shared literary past. In *Arcadia*, however, the result is something much more profound than the recovery of the subterfuge hidden in every reworking or rewording of the past. For in this play Stoppard moves us from paraphrase to paradox.

Oscar Wilde finally makes a long overdue appearance in the Stoppard repertory, but when he does so in *The Invention of Love* he is assigned to a background, cameo role. Center stage goes instead to a quite different literary figure, the English poet A. E. Housman. Wilde, who likes to have the last word but in this play doesn't, merely passes by on the river of time that connects the Oxford of Housman's past to the mythological Styx, as Charon reverentially ferries the author of *A Shropshire Lad* to his final resting place in Hades. The play's narrative makes clear that the underworld journey is in this case entirely appropriate. For Housman in his day was also a famous, if controversial, figure in the British school of Latin and Greek studies; and it is perhaps on the level of classical allusion that Stoppard's manipulation of stage time most keenly affects the emotional center of the play.

Although this work brings together other key players from Oxford's illustrious literary past, including John Ruskin, Walter Pater, and the great Balliol classicist Benjamin Jowett, all of whom we meet in the busy first act, it will be the 41-year-old Wilde who appears in the second who serves as Housman's unlikely *doppelgänger*. His personality shadows Housman, aged from eighteen to twenty-six, played by one actor, just as his presence haunts AEH, aged seventy-seven, played by another (Paul Rhys and John Wood in Richard Eyre's 1997 premiere at the Royal National Theatre). Just as Oscar celebrates his sexuality by literalizing in his own flamboyant way the ardent gospel of Pater's Aesthetic movement, so Housman idealizes his grand, unrequited passion for Moses Jackson by sublimating it in poetry and classical scholarship. Each in his own way has invented "love."

Played in counterpoint, each "invention" has its consequences. In Wilde's case, Stoppard assumes his audience knows what those are, the public humiliation and betrayal dramatized, for example, in two contemporary plays, Moises Kaufman's *Gross Indecency: the three trials of Oscar Wilde* and David Hare's *The Judas Kiss* (both 1998). Yet the construction of A. E. Housman's love, however cerebral and, strictly speaking, from the waist up, may be in the final analysis even more affecting, based as it is on a fatal misreading of a classical myth. Housman should know better; but as we have seen in Stoppard's plays before, there is no accounting for hormones. Poet that he is, he cannot help but overestimate the power of his own song to undo death and rescue love. He forgets that Orpheus succeeds in passing into Hades not by seducing the ferryman, Charon, with his music, but by inadvertently putting him to sleep. Orpheus may sing the praises of his own song as a law unto itself, but he fails to take its proper measure. His evocation of music's seductive powers insists on its absolute supremacy; yet when he looks back, violating the edict not to, he condemns Eurydice to death. This is Orpheus' tragedy, as it is Housman's: not that his powers fail, but that in such self-absorbed form, they cannot succeed. Orpheus imagines an absolute freedom in song that can finally contain love; in the end, like Housman, he loses both.[1]

Stoppard's maturity as a writer, from the theatricality of *Rosencrantz and Guildenstern are Dead* to the somber reflectiveness of *The Invention of Love*, relies on the transformative power of the stage to reinvent and reimagine a past. Clever, witty, irreverent, and above all acrobatic, his best stage effects depend on an audience "there" to meet him (at least) half way. "The show must . . .," as his screenplay for *Shakespeare in Love* splices it, "Go on." Such a cultured and culturally driven "Brit/lit/crit" will not work for slackers. Just how specialized, then, is Stoppard's audience? Look around you the next time you go to the theatre; then decide for yourself whether or not it is full of an intelligentsia (not necessarily effete), the fellow Stoppardian time-travelers we recognize in ourselves.

NOTE

1 See Edward Rothstein, "Even for Death's Escapees, the Myth Says, There Are Rules," *New York Times*, July 19, 1999, p. 23.

13

MICHAEL VANDEN HEUVEL

"Is postmodernism?": Stoppard among/against the postmoderns

A. Tom Stoppard is a postmodernist; and
B. Tom Stoppard refutes postmodernism.
These two things are one.

In my epigram I adopt Wallace Stevens's opening gambit from "Connoisseur of Chaos" for two reasons (which may be one). First, it is necessary to drive home the point early that Stoppard and his plays will frustrate any attempt to impose an either/or logic in terms of their relationships to postmodern ideas and aesthetics. "None of us is classifiable," Stoppard once told David Nathan. "Even the facility to perceive and define two ideas such as classical and romantic in opposition to each other indicates that one shares a little bit of each."[1] The comment was made in the specific context of elucidating *Arcadia* (and this provides the second reason for invoking Stevens's chaotic connoisseur) but Stoppard's work in general, and his relationship to postmodernism in particular, is increasingly informed by this notion, which reaches its fullest expression in his 1993 masterpiece.

Thus, the split/doubled title of this chapter indicates that Stoppard expresses keen interest in certain intellectual, aesthetic, and ideological positions associated with postmodern art and drama, while he is at the same time antipathetic to, and even staunchly critical of, some of the more radical notions and claims of postmodern social theory and its image of the human subject. Stoppard does not, then, fully inhabit the postmodern terrain, but he often travels there and traverses it, speaking the language of the region faultlessly even as he stops occasionally to arraign it with deadpan irony or wit. As he investigates such postmodern issues as the death of the author, the loss of sustaining cultural narratives, the waywardness of language, and the fragmented nature of identity, Stoppard nevertheless exhibits a critical distance and negative capability toward the social, cultural, and aesthetic theories that constitute the loosely confederated discourse of postmodernism. This duality presents both advantages and drawbacks. On the one hand, in accordance with postmodern theory's distrust of totalizing worldviews and conceptual schemes, Stoppard's well-known love of paradox and irreconcilable antinomies ("Paradox and tautology. They don't have to mean anything, lead anywhere, be part of anything else. I just like them. I've got an unhealthy love affair for them"[2]), would seem to nominate his plays as the perfect vehicle for postmodern doubt and "undecidability." In this regard, we might think of Stoppard as exemplifying what Jean Baudrillard refers to as the position of the postmodern subject as "the switching center for all the nodes of culture."

For this reason and others, Stoppard is often mentioned (usually rather casually) in lists of postmodern writers or dramatists,[3] even though he disavows the title. By virtue simply of being a "high" literary stylist, he in many ways would seem a poor example of the prototypical multimedia, cross-genre postmodern performance artist, or of the literary equivalent of a shaman of popular culture. However, building on my title's paraphrase of George Moore's first speech in *Jumpers*, ("Is God?"), I would suggest that, like the dotty professor, we for the moment "leave a space" in regard to the question of Stoppard's stature as a postmodern writer. This is necessary because, for all the Shavian intellectual insouciance Stoppard musters in his plays, the strategy may finally only recuperate what are after all fairly conservative, high-modernist notions regarding contemporary politics, culture, and aesthetics. Here too, one could argue that this actually elevates Stoppard into the pantheon of postmodern artists, for as we shall see, postmodernism has always expressed a reactionary bent in the midst of even its most radical and disorienting theories. But if we conceive of postmodernism as more than a pastiche of modernist styles commenting self-consciously on the artifice of art and life – and I believe it to be so – then we must account for Stoppard's purposes in mimicking postmodern ideas and styles. For now, in regard to Stoppard's investigation of postmodern uncertainty and undecidability, it may suffice to remember James M. Harding's remark that "instability and insecurity are the parents of presumption" who tend to breed offspring mostly capable of "reasserting habitual assumptions."[4] What Harding calls the "comfortable subversions" of nominally postmodern theatre artists (his example is Caryl Churchill) implicate Stoppard, and postmodernism in general, in the debate over whether the postmodern marks a radical reconfiguration of modernism's avant-garde agendas, or whether it simply mimics this subversive discourse to commodify it as *gauchiste* theory that legitimizes the impossibility of reconstructing radical politics and cultural activities. As John Bull argues compellingly (in this volume and in his book *Stage Right*), the collapse of distinctions between mainstream and avant-garde art has seemingly benefited the evolution of the former much more so than the latter, and Stoppard's part in this act of recuperation is central to understanding his complex relation to postmodernism.

"What, then, is postmodernism?" Jean-François Lyotard asked famously and rhetorically in his "The Postmodern Condition: a report on knowledge." Since then, there has been no end of speculation but little consensus as to the meaning or usefulness of the term. However, this must not necessarily lead one to conclude that postmodernism represents, in the words of Stephen Watt, "the bankrupt logic of an empty marker."[5] Lyotard characterized post-modernism itself as coming out of a context of "dissensus," and we can at least agree that the fault lines that differentiate the many positions put forth to theorize the changing global dynamics and cultural and aesthetic practices under the abstract rubric "postmodern" are as complex and meaningful as the common ground on which they are gathered. It is often pointed out, in fact, that the lack of an overarching theory or model of postmodernism that goes unchallenged or which maintains totalizing status is, paradoxically, proof that we live in a postmodern condition of fragments and partial narratives.

Still, one's first confrontation with the dizzying array of postmodernism's institutional histories and developments, philosophical foundations, and its endless archive of cultural and aesthetic practices, is bound to be disorienting.[6] Critics refer to some forms of postmodernism as politically progressive, as opposed to reactionary; mainly aesthetic and formal, as opposed to cultural and activist; aesthetically minimalist, as opposed to spectacularly exuberant; neocolonial and patriarchal, as opposed to postcolonial and postfeminist; as an assertion of boundaries, as opposed to an attempt to transgress and render permeable all borders; and as an extension of a minority, avant-garde culture with its roots in aesthetic modernism, as opposed to a "cultural logic" with a scope as wide as late capitalism itself.

These differences emerge primarily as a function of postmodernism's interdisciplinary scope and breadth. As postmodern social theories interpenetrate cultural theories and activities, and as both inflect postmodern aesthetic practices, these then turn in different ways against the traditions they seek to subvert or deconstruct.[7] Because postmodernism attempts to explode the boundaries between various academic disciplines – social theory, anthropology, ethnography, economics, aesthetics, psychology and even the sciences – such cross-fertilization has been at times healthy, but at other points has occasioned bitter disagreements and some aggressive critiques among academic theorists of postmodernity (most notoriously perhaps Jean Baudrillard's *Forget Foucault*), policy mavens, and the western punditocracy. These differences, in turn, have been presented by the media to mainstream culture as something approaching the battle of ancients and moderns, to the point where it has become commonplace to assume that postmodernism itself describes simply the internecine squabbling of arch-theorists and their graduate student minions. But the earliest formulations of postmodern aesthetics, which came out of architecture, stressed practices of pluralism, hybridity, and "ad-hocism" as the defining feature of the period following the decline of a unified modernist aesthetics. Key to their use of these terms was the provocative notion that such odd blendings of traditional and non- or even anti-traditional styles would not be compelled to operate under a logic of synthesis or proportionality – that one could produce meaningful and expressive forms through a playful and complex mingling of apparently mutually exclusive idioms, none of which was privileged over all others.[8] Even in its latest manifestations, postmodernism is certainly polyglot, but is not thereby incoherent.

Stoppard's mixed response to postmodernism thus may derive, in great part, from the fractured nature of postmodern culture and theory themselves. First, it is generally recognized that the postmodern refers not only to cultural practices and the development of new aesthetic and expressive forms but also to emerging forms of social organization growing out of late capitalism. Like many artists operating within these conditions, Stoppard tends to be more enticed by aesthetic postmodernism than by any wholesale allegiance or antipathy to the economic and social order in which it is grounded. Nevertheless, it would be a mistake to set his plays distinctly apart from their context, as his work resonates with the changing global dynamics effected by new technologies and postcolonial and post-Cold War politics. The socioeconomic context of late capitalism, in which industrial production is displaced by the eminence of information and media technology, and national and statist structures give way to global corporate affiliations and their more open and accelerated movement of capital, has resulted in a radical reconfiguration (although not a complete overturning) of former means of accumulating wealth and power.[9] "Circulation" replaces "concentration" and "consumption" in terms of market strategies, as for example when the worldwide release of films such as the 1999 *Star Wars* "prequel" becomes so thoroughly articulated within product and service tie-ins (fast food outlets, children's toys, game and talk shows, sitcoms, and so on) that it becomes increasingly difficult to see the art product itself as the "center of gravity" within the universe of signs and products it generates. As such decentered markets become more integrated by advanced communication technologies and software, the notion of a core state or national corporation dictating policy and trade is replaced by metaphors of integrated circuits, webs, and systems in which sudden small changes in a single element can cause widespread responses in the loose-knit structure as a whole.

Although postmodernism is often perceived as emanating from the rarefied atmosphere of French and American academies, it is important to remember that both cultural and aesthetic postmodernism are intimately linked to these changing socioeconomic conditions, and that Stoppard as an individual writer is as susceptible to their effects as anyone else. His fascination with contestatory ideas that engage, contradict, and clash without resolving the issues they bring to bear into a stable and totalizing synthesis emerges from postmodernism's central theoretical tenet, that is, the notion of "textuality" and the instability of the sign in general. The notion is first proclaimed in semiotic terms by Barthes in his transition from structuralist thought (in which signifiers – that is, any figurative, gestural, or aural "mark" that stands in for something else – enjoy a relatively stable signifying relation to their referents by virtue of socially generated and maintained systems of codes and structures) to the poststructuralist acceptance of the inherent unsteadiness between signs and the things they name, and the subsequent destabilizing of the sign into what Jacques Derrida would term the *trace* or *différance*. As John Carlos Rowe succinctly summarizes the process:

> The relationship of signifier to signified was revised by Derrida to the irreducible *différance* of signifiers, so that the conceptual or intellectual reference of any speech act was understandable only as the repression or condensation of a potentially endless chain of signifiers. Thus "ideas" and "concepts" had to be reinterpreted as "compositions" of signifiers, and the analytical procedures established by philosophers (especially in the Anglo-American tradition) for understanding complex ideas were transformed at a stroke into rhetorical strategies.[10]

With all forms of human discourse relegated to the level of signifying practice, and with the notion that signification itself will always produce texts incapable of locking on to a "transcendental signfied," or authoritative meaning, the stage was literally set for a rhetorician of Stoppard's rank to produce plays in which meanings are stated, countered, and cross-countered in a dizzying display of linguistic and philosophical paradox. Although little evidence points to the direct influence of post-structuralist theory on Stoppard's plays, this essentially formalist interest in the operations of texts and the means by which they circulate multiple meaning and interpretations has always been of interest to Stoppard. From Rozencrantz and Guildenstern's inability to divine their meaning or place in the text of *Hamlet*, to the skeptical interrogation of visual veracity "after Magritte," to the slippages between textual and lived reality in *The Real Thing* and on to the raucous debates concerning the source of artistic meaning and value in *Travesties*, Stoppard has relentlessly pursued themes relevant to postmodernism's obsession with textual openness and the free(wheeling) play of signification or meaning.

Yet such notions of signs, identities, and meanings in constant circulation and consumption only emerge in concentrated form in the context of late capitalism, and there seems now to be general agreement that postmodernism, as a generic term, must necessarily include the Marxist critic Frederic Jameson's articulation of it as a historical rupture and a "periodizing concept."[11] Stoppard, it seems fair to say, is very much a writer of the late (or "consumer") capitalist phase of history, and some attempts have been made to explain how his plays are "determined" by postmodern means of production.[12] Yet the equation is not so simple, and bears further scrutiny. For instance, even as his plays may mimic the helter-skelter flow of capital, images, and signs that characterize late capitalism, Stoppard is also well situated to analyze and critique such conditions and the effects they produce, because, as many postmodern critics have pointed out, late capitalism and its fetishization of information, signs, and the circulation of images has rendered the contemporary world inherently "theatrical." With postmodernism's claims that foundational meanings and truth are a function of language games and social and cultural practices, the stage is set for a culture of competing and circulating interpretations, each staged with an eye toward gaining its own "audience share." Stoppard, eminently a man of the theatre, has shown a unique capacity to capture this "society of the spectacle" within forms of hypertheatricality that manage both to explicate and to critique the postmodern moment.

Looking at Stoppard's plays may not, then, help one decide if he "is" a postmodern writer or not, but it can reveal a good deal about postmodernity itself: its contours, limits, and its power to affect and alter cultural and aesthetic practice. His work is a record of an artist testing postmodernism's most provocative propositions with keen critical intellect and dialectical skill, pushing his plots, characters, and dialogue toward a thorough investigation of postmodernism's theories of social organization (the breaking down of East/West binaries in *Hapgood* and the dynamics of postcolonial interactions in *In the Native State* and *Indian Ink*), its cultural activities (as practiced by academic philosophers in *Jumpers*, avant-garde artists in *Travesties*, scientists and literary critics in *Hapgood* and *Arcadia*), its modes of knowing and its model of human epistemology and subjectivity in an age of anti-rationalism and uncertainty (*After Magritte*, *The Real Thing*). Few dramatists have addressed with greater rigor and with more expressive theatricality the entire compass of issues that constitute the postmodern terrain, and those catchphrases which now so easily seem to capture the spirit (if not always the scope and depth) of postmodern critique and theory – from Jean-

François Lyotard's eulogy on the death of metanarrative and Roland Barthes's on the "death of the author," to Jameson's definition of postmodern pastiche as "blank irony," to the theoretical extensions of romantic *schauspiel* or "play" (Deleuze and Guattari's schizoanalysis and rhizomatics, Lyotard's gaming and differends, Baudrillard's hyperreality and Judith Butler's performativity), and to the general crisis over representation and its ideological effects – are treated, zestfully and with a trademark mixture of empathy and skepticism, in Stoppard's work. And yet, despite his playing with "play," Stoppard is a deadly serious moral writer unwilling to give himself completely over to the very ideas about which he writes so compellingly.

Stoppard, then, finds himself paradoxically but not unreasonably upholding a kind of humanized postmodernism (or postmodernized humanism). His success at capturing the imagination of the western theatregoing public owes as much to this moderate position between the extremes of the so-called "crises in the humanities" debates as it does to his talent for dialogue. These imbroglios revolve around the attacks launched by traditionalists against postmodernist critiques of modernity, liberalism, nationalism, and their conceptions of subjectivity, and have often been spun in the popular press to indicate that no middle ground exists between postmodern theory and the humanist doctrines they seek to deconstruct. But Stoppard is living and theatrical proof that humanism and postmodernism, like classicism and romanticism, may never exist exclusively at odds with one another: that they, in fact, constitute and animate one another, each "shar[ing] a little bit of each." In fact, one might say that Stoppard has essentially made his career as playwright by having it both ways. He is self-admittedly a "conservative by temperament" who believes that social and cultural evolution "is far too fast" and who convinced at least one interviewer that he was "a somewhat defensive Thatcherite":[13] and so one searches in vain for utopian pronouncements of a coming "third way" or "paradigm shift" to which the name postmodern may be given, especially when that portends an end to modernity's basic humanist and liberal values. Neither does Stoppard express the more stereotypical postmodern future of a dystopian, Baudrillardian "precession of simulacra" producing a "hyperreality" in which the real comes to adopt merely a hallucinatory resemblance to itself. In formal terms, too, his plays are generations removed from the improvisationally based work of such postmodern collectives as the Wooster Group or Pina Bausch's Tanztheater, and one will not find in Stoppard's plays the sustained surrealistic dreamscapes of a Robert Wilson, Suzan-Lori Parks, or John Jeserun. Despite forays into polyglot dialogue in which discourses interrupt, mix with, and alter one another, Stoppard's characters do not speak in the same postmodern babble of tongues as Parks's, nor the pulverized narratives of Heiner Müller or the *mestiza*-speak of the inhabitants of Guillermo Gomez-Pèña's New World Border. The inhabitants of his dramatic world, Stoppard once said, "appear to have been brought up in the same house, have gone to the same school, and have lived together for years before they were released into my plays, so they all have each other's speech rhythms and vocabularies."[14]

The question then becomes, if Stoppard does not walk like or talk like one, is he in fact a postmodernist? Perhaps in order to understand Stoppard's use and abuse of postmodernism, it is necessary to locate which aspects of postmodern society, theory, and aesthetics have caught his attention to the degree that he confronts them, in distinctly postmodern idioms, in order to work through them back to more traditional assumptions and beliefs. A useful model of such an approach is provided by Steven Connor in an essay on "Postmodern Performance," which can be extended to Stoppard's work in addition to *Travesties*, the play Connor takes as his case study for elucidating "some of the problems involved in illustrating the nature of postmodern performance."[15] After noting that a procedure common to Stoppard's plays is to "take closed and self-sufficient worlds and cause them to break in on each other," Connor argues that this activity renders the logic of world systems or structures "arbitrary" (p. 109). Stoppard achieves this sense of indeterminacy via means easily recognizable through the lenses of various postmodern theories. First, the formal structure of *Travesties* is that of postmodern pastiche as it is defined by Jameson; that is, it incorporates a number of potentially contestatory cultural narratives (having to do with high and low culture, the relations between art and society and art and politics) but reduces these conflicts to pure spectacle, unhinged from actual historical referents and devoid of modernist anxiety and overt critical stance toward such mutually antagonistic viewpoints. While virtually every character in the play is happy to spout, recite, or proclaim a manifesto regarding the proper relation of art to politics, none of these absolutely closes off the possibility of the others. The play thus produces a sense of what Jameson calls "hyperspace," a disorienting but not necessary debilitating map of ideas existing without a center of gravity or absolute cartographical code. Interpretation, as Derrida would say, is thus deferred and rendered as a continuous state of difference. As I have argued elsewhere, Stoppard's use of the memory-impaired Henry Carr as the slightly demented compère produces an aporia or lack of narrative/authorial presence in the play in which Carr can be present only to his surrogated memories, rather than to the historical facts of events in Zurich during World War One.[16] For Jameson, this might mean that the play indulges in "blank irony," by which he means the characteristic use of modernist aesthetic experiments in such a way that they are emptied of their power to critique existing social and aesthetic practices. Such insipid ironies, Jameson might argue, prohibit the play from capturing and addressing critically the history of the war and some of modernism's artistic practices (Wildean Art for Art's Sake, Tzara's Dada Anti-Artism), as well as interdicting the play's ability to project a different future (by reducing Lenin to a second writing of history as a figure of farce). However, the aesthetic pay-off of such arbitrariness is an open-ended, dialectical, and theatricalized debate which allows Stoppard to accelerate what Connor calls "the comic engine" of the play, that is, "the coincidence and competition of mutually exclusive ways of being in or ordering the world, as these both interrupt and interpret each other" ("Postmodern Performance," p. 110). To use the language of Lyotard's definition of the "postmodern condition," each of the proposed metanarratives proposed by Joyce, Tzara, and Lenin (as well, Connor reminds us, of the use of *The Importance of Being Earnest* as the frame play and sections of Shakespeare and *Ulysses* as templates for individual scenes) has its absolute authority undermined by what Lyotard refers to as "the differend," defined in his book of that title as a form of dispute "distinguished from litigation . . . a case of conflict between (at least) two parties, that cannot be equitably resolved for lack of a rule of judgment applicable to both arguments. One side's legitimacy does not imply the other's lack of legitimacy."[17] Stoppard has made clear in comments made about the play (but crucially, not overtly *in* the play) that his own sympathies lie with Joyce's position in *Travesties*, but in scenes where litigation is utilized explicitly to resolve the differends (such as Carr's cross-examination of Bennett in the first scene, and of Joyce in the dream recounted at the end of Act 1), such one-sided resolutions are always bound to fail gloriously.

Another decidedly postmodern notion raised by *Travesties*, says Connor, is the manner by which the fantastic dream structure of the play (wherein Carr, Joyce, Lenin, and Tzara may come together and speak the tongue of Oscar Wilde) "intimates self-consciously that it is a forcing of reality into the structure of a game, an imaginary history put together for purposes of spectacle" ("Postmodern Performance," p. 112). This has been of course a Stoppard trademark as far back as *Rosencrantz and Guildenstern Are Dead*, and might easily be used as evidence that Stoppard's concerns go no further than a playful intertextuality in which postmodern art becomes merely the swapping, sampling, and intermingling of existing genres, tropes, and styles in the project of creating a unique *bricolage* which comments self-consciously on the necessary metafictional nature of literature. But Connor astutely points out that Stoppard's intentions are both more serious and more critical. The game structure of *Travesties*, argues Connor, since it includes discussions on the nature of written history and personal remembrance (how it may be textualized by art or by the addled recollections of a biased bureaucrat), as well as the political obligations of any work of art, is set up "in such a way as to suggest that the "other" of theatre – the realities of politics and history that seemingly lie beyond its jurisdiction – has itself been penetrated by theatricality" ("Postmodern Performance," p. 112). The play, then, comments critically on the situation of the "society of the spectacle," in which all cultural activity becomes a kind of high-budget performance of the real, with little regard for "actual" history and the material conditions of the social and political world.

The key here is that, again, Stoppard is having a modernist cake while eating it in postmodern crumbs. In Connor's words:

> For the audience trying to make sense of the play, the emphasis may well fall on the recognition of coincidence and parallel, and the play is amply enough furnished with repetition – of lines, scenes and situations – to reward and reinforce this kind of attention. But, as its title announces, the play is just as fundamentally concerned with dislocation, displacement and mistranslation. Any coherence which the play achieves is against the principle of disarrangement and incompleteness which appear to govern it.
>
> ("Postmodern Performance," p. 110–111)

As Ihab Hassan once wrote, postmodernism is a culture of "unmaking," the characteristics of which include "decreation, disintegration, deconstruction, decentrement, displacement, difference, discontinuity, disjunction, disappearance, decomposition, de-definition, demystification, detotalization, delegitimation."[18] In *Travesties*, the postmodern concern with exploring all things decentered, and thus absent full presence or foundational authority, gets full shrift in the play, even as Stoppard provides basins of order which hint at a source of a center. The play, says Connor, "works to establish predictable rules and patterns which it is necessary for the audience to accept and inhabit for the play's demonstration of unpredictable dislocation to take place" (p. 112): moments, that is, during which characters are self-present to themselves and seem to speak directly and without irony, and episodes of narrative clarity gained by the resolution of certain conflicts. *Travesties* is, then, as Connor argues, exempt from the condition of its own title, "intricately and reliably ordered" (p. 112), the embodiment of "the general principle of dysfunction in the mechanics of communication . . . engineered by a theatrical mechanism which itself whirs and spins with perfect precision" (p. 113). In other words, Stoppard is building a theatrical apparatus that efficiently cranks out an image of the Real as, paradoxically, anything *but* an efficient machine.

While *Travesties* stands as a pinnacle of Stoppard's skill in presenting a dizzyingly undecidable but ordered universe, a series of plays preceding it reveal that such a balance occurred following struggle. John Wood has observed acutely of Stoppard that "Tom has changed over the years. There was an inevitable darkening, like seasoning wood. When I first met him in the sixties, there was a kind of anarchic joy in him, and it's still there, but it contains its own impossibility now. I can't say that life has disappointed Tom, but I think he once thought there must be some kind of system behind the absurdity, and he found out there isn't."[19] *Rosencrantz and Guildenstern Are Dead* has often been discussed as a work of postmodernism, but the absurdist anxiety underlying the frenzied activities of the two courtiers would seem to distinguish the play from a viable embodiment of postmodern ideas and desires. That is, Stoppard deploys Roz and Guil's manic game-playing and verbal inventiveness not to avow a textualized universe of signs and concepts in constant circulation, but to render more poignant the lack of authenticity and presence the two hapless courtiers attempt to overcome. As Derrida wrote, elucidating the concept of poststructuralist "play" in his conclusion to the important essay "Structure, Sign and Play in the Discourses of the Human Sciences":

> Turned towards the lost or impossible presence of the absent origin, this structuralist thematic of broken immediacy is therefore the saddened, *negative*, nostalgic, guilty side of thinking of play whose other side would be the Nietzschean *affirmation*, that is, the joyous affirmation of the play of the world and the innocence of becoming, the affirmation of a world of signs without fault, without truth, and without origin which is offered to an active interpretation. This *affirmation then determines the noncenter otherwise than as the loss of center*.[20]

Burdened with the nostalgic desire for origins certainly felt as lost and irreclaimable, Ros and Guil engage in a deadly game of play that presses home the desire for presence, being, and final truth or signifieds, but ends by affirming nothing. Still, Stoppard is at the same time, like Henry in *The Real Thing*, telling the French that they may have got existentialism "all wrong" by effacing too much the inventive and anarchic aspects of trying to live in good faith. The play thus stands as an early example of a writer attempting to come to terms with the loss of centers (in this case the authoritative text of Shakespeare's play) while at the same time intuiting a post-absurdist response to such lack, but a response nevertheless which cannot yet make the leap to affirming the idea of the "noncenter otherwise than as the loss of center."

Jumpers marks a real turning point in Stoppard's ongoing relationship to postmodernism, as it marks his first full-scale effort both to address the loss of presence, transcendental origins ("Is God?"), and meaningful moral truths while at the same time investing the play with the verbal and theatrical gymnastics that emerge from a world that has experienced, as George Moore says, "presumably a calendar date – a *moment* – when the onus of proof passed from the atheist to the believer, when, quite suddenly, secretly, the noes had it," and in which the agnostic Radical Liberal spokesman for Agriculture may ascend to the Archbishopric of Canterbury (*Jumpers*, p. 25). With the befuddled but dogged George firmly in control of the spectator's empathy, Stoppard exercises great freedom in giving voice and space to the relativistic arguments of Archie and his department of "logical positivists, mainly, with a linguistic analyst or two, a couple of Benthamite Utilitarians . . . Lapsed Kantians and empiricists generally . . . and of course the usual Behaviourists" (*Jumpers*, pp. 50–51). Yet this "not especially talented troupe" of gymnast/philosophers never seriously supplants George's and, eventually, Clegthorpe's and (retroactively to the action of the play) McFee's quest for evidence of moral integrity and ethical order in the universe. Stoppard has contrived a pitched battle between opposing philosophical schools, some representing humanist modernity and others notions at least loosely aligned with postmodern theory, and then reduced it to a farcical series of *contretemps* out of which no clear winner may emerge. Critics often point out that McFee's intended conversion to morality and Clegthorpe's Cranmer-like discovery of a true self just prior to his murder vindicate the "potency and integrity of the intuitive forces" represented by George, indicating the latter's final victory over the relativists.[21] But George is never aware of having vanquished his foes, crying out at the close of the play for the madness to stop and descending, in his last speech, to calling on the deceased rabbit, "Herr Thumper," as witness to his beliefs. And so the victory is at best a Pyrrhic one, with spectators left desiring to come down on the side of George and the angels, but intellectually stimulated by the breezy wit and effortless corruption embodied in Archie. Dotty is saying goodbye to the moon, the once-romantic sphere now tainted by the lack of altruism and moral conscience broadcast to the world when Captain Scott left Astronaut Oates "a tiny receding figure waving forlornly from the featureless waste of the lunar landscape" (*Jumpers*, p. 22). No clear winner emerges in the clash of paradigms, and the result again is a theatricalized differend which cannot be resolved by litigation or literary interpretation. The text of *Jumpers* becomes textualized, in the postmodern sense, and circulates a turbulent mix of signifiers regarding philosophical ideas, personal choices, and presentation of character.

In these plays, then, Stoppard continues to work toward the kind of theatrical machine which Connor describes as efficiently articulating and aesthetically ordering a universe on the verge of losing all structure and predictability. Stoppard registers the loss of stable meaning and decidable moral action by including the presence of characters like George and (in *Travesties*) Old Carr, yet these figures are anything but beyond mockery and derision. At the same time, those who carry the flag of postmodern randomness and instability are likewise deflated in their pretentions: Dotty's madness serves Archie no better than it does George, and the squirming pyramid that so aptly captures Archie's view of reality is coming undone with the conversions and murders of McFee and Clegthorpe (and one doubts that Bones, despite the name, would give more backbone to the structure even if he accepted Archie's bribe to become the Chair of Logic). Behind both positions, however, stands an architect of the chaos, the artist whose grasp of the unpredictable is exactly what allows him to impose a structure of intentionality over the world that he sees as essentially lacking in any kind of totalizing structure.

On the other side of *Travesties*, Stoppard's more recent plays continue to probe the dynamics of stability and instability, pitting against one another (in *Hapgood*) scientists masquerading as spies (or vice versa) in order to extend Heisenberg's philosophical speculations regarding quantum mechanics into the realm of Cold War espionage. The play reveals how even so rigid a binary disposition of power, and its consequent stability, is always undermined by the uncertainties of language, vision, and Eros. *Indian Ink* explores the clash of imperial culture and its aesthetic values with those of subaltern India, contemplating a postmodern, multiculturalist paradigm of new identities and hybrid aesthetic practices emerging from the destabilized condition of a postcolonial world. Most successfully, in *Arcadia* Stoppard finds in chaos science the perfect metaphor to convey his deliberations on the strange dance between order and disorder, and between texts which (like the Platonic letter Bernard seeks to confirm his theory of Byron's duel with Ezra Chater) give up a pure, uncluttered meaning as opposed to those (like Fermat's theorem) which can only be understood as producing competing readings and interpretations. The principles of thermodynamics underlying the content and the structure of the play mimic brilliantly in scientific terms the postmodern notion of what Heiner Müller has called the "entropy of discourse," that is, the manner by which signification assumes a kind of structure of presence, intentionality and interpretability, only to disperse into absence and randomness. The shadow of entropy allows Stoppard to propose various kinds of structure in the world of both the present and past Derbyshire households he depicts, as well as in the structure of his own play, even as such organization and taxonomies are breaking down – literally turning his theatrical apparatus into a steam engine surrendering useful, orderly heat to its environment. Both Thomasina and Valentine adhere to the

10 A scene from the National Theatre 1993 production of *Arcadia* – Harriet Harrison (Chloë Coverly), Bill Nighy (Bernard Nightingale), Felicity Kendal (Hannah Jarvis), Samuel West (Valentine Coverly).

belief that in mathematics one can discover fundamental and unalterable truths, yet each is exploring in their own way the manner in which even equations can leak and become destabilized by certain kinds of repetition. Their quest to discover the order within the turbulence of iterated equations is paralleled by Bernard's and Hannah's respective attempts to (re)write the history of the Croom estate, its landscape designs and its inhabitants, where, similarly, the search for facts and accurate interpretations becomes inevitably a rhetorical exercise, dramatized hilariously in Bernard's spectacularly misguided performance of his conference presentation on Byron.

As the two time periods of the play mix and become increasingly intermingled and confused (the props on the central table sprawling across space and time), the play teeters on the brink of chaos as it is traditionally understood, and how it is often celebrated in postmodern theories of textuality, desire, and social interaction. But Stoppard, always more interested in the interplay of order and disorder than in maintaining a prevailing belief in one or the other, or in reconciling them, draws from nonlinear dynamics the notion that, while disorder is on exhibit everywhere – from Valentine's grouse populations to Noakes's landscape designs (powered by the Newcomen steam engine pounding loudly in the background) to Thomasina's emerging desires for Septimus and the other erotic "attraction[s] that Newton left out" (*Arcadia*, p. 74) – a principal of "self-similarity" provides basins of order and periodicity to the chaos, enriching it and making it signify in unexpected ways. Repetition, the principle against which postmodern theorists like Derrida and Deleuze have launched their notions of *différance* and the rhizome, operates in Stoppard to render his dramatic world orderly, even as the iterations themselves create the f(r)ictional differences that make the story of the play complex and significant.

Stoppard's evolution toward a compromise formation with postmodernism, then, reaches it fullest expression in a play that is largely about evolution, but in the nonlinear evolution of dynamical systems in which both regularity and turbulence interact to drive time and life forward into an unpredictable future. While maintaining faith in the postmodern slippages and flux of language, signs, history, identities, and interpretations, Stoppard nevertheless insists that when structure and stability emerge, attention must be paid. Registering the breakdowns in cultural narratives, he holds out the possibility that these may evolve into breakthroughs.

NOTES

1 Quoted in David Nathan, "In a Country Garden (if it is a Garden)," *Sunday Telegraph*, 28 March 1993, reprinted in Paul Delaney, ed., *Stoppard in Conversation* (Ann Arbor: University of Michigan Press, 1994), pp. 263–64.

2 Quoted in Stephen Schiff, "Full Stoppard," *Vanity Fair*, 52.5 (May 1989), reprinted in Delaney, ed., *Stoppard in Conversation*, p. 221.

3 See for example Rodney Simard, *Postmodern Drama: contemporary playwrights in America and Britain* (New York and London: University Press of America, 1984). Stephen Watt provides an overview of the neglect of dramatic writers in the postmodern canon in *Postmodern/Drama: reading the contemporary stage* (Ann Arbor: University of Michigan Press, 1998).

4 James M Harding, "Cloud Cover: (re)dressing desire and comfortable subversions in Caryl Churchill's *Cloud Nine*," *PMLA*, 113.2 (March 1998), p. 266.

5 See Watt, *Postmodern/Drama*, pp. 15–40.

6 The most concise history of postmodern theory is in Steven Best and Douglas Kellner, *Postmodern Theory: critical interrogations* (New York: Guilford Press, 1991).

7 The point is made most compellingly in Clifford Geertz, "Blurred Genres: the reconfiguration of social thought," *American Scholar*, 37 (Spring 1968) pp. 168–177.

8 See for instance Robert Ventura, *Complexity and Contradiction in Postmodern Architecture*, 2nd edn (New York: Museum of Modern Art and Graham Foundation, 1972).

9 See for instance Manuel Castells, *The Rise of the Network Society* (London: Basil Blackwell, 1996).

10 John Carlos Rowe, "Postmodernist Studies," in Stephen Greenblatt and Giles Gunn, eds., *Redrawing the Boundaries* (New York: MLA, 1992), p. 189.

11 Frederic Jameson, *Postmodernism, or the cultural logic of late capitalism* (Durham: Duke University Press, 1991), p. 3.

12 John Bull, *Stage Right: crisis and recovery in British contemporary mainstream theatre* (London: Macmillan, 1994), especially pp. 192–206.

13 Quoted in Schiff, "Full Stoppard," pp. 221–222.

14 Quoted ibid.

15 Steven Connor, "Postmodern Performance," in *Postmodernism and Politics*, ed. Jonathan Arac (Minneapolis: University of Minnesota Press, 1986): pp. 107–122.

16 Michael Vanden Heuvel, "Complementary Spaces: realism, performance and a new dialogics of theatre," *Theatre Journal*, 441 (March 1992), pp. 47–58.

17 Jean-François Lyotard, *The Differend* (Minneapolis: University of Minnesota Press, 1988), p. ix.

18 Ihab Hassan, *The Postmodern Turn: essays in postmodern theory and culture* (Columbus: Ohio State University Press, 1987), p. 92.

19 Quoted in Schiff, "Full Stoppard," pp. 223–224.

20 Jacques Derrida, *Writing and Difference*, trans. Alan Bass (Chicago: University of Chicago Press, 1978), p. 292.

21 See for example Eric Salmon, "Faith in Tom Stoppard," *Queen's Quarterly*, 89 (1976), pp. 215–232.

14

MELISSA MILLER

The Tom Stoppard Collection at the Harry J. Ransom Humanities Research Center

The archive of the Tom Stoppard papers at the Harry J. Ransom Humanities Research Center, University of Austin, Texas, has become the primary location for scholarly holdings relating to the playwright and his work. With an array of written and visual materials representing the writer's work over a broad span of his creative life, this archive is both extensive in range and well contextualized, featuring holdings on related figures such as Stoppard's contemporary David Hare, the absurdists James Saunders and N. F. Simpson, and others. The Ransom Center holdings document the creative process and reveal the responses of artists to forms and innovations that have gone before. For example, the Ransom Center's Beckett papers, as well as the archive of the producer Sir Donald Albery, reveal much relating to the ground-breaking development of *Waiting for Godot*, just as the John Osborne papers, Royal Court papers, and others provide an equally significant context for other artists and historical moments.

A brief examination of the box and folder listings of materials held within the Stoppard papers suggests the variety of inquiry supported by this holding. The listings suggest materials from concept work, through production revisions, through variant treatments for alternate media, as well as the post-production commentary of critics and correspondents. One example that speaks directly to the archive's capacity to yield evidence of the creative process derives from a meeting summary for work on *Squaring the Circle: Poland 1980–1981*. The summary records the company's efforts to create "drama, not documentary." While entertaining disclaimers and dramatic devices, Stoppard develops an idea for a "composite character, probably not a radical, to act as a voice. Perhaps there should be a frame within a frame. The composite character would have a role and observe the inner frame action from the outside one." Other examples include notes developed for the production company of *The Real Thing* and crib notes for *Hapgood*. These clarify production style by elaborating points of interpretation. In addition, the archive encompasses translated notes from Václav Havel to the company performing *Largo Desolato* that provide ground work crucial for approaching the production of translated work, destined for reception by English-speaking audiences. The archive includes Stoppard's original works, translations, adaptations from literature and myth, from intertextual sources, and from historic events, as well as some work by others.

Stoppard's works have occasionally been characterized as centered on static ideas at the expense of character development or emotional expression. Yet, the archival holdings suggest a record imbued with the process of incarnating an idea: a record of processes in which ideas become charged with the personal cost of political exercise. Among the evidence of process made tangible are pages that may include graphic musings strewn with bishops' croziers and Gothic arches, or diagrams such as the one for the espionage exchange in *Hapgood*. Similarly, the processes of developing work for stage, radio, and screen include consultations with experts on points of scientific or philosophic theory and practice, and some of these explorations form chains of correspondence in the archive. The papers suggest a playwright's traffic with the substance of lives and situations created for the stage rather than cold analysis and disembodied ideas.

The archive has been arranged in a sequence of five series (Works; Works About Stoppard; Correspondence; Legal and Personal Material; and, Works by Other Authors) with subseries citing the titles of plays when correspondence relates directly to a given play. The scope notes, biographical notes, and expanded notations on the arrangement of the archive are all available on site at the Reading Room, as well as on the Research Center website. A quick perusal of the folder lists indicates that this archive covers the full range of the artist's work for narrative publication, stage, and radio, as well as for television studios, the European cinema, and Hollywood. As the definitive holding of Tom Stoppard's papers, this would suggest a sort of completeness. Still, researchers in the performing arts will always remain cognizant of the elusive detail: the rehearsals, telephone conversations, and other aspects of process inherent to work for performance, which by the nature of the exchange have gone unrecorded. Such elements of process leave tantalizing gaps, such as the note: "I have an idea, however, which I will explain orally." No one familiar with Stoppard's *Arcadia* could resist such an invitation to the archive. The possibilities are infinite, the material extensive, and the invitation, open.

The finding aid for the Stoppard Archive and listings for many holdings, are accessible at website: http://www.lib.utexas.edu/Libs/HRC/HRHRC/. The Center's website provides current contact data, as well as information on fellowship programs, exhibitions, and public programming. The finding aid is periodically updated to encompass recently catalogued additions.

Selected bibliography

The resources which follow represent a limited selection of scholarly, documentary, or production records on Tom Stoppard and his work, with attention to covering the several decades of his career. Space limits have confined this bibliography to suggestive rather than comprehensive or definitive listings.

PRIMARY WORKS

Collections

Four Plays for Radio. London and Boston: Faber and Faber, 1984. Contents: *Artist Descending a Staircase, Where Are They Now?, If You're Glad I'll Be Frank, Albert's Bridge.*

Plays. London and Boston: Faber and Faber, 1996. Contemporary Classics series. Vol. I, *The Real Inspector Hound, After Magritte, Dirty Linen, New-Found-Land, Dogg's Hamlet, Cahoot's Macbeth.* Vol. II, *The Dissolution of Dominic Boot, "M" Is For Moon Among Other Things, If You're Glad I'll Be Frank, Albert's Bridge, Where Are They Now?, Artist Descending a Staircase, The Dog It Was That Died.* Vol. III, *A Separate Peace, Teeth, Another Moon Called Earth, Neutral Ground, Professional Foul, Squaring the Circle.* Vol. IV, *Dalliance, Undiscovered Country, Rough Crossing, On the Razzle, The Seagull.* Vol. V, *Arcadia, The Real Thing, Night and Day, Indian Ink, Hapgood.*

The Real Inspector Hound and other entertainments. London and Boston: Faber and Faber, 1993. Contents: *The Real Inspector Hound, After Magritte, Dirty Linen, New-Found-Land, Dirty Linen* (concluded), *Dogg's Hamlet, Cahoot's Macbeth.*

Stoppard: the plays for radio 1964–1983. London and Boston: Faber and Faber, 1990. Contents: *The Dissolution of Dominic Boot, "M" Is For Moon Among Other Things, If You're Glad I'll Be Frank, Albert's Bridge, Where Are They Now?, Artist Descending a Staircase, The Dog It Was That Died.*

Stoppard: the plays for radio, 1964–1991. London and Boston: Faber and Faber, 1994; previous edn 1990.

Stoppard: The television plays, 1965–1984. London and Boston: Faber and Faber, 1993. Contents: *A Separate Peace, Teeth, Another Moon Called Earth, Neutral Ground, Professional Foul, Squaring the Circle.*

Books

After Magritte. London and Boston: Faber and Faber, 1971; New York: Samuel French, 1971.

Albert's Bridge. London and New York: Samuel French, 1969. [Stage adaptation of radio play.]

Albert's Bridge. London and Boston: Faber and Faber, 1970; new edn.

Albert's Bridge; a radio play. New York, Samuel French, 1969.

Albert's Bridge; and, If You're Glad I'll Be Frank: two plays for radio. London and Boston: Faber and Faber, 1969.

Albert's Bridge and other plays. New York: Grove Press, distributed by Random House, 1st edn 1977. Contents: *Albert's Bridge, If You're Glad I'll Be Frank, Artist Descending a Staircase, Where Are They Now?, A Separate Peace.*

Arcadia. London and Boston: Faber and Faber, 1993.

Artist Descending a Staircase. London and Boston: Faber and Faber, 1988.

Artist Descending a Staircase, and, Where Are They Now? Two plays for radio. London and Boston: Faber and Faber, 1973.

The Battle of Brazil; with the director's-cut screenplay complete and updated by Terry Gilliam, Tom Stoppard, and Charles McKeown. Jack Mathews. New York: Applause Books; Huntington, Cambs: A&C Black; revised edn, 1998.

Dalliance and Undiscovered Country. Adapted from Arthur Schnitzler. London and Boston: Faber and Faber, 1986.

Dirty linen; and, New-Found-Land. New York: Grove Press, distributed by Random House, 1st edn, first printing, 1976; Book Club edition, 1976; London and Boston: Faber and Faber, 1976; London: Samuel French, "French's Acting Edition," 1976; London: Inter-Action, Ambiance/Almost Free Playscripts, 1976.

The Dog It Was that Died, and other plays. London and Boston: Faber and Faber, 1983. Contents: *The Dog It Was That Died, The Dissolution of Dominic Boot, "M" Is For Moon Among Other Things, Teeth, Another Moon Called Earth, Neutral Ground, A Separate Peace.*

Dogg's Hamlet, Cahoot's Macbeth. London and Boston: Faber and Faber, 1980.

Enter a Free Man. New York: Grove Press, distributed by Random House, 1972, 1968; London and Boston: Faber and Faber, 1968; London and Boston: Faber and Faber, (1991 printing); Samuel French. 1968.

Every Good Boy Deserves Favor; and, Professional Foul. New York: Grove Press, distributed by Random House, 1st edn, first printing, 1978.

Every Good Boy Deserves Favour: a play for actors and orchestra, and Professional Foul: a play for television. London and Boston: Faber, 1978; New York: Grove Press, distributed by Random House, 1st Evergreen edn, second printing. 1978.

Every Good Boy Deserves Favour: a play for actors and orchestra. Tom Stoppard and Andre Previn. New York: Wilhelm Hansen/Chester. 1982. Score: large (orchestra) version; does not include words. Notes by André Previn and Tom Stoppard.

The Fifteen Minute Hamlet. London and New York: Samuel French, 1976.

Glynn Boyd Harte: a spring collection: coloured pencil drawings, 5 April–1 May, 1976. Introduction by Tom Stoppard. London: Thumb Gallery, 1976.

Hapgood. London and Boston: Faber and Faber, 1988; London and Boston: Faber and Faber, 1994. Reprinted with corrections 1994.

If You're Glad I'll Be Frank. London and New York: Samuel French, 1969.

If You're Glad I'll Be Frank: a play for radio. London and Boston: Faber and Faber, new edn, 1976.

In the Native State. London and Boston: Faber and Faber, 1991.

Indian Ink. London and Boston: Faber and Faber, 1995.

The Invention of Love. London and Boston: Faber and Faber, 1997.

Jumpers. New York: Grove Press, 1972; London and Boston: Faber and Faber, 1972; London and Boston: Faber and Faber; revised edn, 1986.

Largo Desolato: a play in seven scenes. Vaclav Havel; English version by Tom Stoppard. London and Boston: Faber and Faber, 1987, 1984.

Lord Malquist and Mr. Moon. London: Blond, 1966; New York: Knopf, distributed by Random House, 1st American edn, 1968.

Night and Day. London and Boston: Faber, 1978; New York: Grove Press, distributed by Random House, 1st edn, 1979; New York: Grove Press, Book Club edition, 1979.

On the Razzle. Adapted from "Einen Jux will er sich machen," by Johann Nestroy. London and Boston: Faber and Faber, 1981; reprinted with corrections 1982.

The Real Inspector Hound. London and Boston: Faber, 1968; London and New York Samuel French, 1968; New York: Grove Press, 1968.

The Real Inspector Hound and After Magritte. New York: Grove Weidenfeld, 1st Evergreen edn, 1975.

The Real Thing. London and Boston: Faber and Faber, 1982; London and Boston: Faber and Faber, reprinted with revisions, 1983; London and Boston: Faber and Faber, Book Club edn, reprinted with revisions, 1983; Boston: Faber and Faber, Broadway edition, 1984.

Rosencrantz and Guildenstern Are Dead; consulting editor Henry Popkin. New York: Grove Weidenfeld, 1967; New York: Grove Press, 1st Evergreen Black Cat edn, 1968.

Rosencrantz and Guildenstern Are Dead. London and Boston: Faber and Faber, 1967; New York: Samuel French, 1967; London and Boston: Faber and Faber, 1980 printing, 1968.

Rosencrantz and Guildenstern are Dead, the film. London and Boston: Faber and Faber, 1991.

Rough Crossing; freely adapted from Ferenc Molnar's "Play at the castle." London and Boston: Faber and Faber, 1985.

Rough Crossing: adapted from "Play at the Castle" by Ferenc Molnar; and, On the Razzle: adapted from "Einen Jux will er sich machen" by Johann Nestroy. London and Boston: Faber and Faber, 1991.

The Seagull; a new version by Tom Stoppard. London and Boston: Faber and Faber, 1997.

A Separate Peace. London and New York: Samuel Samuel French, 1969.

Shakespeare in Love. By Marc Norman and Tom Stoppard. London and Boston: Faber and Faber, 1999. [Issued as screenplay.]

Squaring the Circle, Every Good Boy Deserves Favour, Professional Foul. London and Boston: Faber and Faber, 1984.

Travesties. London and Boston: Faber and Faber, 1975; New York: Grove Press, 1st Evergreen edn, distributed by Random House, 1975; New York: Grove Press, 1st Evergreen edn, second printing, distributed by Random House, 1975.

Undiscovered Country / English version by Tom Stoppard of Arthur Schnitzler's "Das Weite Land." London and Boston: Faber and Faber, 1980; London and Boston: Faber and Faber, Book Club edn, 1980.

Collected interviews

Conversations with Tom Stoppard. Edited by Mel Gussow. London: Nick Hern, 1995.

Tom Stoppard in Conversation. Edited by Paul Delaney. Ann Arbor: University of Michigan Press, 1994.

SECONDARY WORKS

Biography

Nadel, Ira. *The Invention of Tom Stoppard*. London: Methuen, 2001; New York: St. Martin's Press, 2001.

Bibliographies and checklists

Bratt, David. *Tom Stoppard: a reference guide*. Boston: G. K. Hall, 1982.

Critical studies: independent volumes and volumes within series

Andretta, Richard A. *Tom Stoppard: an analytical study of his plays*. New Delhi: Har-Anand Publications [in association with Vikas Publishing House], 1992.

Bigsby, C. W. E. *Tom Stoppard*. British Council series on Writers and their Work, ed. Ian Scott-Kilvert. Hayden: Longman, 1976.

Billington, Michael. *Stoppard: the playwright*. London: Methuen, 1987.

Brassell, Tim. *Tom Stoppard: an assessment*. New York: St. Martin's Press, 1985.

Cahn, Victor L. *Beyond Absurdity: the plays of Tom Stoppard*. Rutherford, Conn.: Farleigh Dickinson University Press, 1979.

Corballis, Richard. *Stoppard: the mystery and the clockwork*. New York: Methuen, 1984.

Dean, Joan Fitzpatrick. *Tom Stoppard: comedy as a moral matrix*. Literary Frontiers edn. Columbia, Miss.: University of Missouri Press, 1981.

Delaney, Paul. *Tom Stoppard: the moral vision of the major plays*. New York: St. Martin's Press, 1990.

Fleming, John. *Tom Stoppard: front and center*. Literary Modernism series Editor. Thomas F. Staley. Austin: University of Texas Press, 2000.

Gordon, Robert. *Rosencrantz and Gildenstern are Dead, Jumpers and The Real Thing: text and performance*. London: Macmillan, 1991.

Harty, John, III, ed. *Tom Stoppard: a casebook*. New York: Garland, 1988.

Hayman, Ronald. *Tom Stoppard*. Contemporary Playwrights series. London: Heinemann, 1977. The fourth edn (1982) adds a section after the second interview (1976) to address plays from *Night and Day* through *On the Razzle*; converts chronology to a "Biographic Outline."

Jenkins, Anthony. *The Theatre of Tom Stoppard*. Cambridge: Cambridge University Press, 1987.

Jenkins, Anthony, ed. *Critical Essays on Tom Stoppard*. Boston: G. K. Hall, 1990.

Kelly, Katherine E. *Tom Stoppard and the Craft of Comedy: medium and genre at play*. Ann Arbor: University of Michigan Press, 1991.

Londre, Felicia Hardison. *Tom Stoppard*. Modern Literature series. Philip Winsor, general editor. New York: Frederick Unger, 1981.

Page, Malcolm. *File on Stoppard*. Writer-Files series. Simon Trussler, general editor. London: Methuen, 1986.

Rusinko, Susan. *Tom Stoppard*. Twayne's English Authors series, 4/9. Kinley E. Roby, editor. Boston: Twayne, a division of G. K. Hall, 1986.

Sammells, Neil. *Tom Stoppard: the artist as critic*. Basingstoke: Macmillan, 1988.

Whitaker, Thomas R. *Tom Stoppard*. Grove Press Modern Dramatists series. New York: Grove Press, 1983.

Critical studies: journals

Abbotson, Susan C. W. "Stoppard's (Re)vision of Rosencrantz and Guildenstern: a lesson in moral responsibility." *English Studies*. Volume 79, number 2, March 1998.

Arndt, Susanne. "'We're all Free to do as We're Told': gender and ideology in Tom Stoppard's *The Real Thing*." *Modern Drama*. Volume 40, number 4, winter, 1997.

Delaney, Paul. "Structure and Anarchy in Tom Stoppard." *PMLA*. Volume 106, number 5, October 1991.

Demastes, William. "Re-Inspecting the Crack in the Chimney: chaos theory from Ibsen to Stoppard." *New Theatre Quarterly*. Volume 10, number 39, August 1994.

Freeman, John. "Holding up the Mirror to Mind's Nature: reading Rosencrantz 'Beyond Absurdity.'" *MLR*. Volume 91, number 1, January 1996.

Guaspari, David. "Stoppard's *Arcadia*." *Antioch Review*. Volume 54, number 2, spring 1996.

Hynes, Joseph. "Tom Stoppard's Lighted Match." *Virginia Quarterly Review*. Volume 71, number 4, autumn, 1995.

Kelly, Katherine E. "Tom Stoppard Journalist: through the stage door." *Modern Drama*. Volume 33, number 3, September 1990.
"Tom Stoppard Radioactive: a sounding of the radio plays." *Modern Drama*. Volume 32, number 3, September 1989.

MacKenzie, Ian. "Tom Stoppard: the monological imagination." *Modern Drama*. Volume 32, number 4, December 1989.

Meyer, Kinereth. "'It is Written': Tom Stoppard and the drama of the intertext." *Comparative Drama*. Volume 23, number 2, summer 1989.

Rodd, David. "Carr's View on Art and Politics in Tom Stoppard's *Travesties*." *Modern Drama*. Volume 29 (1983).

Ronnick, Michelle Valerie. "Tom Stoppard's *Arcadia*, Hermes' tortoise and Apollo's lyre." *Classical and Modern Literature: a quarterly*. Volume 16, number 2, winter 1996.

Thomson, Leslie. "The Subtext of *The Real Thing*: it's 'all right.'" *Modern Drama*. Volume 30, number 4, December 1987.
"'The Curve Itself' in *Jumpers*." *Modern Drama*. Volume 33, number 4, December 1990.

Werner, C. "Stoppard's Critical Travesty, or Who Vindicates Whom, and Why . . ." *Arizona Quarterly*. Volume 35 (1978).

Zinman, Toby Silverman. "Blizintsy/Dvojniki; Twins/Doubles; Hapgood/Hapgood." *Modern Drama*. Volume 34, number 2, June 1991.

Critical studies: book sections

Bull, John. "Tom Stoppard." *Stage Right*. London: Methuen, 1994.

Innes, Christopher. "Tom Stoppard: theatricality and the comedy of ideas." *Modern*

British Drama: 1890–1990. Cambridge and New York: Cambridge University Press, 1992.

Rusinko, Susan. "Tom Stoppard: parodic stylist." *British Drama: 1950 to the present, a critical history.* Twayne's Critical History of British Drama. Kinley E. Roby, series editor. Boston: Twayne, a division of G. K. Hall, 1989.

INDEX

Note: works of literature are listed under their authors' names, except for plays by Tom Stoppard. *R&GAD* in the index stands for *Rosencrantz and Guildenstern Are Dead* (the play); TS stands for Sir Tom Stoppard.